AF505802

Financing Referendum Campaigns

Also by Karin Gilland Lutz

RESEARCH METHODS IN POLITICS (*co-author with Peter Burnham, Wyn Grant and Zig Layton-Henry*)

Also by Simon Hug

ALTERING PARTY SYSTEMS: Strategic Behaviour and the Emergence of New Political Parties in Western Democracies

ECONOMIC MODELS IN POLITICS AND ECONOMICS: A Dialogue (*co-editor with Lars Feld*)

NOUVELLES VALEURS ET NOUVEAUX CLIVAGES EN SUISSE (*co-editor with Pascal Sciarini*)

PARTIES AND PARTY SYSTEMS: A Biblio-graphic Guide to the Literature on Parties and Party Systems in Europe since 1945 (*co-author with Stefano Bartolini and Daniele Caramani*)

POLICY-MAKING PROCESSES AND THE EUROPEAN CONSTITUTION: A Comparative Study of Member States and Accession Countries (*co-editor with Thomas König*)

TAX EVASION, TRUST, AND STATE CAPACITIES (*co-editor with Nicolas Hayoz*)

VOICES OF EUROPE: Citizens, Referendums and European Integration

Financing Referendum Campaigns

Edited by

Karin Gilland Lutz
Center for Comparative and International Studies
ETH Zürich, Switzerland

and

Simon Hug
Professor of Political Science
University of Geneva, Switzerland

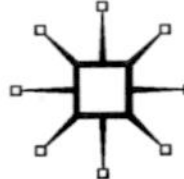

Editorial matter, selection, introduction and conclusion © Karin Gilland Lutz and Simon Hug 2010
All remaining chapters ©respective authors 2010

All rights reserved. No reproduction, copy or transmission of this publication may be made without written permission.

No portion of this publication may be reproduced, copied or transmitted save with written permission or in accordance with the provisions of the Copyright, Designs and Patents Act 1988, or under the terms of any licence permitting limited copying issued by the Copyright Licensing Agency, Saffron House, 6–10 Kirby Street, London EC1N 8TS.

Any person who does any unauthorized act in relation to this publication may be liable to criminal prosecution and civil claims for damages.

The authors have asserted their rights to be identified as the authors of this work in accordance with the Copyright, Designs and Patents Act 1988.

First published 2010 by
PALGRAVE MACMILLAN

Palgrave Macmillan in the UK is an imprint of Macmillan Publishers Limited, registered in England, company number 785998, of Houndmills, Basingstoke, Hampshire RG21 6XS.

Palgrave Macmillan in the US is a division of St Martin's Press LLC, 175 Fifth Avenue, New York, NY 10010.

Palgrave Macmillan is the global academic imprint of the above companies and has companies and representatives throughout the world.

Palgrave® and Macmillan® are registered trademarks in the United States, the United Kingdom, Europe and other countries.

ISBN: 978–0–230–57933–0   hardback

This book is printed on paper suitable for recycling and made from fully managed and sustained forest sources. Logging, pulping and manufacturing processes are expected to conform to the environmental regulations of the country of origin.

A catalogue record for this book is available from the British Library.

A catalog record for this book is available from the Library of Congress.

10   9   8   7   6   5   4   3   2   1
19 18 17 16 15 14 13 12 11 10

Printed and bound in Great Britain by
CPI Antony Rowe, Chippenham and Eastbourne

Contents

List of Tables

List of Figures

Notes on the Contributors

Daunis Auers defended his doctoral dissertation at the School of Slavonic and East European Studies at University College London and is currently Assistant Professor of Comparative Politics at the Department of Political Science, University of Latvia. He was a Fulbright Scholar at the University of California-Berkeley in the 2005–2006 academic year. His most recent published research has focused on political parties and movements in the Baltic States, particularly extreme right movements ('Explaining the Electoral Failure of Extreme Right Parties in Estonia and Latvia' (with Andres Kasekamp), *Journal of Contemporary European Studies*, 2009) and Green parties ('Green, Black, and Brown: Uncovering Latvia's Environmental Economics' (with David Galbreath), *Journal of Baltic Studies*, 2009).

Flavia Carbonell Bellolio is Lecturer and Researcher at the Faculty of Law of University Alberto Hurtado (Santiago, Chile). She is currently finishing her PhD at University Carlos III, Madrid. Her main research interests are legal argumentation and interpretation, particularly applied to constitutional courts and to the European Court of Justice, a field in which she has published several articles and made a number of contributions in edited books.

Navraj Singh Ghaleigh has been Lecturer in Public Law at Edinburgh since 2003. Previously a barrister in London and Lecturer at King's London, he undertook his graduate work at the University of Cambridge, the European University Institute (Florence) and the University of California, Berkeley (where he was a Fulbright Scholar). Navraj's electoral law research (and teaching) focusses on party and election funding, direct democracy and the implications of new technologies for the electoral process. His work has been widely cited and reviewed in scholarly publications, the quality press, including the *Times Literary Supplement* and the *Financial Times*, and parliamentary reports. He has also advised various regulatory agencies, foreign governments and international organizations on issues in party funding law.

Karin Gilland Lutz holds a PhD in political science from Trinity College, Dublin. Her current affiliation is with the Center for Comparative and International Studies, University of Zurich/ETH Zurich. Her major research interest in recent times has been the policy effects of referendums.

Francis Hamon is a Professor Emeritus of Public Law and Political Science at the Paris Eleventh University. He is the co-author of a well-known manual on constitutional law. He has also published a book on the referendum from a comparative point of view, as well as many articles on that subject.

Sara Binzer Hobolt is Lecturer in Comparative European Politics at the University of Oxford and a Fellow of Lincoln College, Oxford. She has published widely on direct democracy, voting behaviour and political parties in international scientific journals, such as the *British Journal of Political Science, Comparative Political Studies, Electoral Studies*, the *European Journal of Political Research, European Union Politics* and *Political Studies*. She is the author of the book *Europe in Question: Referendums on European Integration* (2009).

Simon Hug teaches Political Science at the University of Geneva. His research focuses on the effect of institutions on policy outcomes. His publications on referendums have appeared or are forthcoming in the *European Journal of Political Research, Comparative Political Studies, Constitutional Political Economy, European Union Politics, International Organization*, the *Journal of Theoretical Politics, Quality & Quantity*, the *Review of International Organizations* and in the volume *Voices of Europe* (2002).

Richard Johnston holds the Canada Research Chair in Elections, Public Opinion, and Representation and is Director of the Centre for the Study of Democratic Institutions at the University of British Columbia. He is author or co-author of five books and of over 60 journal articles and book chapters and is co-editor of three books. He was Principal Investigator of the 1988 and 1992–3 Canadian Election Studies and Research Director for the 2008 National Annenberg Election Survey at the University of Pennsylvania.

Algis Krupavicius is Professor and Director of Policy and Public Administration Institute, Kaunas University of Technology. His main research areas are the following: comparative politics, political parties and electoral studies, and quantitative and qualitative methods in social sciences. Among his most recent publications is a book he has co-edited, *Civil Service in Lithuania: Past and Present* (2007), and a number of book chapters, including 'The End of Communism and the New Party System', in Jean Blondel et al., *Governing New European Democracies* (2007),

'Semi-presidentialism in Lithuania: Origins, Development and Challenges', in Elgie and Moestrup (eds), *Semi-presidentialism in Central and Eastern Europe* (2008), 'La Lituanie' in De Waele and Magnette (eds), *Les démocraties européennes: Approche comparee des systemes politiques nationaux* (2008).

Irène Renfer is a former assistant of the Centre for Research on Direct Democracy (c2d). She's now assistant of the Constitutional Law Department of the University of Geneva where she is completing her doctoral thesis on direct democracy in Latin America.

Roland Ricci is Professor of Public Law at the University Paris 13. He also teaches at the Paris 8 University (Vincennes- Saint Denis) in the Masters programme 'Contemporary Systems of Law and Cultural Diversities'. He performs his research in the areas of the theory of law, comparative law, constitutional and administrative law at the Paris 8 research centre: 'Forces of Law: Paradoxes, Comparisons, Experimentations'.

Jüri Ruus is Senior Researcher (PhD) at the International and Social Research Institute, Tallinn University, Estonia. His main research interests are in the areas of democratization, regime transitions and political elites. His publications include 'Democracy and Change of Regime – Continuity of Elites? The Case of Estonia', in *East European Politics and Societies*; and 'The Resurgence of Professionalism: Estonian Elites between Continuity and Change', in Sten Berglund and Kjetil Duvold (eds), *Baltic Democracy at the Crossroads: An Elite Perspective* (2003).

Uwe Serdült is currently vice-director of the Centre for Research on Direct Democracy (c2d) at the newly established Zentrum für Demokratie Aarau (ZDA) and lecturer for the Master of Arts in Comparative and International Studies, offered jointly by the university and the ETH Zurich. His research interests include direct and electronic democracy, decision-making processes and structures, institutional change and comparative public policy.

Daniel A. Smith is Associate Professor of Political Science and Interim Director of the Political Campaigning Program at the University of Florida. He has published extensively on the process and politics of direct democracy in the American states. He is the (co)author of several books, including *Tax Crusaders and the Politics of Direct Democracy* (1998), *Educated by Initiative* (2004) and *State and Local Politics: Institutions and Reform* (2008).

Thomas Stratmann is Professor of Economics at George Mason University, and resident scholar at the Center for the Study of Public Choice. He has worked extensively on campaign finance issues, including an analysis of impact of campaign contributions on congressional decisions, the impact of campaign spending on election campaigns and referendums, campaign finance reform, legislative politics, and interest groups. His research as been published in the leading economics and political science journals.

Tobias Zellweger is a former assistant of the Centre for Research on Direct Democracy (c2d) and of the Constitutional Law Department of the University of Geneva. His doctoral thesis on transborder cooperation has been published in 2008. Zellweger is currently working for a Geneva-based law firm with a strong interest in public law.

Preface

This aim of this book is to bring together both country experts and scholars interested in the role of money in referendum campaigns from either a theoretical or an empirical perspective. As is suggested by the chapters in this volume, understanding the spending regulations of referendum campaigns is an important but largely neglected topic in the comparative literature. Hence, this volume offers an initial systematic overview of such regulations in countries where referendums are staged with some degree of regularity.

In the process that has generated this volume we incurred a number of substantial debts. First, none of this would have been possible without the generous support of the Swiss National Science Foundation, the Center for Comparative and International Studies (CIS) and the Institute for Political Science at the University of Zurich, the Schweizerische Akademie der Geistes – und Sozialwissenschaften (SAGW), the Vereinigung akademischer Mittelbau der Universität Zürich (VAUZ) and the Zürcher Universitätsverein through its *Hochschulstiftung*. We also benefited from the support of the Centre for Research on Direct Democracy (c2d), especially its vice-director Uwe Serdült.

We are also heavily indebted to Amy Lankester-Owen and Gemma d'Arcy Hughes at Palgrave Macmillan, who helped us bring this project to fruition. Finally, Joanne Richards deserves our gratitude for putting the final touches to the manuscript.

KARIN GILLAND LUTZ
SIMON HUG

1
Introduction

Karin Gilland Lutz and Simon Hug

All direct democratic political institutions, which we will subsume under the term referendums in what follows, have the common feature that they in some sense allow the voters to make decisions 'directly', bypassing other political structures, channels and processes – in short, bypassing representative democracy. Taking in the consequences of this, one has to admit that referendums can be a very powerful tool. Nevertheless, referendums form a set of political institutions that are usually associated with only a small handful of countries, Switzerland and certain US states such as California being among the most frequently mentioned in this context. In reality, however, many more countries possess institutions allowing for referendums. In this context it is notable, too, that the wave of democratization in Europe in the last 15–20 years involved the writing of new constitutions foreseeing referendums as part of the new political set-up.

Having the tools is one thing, using them is arguably another. Nevertheless, countries whose constitutions provide for referendums but where such votes rarely take place are interesting to those who want to understand politics today, because the possibility cannot be excluded that the politicians' awareness of the potential use of these tools influences the choices they make; they know that any political project they want to realize has to have a realistic chance of surviving a vote. Such indirect effects of referendums are perhaps too intangible to be observed, but nevertheless add to the direct effects of the outcome of referendum votes. What adds complexity to such lines of thought is the richness of referendum institutions world-wide. Among other things, there is the question of who may launch a vote (the president? the parliament? several thousand voters? is it simply required by the constitution?). There is also the question of on what issues votes may be held (all issues? issues that are in some sense of 'national importance'? constitutional amendments?). And then there is the question that is at the centre of this book: the question of financing.

Many critics of referendum institutions lament the excessive role money plays in referendum campaigns. Others argue that rules regulating the financing of referendum campaigns, particularly those that lead to transparency, might actually help voters to make more informed decisions. These insights are, however, almost exclusively based on theoretical models or empirical results stemming from experiences at the state level in the United States. In other contexts where referendums are used, we know very little about the rules regulating the financing of referendum campaigns and the effect on them of both money and the rules under which they are carried out. At a theoretical and/or normative level, the most immediate reaction to the possible influence of money might often be to presume that it is negative, along the lines of 'money is the root of all evil'. However, on reflection it might also be considered plausible that on the condition that voters have the chance to inform themselves of who sponsors what in a referendum contest, this information might in fact aid them in making their vote decision.

The financial aspects of electoral institutions have been very well researched in relation to normal elections (see, for instance, Clawson, Weller, and Neustadtl, 1998; Erikson and Palfrey, 1998, 2000; Carty and Eagles, 1999; Fisher, 1999; Anderson, 2000; West, 2000; Benoit and Marsh, 2004), but not with respect to referendums. This is particularly striking, given that a commonly voiced argument in favour of referendums is the supposedly unrivalled legitimacy of decisions made in this way, as opposed to decisions made through representative processes or indeed other forms of decision-making processes common to modern democracies. Decisions made directly by the people, so the argument goes, are quite simply of a different, better democratic quality, because there are no processes or actors between the people and the decision that could bias, or in any way shape, the eventual decision.

This argument obviously rests on the assumption that referendum institutions are 'pure' in a way that most observers would probably agree they clearly are not: on the one hand, we see the same actors engage in representative as in referendum processes (political parties, interest groups, and so on); on the other hand, referendum decisions often have immediate consequences for specific industries and economic interests, which therefore quite rationally want to engage in the process in order to protect their interests. Whether referendum institutions are indeed 'purer' than other forms of decision making is ultimately a question that can only be answered empirically, by analyzing the specific institutions that regulate this type of decision making.

In this vein, the purpose of the present book is, first, to provide systematic information in this area; to the authors' knowledge there is no single source of comprehensive information on the regulations applying to the financing of referendum campaigns, although financing regulations cannot be assumed to be neutral institutional parameters. Secondly, the book also wishes to make a contribution to the understanding of how different financial regulations affect referendums, either in particular country contexts, or more generally.

These two purposes rest on the assumption that the use of referendums to make decisions has the power to shape politics, and is thus worthy of detailed investigation. That referendums indeed have this effect appears beyond question, considering the amount of research coming to this conclusion. However, there are also studies that reach the opposite conclusion. This research literature focuses primarily on the US states, where it has been shown that public debt and tax levels are lower whereas the gross domestic product is higher in states with referendum institutions than in other states (see, for instance, Kirchgässner, Feld, and Savioz, 1999; Matsusaka, 2004 – although Besley and Case, 2003 and Camobreco, 1998 come to other conclusions). In policy areas of a 'moral' nature, such as minority rights (Gamble, 1997; Donovan and Bowler, 1998; Frey and Gotte, 1998) and abortion (Gerber, 1996), effects of referendum institutions on policy making have also been identified.

Beyond the US context, Switzerland is a much-studied case of referendums, where cantonal differences (parallel to the comparison of US states on the other side of the Atlantic) with regard to the use of referendum votes have been shown to have a systematic effect on health politics (Vatter and Rüefli, 2003), and moreover Fischer (2005) shows that the use of referendums is associated with lower levels of social spending and redistribution. Moreover, in Switzerland as in other countries, recent years have shown that referendums at the national level have a clear effect on the shape that European integration is taking.

Focusing more specifically on studies concerning the financing of referendums, of which there are comparatively few, Hertig (1982) analyzed 20 votes in Switzerland and drew the conclusion that dominating the campaign – which obviously requires financial muscle – means almost certain victory, although the effect is asymmetric and appears stronger for 'No' campaigns (the defenders of the status quo) than for 'Yes' campaigns. Hertig also comments that this conclusion has been drawn with respect to the USA, too, something that more recent US studies confirm

(Smith, 1998; Broder, 2000). Broder wrote that '[m]oney does not always prevail in initiative fights, but it is almost always a major – even dominant – factor. [...] Just as in presidential campaigns, the first test for any contender is the ability to raise the needed money' (Broder, 2000: 163). More systematic studies (e.g. Gerber, 1996) come to more nuanced conclusions on the role of money in referendum campaigns.

Apart from the more systematic studies on the United States and the initial forays in Switzerland, few studies deal with the ways in which referendum campaigns are financed and how these financial aspects are regulated. The bulk of this volume constitutes a systematic overview of a range of countries, showing how referendum campaigns are financed and regulated in each case. As a backdrop, each country chapter covers the history of how and when institutions allowing for referendums were introduced, their legal basis, the frequency of use of these institutions, and the kinds of issues that are voted upon. On this basis, the chapters set out what financial regulations there are, as well as any significant changes to them and the reasons for or public discourse associated with such changes. The regulations for referendum campaigns are briefly compared with those applying to election campaigns. Each country chapter also contains a discussion of any observable or potential effects of these regulations (or studies having dealt with them) specifically, and the more general effects of campaign expenditure.

For instance, Richard Johnston shows that in Canada, referendum votes have come in two waves. The first wave tended to concern issues of moral relevance and had strong US parallels. The second wave also had US parallels but concerned the country's protracted constitutional crisis. Here, the real cause of the votes that took place was Quebecois provincial politics. The chapter comments on the different provincial approaches to financial regulation in Canada and also sets the country in its 'Westminster' context, which highlights the awkward fit of referendums and highly centralized (within a given federal or provincial arena) decision-making structures. This, Johnson argues, makes the system susceptible to strategic manipulation.

Daniel A. Smith surveys the US states from the perspective of financial regulations, and comments on the increasingly important role money plays in campaigns. After providing a brief historical background on the adoption and usage of the initiative in US states, this chapter examines state regulations and the precedent-setting legal decisions that have shaped campaign financing. While some states in the past tried to regulate financial contributions to campaigns, regulations of ballot measure financing have been sharply curtailed by the federal courts. As a result, the setting is reasonably *laissez-faire*. The chapter concludes with a discussion of the scholarly research examining the impact of campaign financing on the outcomes of ballot initiatives. Since scholars have begun examining the relationship, they have found that money does have an impact on initiative outcomes, although a contingent one.

Denmark is one of a handful of European countries that make regular use of referendums. In her contribution to the volume Sara Binzer Hobolt points out that there are few legal limits or restrictions on spending there, but that the Danish state nevertheless has considerable influence over campaign expenditure and in particular over the 'resource balance' between the two sides in a campaign.

The three Baltic States – Estonia, Latvia and Lithuania – are dealt with in the following chapter. The authors, Jüri Ruus, Daunis Auers and Algis Krupavicius, cover the legal and historical background of the three Baltic States and provide an in-depth presentation of their financing rules and regulations. The authors note that while there are no specific regulations in any of the three countries, in Lithuania the campaign finances are regulated by a law covering all political campaigns.

In France, Francis Hamon shows that the 'Yes' side usually has an advantage in terms of finance, but that this can have adverse effects for the French president (who has the right to call a vote). Usually there is the sense that voters either vote for or against the president rather than for or against this or that policy proposal. More balanced campaigns, Hamon proposes, with equal means for both sides, would better serve democracy by arousing interest for the subject and encouraging the people to focus on the question itself.

The Irish Constitution of 1937 foresees two types of referendum, but only one of them has ever been used, and over the years, referendums have been used to settle various types of issues, including Ireland's participation in European integration and moral issues like divorce and abortion legislation. However, as Karin Gilland Lutz remarks in her chapter, only in the 1990s and the first few years of the new millennium did financial issues become part of the Irish discourse on referendums. It may be too early as yet to make a definitive statement on the effect of these regulations, which nonetheless at first glance appear to be potentially quite weak.

Italy, like Ireland, is a country where many votes take place. Roland Ricci draws attention to the fact that referendums became a central juridical and political institution at the promulgation of the Italian Constitution of 1948. Referendums continued to play a major role during the political crises of the 1980s and 1990s. There are rules for financial spending in referendum votes, however, and there are different normative authorities that come into play.

Carlos Closa Montero and Flavia Carbonell Bellolio write that in Spain, the financial regulations in the context of referendums vary depending on the type of vote and on the institutional or non-institutional character of the campaign. While the state provides full financing for institutional campaigns, it grants only limited resources (free spaces in public media) for the financing of non-institutional campaigns. Consequently, other actors cover the rest of the campaign expenditure, for which there are no clear limits or control mechanisms. Yet, since in some cases funding is distributed according to the representation of political parties in parliament, strong political parties are in a better position to carry out non-institutional campaigns than other actors. Some of these problems, including the lack of uniformity, lack of clarity and the incompleteness of these financial regulations, are reflected in the practice of enacting particular complementary norms to provide extraordinary economic aids for specific consultative processes, especially in the case of national consultative referendums.

In Switzerland there is no shortage of direct democratic votes, but, as Uwe Serdült shows in his chapter, in terms of financial regulations in this area, Switzerland is not especially developed. In contrast, the United Kingdom has a very limited experience in conducting votes, but as Navraj Ghaleigh shows in his chapter, since 2000 the UK's party and campaign finance regime has undergone wholesale reform. This chapter examines in detail the experience since that reform. Further, with highly contentious votes (concerning Scottish independence and the 'European' question) on the horizon, there are potential tensions between the financing of these votes and mooted reforms to the entirety of the party finance regime.

In addition to the country chapters, this volume contains one chapter that deals with the theoretical premises of much of the research on the effects of finances in referendum campaigns. In this chapter, Thomas Stratmann points out that scholarly work on the role of money in referendum votes is primarily empirical, and that there is a general perception that interest groups control the initiative process. Stratmann discusses theoretical considerations of how interest groups can influence ballot measure elections through their campaign spending, and argues that some types of campaign spending may increase welfare, while other types of spending may not.

Another chapter, written by Tobias Zellweger, Uwe Serdült and Irène Renfer, presents the results of a systematic inventory of rules applying to referendum campaigns. These two authors take as their point of departure the fact that in recent times, the use of referendums at the national (as opposed to local or regional) level has become more frequent internationally. The authors focus specifically on Europe and Latin America and argue that with the increased frequency of use, there is also a growing need to ensure that such votes meet with minimum democratic requirements. In order to define such a referendum standard, the Council of Europe's Venice Commission adopted the Code of Good Practice on Referendums in March 2007. This standard is the yardstick against which Serdült and Zellweger analyze national-level regulations, focusing on aspects of campaign finance and rules concerning media access. Beginning with a presentation of the relevant regulation in Switzerland, the chapter turns to regulations in Council of Europe member states as well as Latin American countries.

References

Anderson, A. (ed.) (2000) *Political Money: Deregulating American Politics* (Stanford, CA: Hoover Institute Press).

Benoit, K. and M. Marsh (2004) 'Campaign Spending in the Local Government Elections of 1999', *Irish Political Studies*, 18(2): 1–22.

Besley, T. and A. Case (2003) 'Political Institutions and Policy Choices: Evidence from the United States', *Journal of Economic Literature*, 41(1): 7–74.

Broder, D. (2000) *Democracy Derailed: Initiative Campaigns and the Power of Money* (New York: James H. Silberman Book/Harcourt).

Camobreco, J.F. (1998) 'Preferences, Fiscal Policies, and the Initiative Process', *Journal of Politics*, 60(August 3): 819–29.

Carty, R.K. and M. Eagles (1999) 'Do Local Campaigns Matter? Campaign Spending, the Local Canvass and Party Support in Canada', *Electoral Studies*, 18(1): 69–87.

Clawson, D., M. Weller and A. Neustadtl (1998) *Dollars and Votes: How Business Campaign Contributions Subvert Democracy* (Philadelphia: Temple University Press).

Donovan, T. and S. Bowler (1998) 'Direct Democracy and Minority Rights: An Extension', *American Journal of Political Science*, 42(3): 1020–4.

Erikson, R. and T.R. Palfrey (1998) 'Campaign Spending and Incumbency: An Alternative Simultaneous Equation Approach', *Journal of Politics*, 60 (May): 355–73.

Erikson, R. and T.R. Palfrey (2000) 'Equilibria in Campaign Spending Games: Theory and Data', *American Political Science Review*, 94(3): 595–609.

Fischer, J. (2005) *The Impact of Direct Democracy on Society.* Dissertation of the University of St Gallen (Bamberg: Difo-Druck GmbH).

Fisher, J. (1999) 'Party Expenditure and Electoral Prospects: A National Level Analysis of Britain', *Electoral Studies*, 18(4): 519–32.

Frey, B.S. and L. Gotte (1998) 'Does the Popular Vote Destroy Civil Rights?', *American Journal of Political Science*, **42**(4): 1343–8.

Gamble, B.S. (1997) 'Putting Civil Rights to a Popular Vote', *American Journal of Political Science*, **41**(1): 245–69.

Gerber, E. (1996) 'Legislative Response to the Threat of Popular Initiatives', *American Journal of Political Science*, **40**(1): 99–128.

Hertig, H.P. (1982) 'Sind Abstimmungserfolge Käuflich? – Elemente der Meinungs-bildung bei Eidgenössischen Abstimmungen', *Annuaire Suisse de Science Politique*, **22**(1): 35–58.

Kirchgässner, Gebhard, Lars Feld and Marcel R. Savioz (1999) *Die Direkte Demokratie der Schweiz: Modern, erfolgreich, Entwicklungs-und Exportfähig* (Basel: Helbing und Lichtenhahn).

Matsusaka, J.G. (2004) *For the Many or the Few: How the Initiative Process Changes American Government* (Chicago: Chicago University Press).

Smith, D. (1998) *Tax Crusaders and the Politics of Direct Democracy* (New York: Routledge).

Vatter, A. and C. Rüefli (2003) 'Do Political Factors Matter for Health Care Expenditure?', *Journal of Public Policy*, **23**(3): 325–47.

West, D. (2000) *Checkbook Democracy: How Money Corrupts Political Campaigns* (Boston: Northeastern University Press).

2
Campaign Spending and Ballot Measures

Thomas Stratmann

2.1 Introduction

Scholarly work on the role of money in ballot measure campaigns is primarily empirical. Ballot measures are either initiatives, which are drafted by citizens, or referendums, which are written by government officials. There is a perception that interest groups control the initiative process (Broder, 2000). This chapter discusses some theoretical considerations addressing how interest groups can influence ballot measure elections through their campaign spending. Some types of campaign spending on ballot measure elections may increase welfare, while other types of spending may not. I will then describe whether the evidence is consistent with either of these theoretical models.

2.2 Quantitative importance of campaign spending on ballot measures

Real campaign spending on ballot measures has been rising steadily for decades, and reached new heights in the 1990s (Smith, 2000). In 1992, $117 million was spent in 21 states on supporting and opposing measures on ballots (Magleby, 1984) while in 1998 interest groups spent close to $400 million in 44 states (Gerber, 1999). In comparison, in the 2000 Presidential Elections, the total amount spent by all of the presidential candidates, for both the primary and the general election, was $326 million. Candidates for the US House and the US Senate spent $740 million on their campaigns for the 1998 election.

For the November 2004 election, $400 million was spent on 59 initiatives on the ballots in 18 states (Smith, 2006). $269 million of this amount was spent on ten campaigns. In comparison, Senate and House candidates spent $911 million in primary and general election races in 2004.[1] Presidential candidates Bush and Kerry spent $493 million combined on their 2004 presidential campaigns, although this does not include spending by parties and others in support of these candidates.[2]

Californians spend more money on passing or defeating ballot measures than the citizens of any other state. For example, in 2004 gambling interests spent $100 million in California to influence the passage of two propositions alone (Smith, 2006). This was about one quarter of what George W. Bush and John Kerry each spent in their 2004 presidential campaigns (Matsusaka, 2004).

2.3   Median voter model and ballot measures

In a representative democracy, the electoral outcome is most often predicted by the median voter model (Downs, 1957; Hotelling, 1929). In this model, platforms converge to the ideal of the median voter, and the winning candidate faithfully implements the policy preferred by this voter. Many scholars have pointed out that representative democracy involves a principal–agent problem. The agent, namely the politician, has some leeway, and may deviate from the preferences of the principals, the voters (Kau and Rubin, 1979; Kalt and Zupan, 1984; Peltzman, 1984).

This leeway arises because elections occur only periodically. Politicians have some reason to believe that by the time of the next election, voters will have forgotten what happened earlier in the term. Politicians may exploit the voters' short memory to deviate from voter preferences early in their term in office. There is some evidence in support of this hypothesis. Stratmann (2000), for example, shows that US Senators exhibit different voting patterns at different times during their terms. But perhaps more importantly, politicians have some leeway as a result of the free-rider problem. Each individual voter does not have sufficient incentive to monitor whether politicians are executing the wishes of the median voter; the costs of monitoring exceed the benefits.

The principal–agent problem provides a theoretical explanation for the use of direct democracy: via ballot measures, policy may be closer to the ideal point of the median voter. This is because voters may overturn the decisions of legislators. Further, legislators, when faced with the possibility of a ballot measure, may deviate to only a slight extent from the preferred position of the median voter in the first place (Gerber, 1999). The threat of an initiative may give the legislator an incentive to implement policies that are close to the policy preferred by the median voter. Therefore, ballot measures may bring political outcomes closer to that of the median voter.

However, ballot measures do not ensure the median voter outcome. The ballot measure proposed by an interest group may not coincide with the position of the median voter, and the status quo, the chosen alternative when the measure is rejected, may not be at the median voter's ideal point either. Further, the presence of direct democracy may lead to political outcomes that are worse for the median voter than if the direct democracy option did not exist. For example, Gerber and Lupia (1995) and Matsusaka and McCarty (2001) show that if the legislature is uncertain about the voters' ideal position, legislators may implement policies closer to that of extreme groups if these groups threaten to put a measure on the ballot. As a consequence of the legislature's actions, the median voter is worse off.[3]

In sum, there are some theoretical reasons why direct democracy may produce outcomes that are preferred by the median voter, and some why it may not. It is an empirical task to determine whether policy outcomes in the presence of direct democracy are more likely to lead to median voter outcomes than if no option for direct democracy is available.

2.4 The role of campaign advertising in a direct democracy

One can think of ballot measures in a uni-dimensional space where one point in this space is the policy status quo, and the other is the policy proposed by the ballot measure. The policy chosen will be that which is closest to the median voter. Assuming all voters cast a ballot, and that all voters are fully informed, it is not clear what role campaign expenditures play. In order for campaign expenditures to have a role, we need to relax one or both of the two assumptions.

One type of advertising may be called *informative* (Mueller and Stratmann, 1994). Informative campaign spending educates voters about the position of the proposed policy (X) on the single-dimensional space, and it can also provide information about the position of the status quo (S). Suppose there are two interest groups, one group s, which supports the status quo, and group x, which supports the ballot measure. If uninformed voters abstain, each group has an incentive to inform voters with ideal points closest to the groups' preferred policy.

With informative advertising, opponents and supporters of ballot propositions inform the voter of the position of the status quo and the proposition on the single dimension. The voter then compares his ideal point to the points where the status quo and the ballot proposition are located and makes his decision. Informative advertising assures that the option closest to the ideal point of the median voter wins. Informative campaigning by both interest groups increases the likelihood that the policy closest to the median voter will be chosen.

Informative advertising may be more important in ballot measure campaigns than in races for well-known offices, like the Presidency, Governorships, or Senate seats. This is because voters often have little information about the consequences of ballot measures, while they are more likely to be familiar with candidates. Moreover, even if there were no campaign advertisements by candidates in races for a seat in the Senate, for example, voters know the candidate's party affiliation, which they can use as an information cue to determine their vote.

If there are two opposing organized groups, and advertising is informative and the groups know the voters' ideal points, it is not clear that both groups will advertise. Suppose that initially no voter is informed. This provides one group with an incentive to spend resources on informative advertising, while the other group will spend no resources.

For illustrative purposes, assume that policy X is closer to the preferences of the median voter than the status quo S. Suppose group x provides informative advertisements. In that case the group s has no incentive to advertise because a majority of voters will favour the policy advanced by the other group. Thus, in equilibrium only one group – the group closest to the median voter – will advertise. Alternatively, suppose group s, whose alternative is further away from the median voter, advertises first. In this case opposition group x will advertise, and again proposal X will win. Thus group s would have been better off spending no resources. Assuming that the preferences of the voters are known, one group will spend no resources on informative advertising.

The previous example assumed that there were interest groups on both sides of the issue. The benefits of informative advertising can vanish if only one group is organized. Suppose, for example, that group s is organized, group x is not, and s is farther away from the median voter's ideal point than the status quo S. In this example, group s targets its advertisement to the voters close to S. The status quo S, the inferior alternative, will win.

When there is interest group competition, informative advertising implies only one group, namely the group whose preferred policy is closest to the median voter, will advertise. However, we sometimes observe that both groups advertise.

With informative advertising, an advertiser increases his support among voters close to his position, but decreases it among voters closer to the alternative. He would prefer to increase the probability that all voters will vote for his preferred outcome. Drawing an analogy to consumer advertising, Mueller and Stratmann (1994) introduce the concept of persuasive advertising, borrowed from the consumer advertising literature. In the context of candidate elections, persuasive advertising implies advertising on a dimension that is preferred by all voters, like honesty or competence. For example, persuasive advertising would point out that the candidate is honest and competent. In ballot measure campaigns, advertisers may try to persuade voters about the result of their initiative, if adopted. Whereas informative advertising addresses positive analysis of the initiative (what, specifically, does the initiative do?), persuasive advertising focuses on normative analysis (what will be the non-proximate effect of this policy?). For example, an advertisement may argue that an increase in teacher pay will result in better teachers in public schools and should be supported on these grounds.

An alternative way of thinking about persuasive advertising is that there are two types of voters, 'informed' voters, and 'uninformed' or 'impressionable' voters (McKelvey and Ordeshook, 1987; Baron, 1994), and that advertising is directed towards impressionable voters.

Advertising to target impressionable voters may be more pronounced on complex issues, like insurance regulation, as opposed to simple or emotional issues on which many voters have already formed an opinion, like abortion. It may also be more common when the status quo is not very different from the proposed measure, and therefore many voters are indifferent between the two alternatives.

An additional role of campaign spending is that it reduces uncertainty about the effect of measures. This role is related to informative advertising. Reducing uncertainty is especially important for groups that want to change the status quo. Often voters will feel more uncertain about the effects of a new policy than the effects of maintaining the status quo. Spending may lead a risk-averse voter to vote for the measure (Morton, 2006).

Groups may also campaign to mobilize some parts of the electorate. These groups spend money with the goal of increasing the probability that their supporters turn out on election day. Increasing voter turnout among supporters increases the likelihood of victory, and it is therefore not surprising that political advertising serves this purpose as well.

An additional reason for spending is negative advertising. Negative advertising presents information about the opposition. This is done with the intention of reducing the likelihood that a voter will favour the opposing side. In some cases, it may be thought of as a variant of persuasive advertising. For example, negative advertising can draw attention to the ill effects of the proposed policy or to the hidden agenda of those supporting it.

While the effects discussed in this section are largely positive and tend to enhance welfare by bringing the outcome closer to that preferred to the median voter, many observers are concerned that special interests have an overly strong influence on the initiative process. For example, journalist David Broder (2000: 243) argues that '[T]he experience with the initiative process at the state level in the last two decades is that wealthy individuals and special interests ... have learned all too well how to subvert the process to their own purposes.'

There are several reasons to believe that this may be the case. First, some groups are more organized than others. Groups with diffuse interests, such as consumers, do not tend to be organized. However, groups who benefit greatly from particular policies have a greater incentive to overcome the free-rider problem and thus tend to be organized. Consequently, if advertising is not purely informative, but also has another dimension, such as deception or the selective mobilization of voters (the latter being of concern if there is only one side of the issue being advertised), the outcome chosen may not be the one preferred by the median voter. Secondly, and related to the first point, some groups are better at mobilizing support. If these groups persuade more people to vote, outcomes will be skewed in their favour. Thirdly, the threat of a ballot measure may induce legislators to enact laws that are supported by special interests, but not supported by the median voter. Fourth, deceptive campaigning may change the minds of uninformed voters who end up voting against their own interests. Deceptive advertising is especially problematic when the opposition group is unorganized, and lacks the resources to point out the deception.

2.5   Evidence

There is little direct evidence linking campaign spending to the level of knowledge or the competency of voters. One potential, albeit poor measure of whether campaign spending provides information is whether voters are aware of the ballot measure. Some evidence points to the fact that campaign spending makes voters aware of ballot measures. Nicholson (2003) studies ballot elections in California between 1956 and 2000 and finds that campaign spending leads to greater ballot measure awareness. Using awareness questions from the California Field Poll, he finds that negative spending increased voter awareness while positive spending had no effect on awareness. Bowler and Donovan (1998) find that campaign spending has a small but statistically significant positive effect on voter awareness on ballot measures.

In unpublished work, I examine whether television advertising on ballot measures in California between 2000 and 2004 acted to raise the levels of awareness. Using Field Poll data, I show that voter awareness of ballot propositions increases when groups increase their television advertising.

Evidence linking competency and campaign spending is even harder to come by than that linking awareness (as a measure of being informed) and campaign spending. Even so, voters may get information cues on how to vote from endorsements of ballot measures. They can use these cues to economize on information costs as they decide how to vote. For example, an environmentalist can cast a pro-environment vote by knowing that Greenpeace is campaigning for passage of the measure. Work by Lupia (1994) shows that voters use information cues to vote in their own best interest. Based on exit poll votes, this work classifies voters as informed and uninformed. The findings indicate that uninformed voters were able to mimic the voting behaviour of informed voters, based on information cues. For example, knowing whether someone like Ralph Nader opposed a measure was sufficient to cast a vote mimicking the voting pattern of informed voters.

I am not aware of empirical evidence that speaks directly to the hypothesis that campaign spending mobilizes supporters. There is some work that shows that turnout in candidate elections is higher when initiatives and referenda are also on the ballot. For example, Tolbert and Smith (2005) analyze the impact of ballot initiative use on voter turnout from 1980 through 2002. They find that ballot initiatives increase turnout in midterm as well as presidential elections. Although studies that examine the effect of ballot measures on overall turnout do not directly link turnout to spending on ballot measures, presumably the reason why turnout is higher is because voters are aware of the ballot measures. This may be due to campaign spending.

Many commentators are concerned with the influence of campaign spending on outcomes and therefore support regulations to mitigate its potentially detrimental effects. Below is an examination of the evidence regarding the effectiveness of campaign spending.

Evidence suggests that it is more likely that laws are enacted that reflect the wishes of the majority when there is direct democracy. For example, Gerber (1999) finds that among all states where a majority preferred the introduction of parental notification laws and death penalty laws, those states with a direct democracy option were more likely to adopt these policies. Similarly, Matsusaka finds that initiative states were more likely to adopt fiscal policies that were preferred by the majority than non-initiative states. Finally, opinion polls have shown that voters uniformly like term limits. The sum of evidence suggests that states with the direct democracy option have laws and policies that are closer to the desires of the majority of voters than those states that do not have that option. These findings suggest that, at least on average, interest groups do not have a detrimental effect on policy outcomes.

The older literature on the effects of campaign spending on initiatives calculates whether the side that spent more is also more likely to obtain a majority vote for their cause (Lee, 1978; Lowenstein, 1982; Shockley, 1980; Zisk, 1987). Lowenstein (1982), for example, examines ballots where 'spending on either the affirmative or the negative side ... exceeds $250,000 and ... is at least twice as high as the spending on the opposing side' (Lowenstein, 1982: 513). Using this selection criterion, he finds that spending in support of a measure was successful in getting these measures passed in 67 per cent of the cases. Conversely, opposing committees were successful in defeating measures in 90 per cent of the cases. Findings similar to those in Lowenstein (1982) have been reported by Shockley (1980), Lydenberg (1983), Magleby (1984), Owens and Wade (1986), Zisk (1987), Price (1988) and Bowler and Donovan (1998). More recent evidence comes from Garrett and Gerber (2001) who examine the Californian experience between 1992 and 1998. During this time period, one-sided supporting spending was successful in passing the initiative in 75 per cent of the cases, and one-sided opposition spending saw initiatives passed in 31 per cent of the cases.

I analyzed one-sided spending using Lowenstein's (1982) criteria and adjusted his criterion of $250,000 for inflation (Stratmann, 2005). Between the California 2000 primary and the 2004 primary, 24 ballot measures featured one side exceeding spending by the other side by $575,000 (Table 2.1). For 20 of these ballot measures, the supporting side significantly outspent the opposing side and the measure passed in 15 cases, bringing the success rate to 75 per cent. In four cases, the opposing side outspent the supporting side and all of these initiatives failed, generating a success rate of 100 per cent.

The findings in Table 2.1 provide some support for the hypothesis advanced in much of the literature: when the opposing side outspends the supporting side, it will most likely defeat the ballot initiative. This seems to answer the question of whether the amount of money spent is important for determining election outcomes. A group is more likely to win if it vastly outspends its opponents.

Table 2.1   Expenditures and ballot proposition outcomes

	One-sided supporting spending	One-sided opposition spending
Proposition passes	15	0
Proposition fails	5	4

While these numbers suggest a link between spending and outcomes, they do not imply that more money has bought the outcome in 79 per cent of the measures (19 out of 24). The supporting or opposing side may have outspent the other side because the measure was inherently popular or unpopular and thus was able to generate more funds.

Gerber (1999) classifies groups according to their membership characteristics. She defines economic interest groups as those who have primarily organizational representatives as members. She defines citizens' groups as those who have autonomous individuals as members. Put differently, citizens' groups are those which receive their support from personal and monetary resources, and economic groups are those that are solely reliant on monetary resources. Businesses and corporations are considered economic interest groups. Trade unions and citizen interest groups are included in the citizens' group category. She defines professional interest groups, such as the California Trial Lawyers Association, as a hybrid group.

Gerber's (1999) economic interest groups are effective in blocking the passage of ballot measures; they are especially effective in maintaining the status quo. However, she does not find evidence that these groups effectively use ballot measures to change the status quo. She finds that '… economic interest groups are severely limited in their ability to pass new laws by initiative. Simply put, money is necessary but not sufficient for success at the ballot box.' Citizens' groups, in contrast, are more effective in using ballot measures to alter the status quo. Gerber suggests the fact that citizens' groups are more effective than economic interest groups is consistent with the model, which claims that citizen interest groups have an advantage over economic interest groups because the latter lack personal resources.

A related finding is that during the period 1986–96 while 40 per cent of all initiatives on the Californian ballot passed, only 14 per cent of the initiatives promoted by special interests did. The authors conclude that the latter, 'are indeed the hardest initiatives to market in California, and that money spent by proponents in this arena is largely wasted'

(Donovan, Bowler, McCuan, and Fernandez, 1998). These findings suggest that economic interest groups have been influential in blocking initiatives they oppose, but that they cannot purchase their preferred changes in the status quo.

The studies described in the previous section have tried to establish a correlation between spending and initiative outcomes. However, it is not clear that the research designs employed have isolated the causal effect of campaign spending on ballot measure outcomes. One interpretation of these results is that opposition campaign expenditures lead to the failure of initiatives, but it is equally likely that a very unpopular initiative attracts a lot of negative advertising. In this example, the pre-existing opposition to the measure attracts advertising and causes the defeat of the measure – not the large amounts of negative spending. Alternatively, a committee supporting a measure that already had a large amount of popular support may receive many campaign contributions. The committee spends the contributions on advertising and the measure passes. However, in this example it is not the expenditures that led to passage. Rather, pre-existing support determined both large amounts of campaign spending and passage.

Stratmann (2006) analyzes 18 initiatives between 2000 and 2004 in California and uses an estimation technique that can address this causality issue. Within California there are several television markets and the number of television advertisements differs from market to market. Using this variation, Stratmann (2005, 2006) examines the effect of TV campaign advertising on voting decisions in Californian counties. Taking account of the endogeneity of campaign spending, his findings contrast with the findings in previous studies. He finds that supporting spending is at least as productive as opposition spending – in some cases, supporting spending is significantly more productive than spending by the other side. For example, examining the effect of advertising on the vote percentage favouring passage, he reports that 100 extra supporting television advertisements increase the ballot's supporting vote percentage between 1 and 2 percentage points. The findings indicate that for the most part, positive and negative advertising is equally productive.

Does television advertising have a big effect on the outcome of ballot measure elections? By some measures the answer is 'No'. For example, one set of estimates suggests that an additional 100 supporting advertisements increases the percentage of votes in favour by 1.1 percentage points and that a one standard deviation increase raises the vote share by 4.4 percentage points. A corresponding increase in opposing advertising lowers the vote share by 0.6 percentage points and 2.2 percentage points, respectively. Given the advertising means, the point estimates imply that the supporting side must increase its advertising by 18 per cent relative to the mean in order to obtain a 1.1 percentage point increase in the percentage of voters favoring passage. The opposing side must increase its advertising by 20 per cent to obtain a 0.6 percentage point increase in voter support.

Instead of using indicators to control for endogeneity, an alternative way of addressing the simultaneity problem between ballot measure outcomes and spending is via instrumental variables (Figueiredo, 2005).

The results in Stratmann (2006) are more comforting with respect to the concern that interest groups have a disproportionate influence on initiatives and referenda. The results show that the effect of interest groups on outcomes is somewhat offsetting. Although spending taken by itself has an influence on whether a ballot proposition is passed or defeated, the results suggest that the other side can adopt a counter campaign and thereby partially – and sometimes completely – offset the influence of the other group. These results suggest that if only one side spends, it has the advantage. However, if both sides spend, the spending of one is largely offset by the other.

2.6 Conclusion

On one side of the debate regarding money in ballot measure campaigns are those who are concerned that interest groups have too much influence in the process (Briffault, 1997; Shockley, 1985). This side of the debate is concerned with the influence of money on outcomes. Spending by wealthy or well-funded interests may offer an advantage with respect to the passage or defeat of ballot measures over those who do not have the financial means to present their views though an advertising campaign. Some claim that if those who spend are more likely to win, then those without the financial means to compete are limited in their political participation. Broder (2000: 1), for example, suggests that the initiative process 'has become the favored tool of millionaires and interest groups to use their wealth to achieve their own policy goals.' Broder (2000: 18) continues to argue that 'initiative campaigns have become a money game, where average citizens are subjected to advertising blitzes of distortions and half-truths and are left to figure out for themselves which interest groups pose the greatest threats to their self-interest'.

Overall, it appears that direct democracy benefits the many, not the few (Matsusaka, 2004). Direct democracy affects policy. It does not appear that, at least on average, interest groups have successfully pushed for policies that benefit the few.

Early work showed that money may be most successful in maintaining the status quo. Later work showed that economic groups are more successful than citizen groups in maintaining the status quo, and that citizen groups are more successful in pushing for a change in the status quo. Overall, the academic literature has found little evidence that interest groups can purchase their preferred policies through the initiative process and that money has only a small influence on whether initiatives pass.

Evidence that the side that spends more money is also more likely to win does not necessarily imply an inequality in access to political participation. The reason that the winning side outspends the other side may simply reflect that the winning side represents the views of the majority and thus was able to attract many funds. Recent work has shown that campaign spending for both sides is equally effective, but that this effect is small (Stratmann, 2006). Campaign spending can have benefits such as informing voters and reducing uncertainty, but if it is deceptive and no opposition group is formed, the outcome may not be the one preferred by the median voter.

Notes

1. http://www.fec.gov/press/press2004/20050103canstat/20050103canstat.html.
2. http://www.fec.gov/press/press2005/20050203pressum/presdisb2004full.pdf. According to the Federal Election Commission, '[f]inancial activity of 2004 presidential candidates and national conventions totaled more than $1 billion, 56 per cent more than comparable activity during the 2000 campaign.': http://www.fec.gov/press/press2005/20050203pressum/20050203pressum.html.
3. This discussion is based on Matsusaka (2005).

References

Baron, D. (1994) 'Electoral Competition with Informed and Uninformed Voters', *American Political Science Review*, **88**: 33–47.

Bowler, S. and T. Donovan (1998) *Demanding Choices: Opinion and Voting in Direct Democracy* (Ann Arbor: University of Michigan Press).

Briffault, R. (1997) 'Ballot Propositions and Campaign Finance Reform', 1 *New York Journal of Legislation & Public Policy*, **41**: 43–4.

Broder, D.S. (2000) *Democracy Derailed: Initiative Campaigns and the Power of Money* (New York: Harcourt).

Donovan, T., S. Bowler, D. McCuan and K. Fernandez (1998) 'Contending Players and Strategies: Opposition Advantages in Initiative Elections', in S. Bowler, T. Donovan and C.J. Tolbert (eds), *Citizens as Legislators: Direct Democracy in the United States* (Columbus, OH: Ohio State University Press).

Downs, A. (1957) *An Economic Theory of Democracy* (New York: Harper & Row).

Figueiredo, J.M. de (2005) 'How Much Does Money Matter in a Direct Democracy?', **78** *Southern California Law Review*, 1065–73.

Garrett, E. and E.R. Gerber (2001) 'Money in the Initiative and Referendum Process: Evidence of Its Effects and Prospects for Reform', in M.D. Waters (ed.), *The Battle over Citizen Lawmaking* (Durham, NC: Carolina Academic Press), pp. 73–96.

Gerber, E.R (1999) *The Populist Paradox: Interest Group Influence and the Promise of Direct Legislation* (Princeton, NJ: Princeton University Press).

Gerber, E.R. and A. Lupia (1995) 'Campaign Competition and Policy Responsiveness in Direct Legislation Elections', *Political Behavior*, **17**(2): 287–306.

Hotelling, H. (1929) 'Stability in Competition', *Economic Journal*, March, **39**: 41–57.

Kalt, J.P. and M.A. Zupan (1984) 'Capture and Ideology in the Economic Theory of Politics', *American Economic Review*, **74**(3): 279–300.

Kau, J.B. and P.H. Rubin (1979) 'Self Interest, Ideology, and Logrolling in Congressional Voting', *Journal of Law and Economics*, **22**(2): 365–84.

Lee, E. (1978) 'California', in David Butler and Austin Ranney (eds), *Referendums: A Comparative Study of Practice and Theory* (Washington, DC: AEI Press).

Lowenstein, D.H. (1982) 'Campaign Spending and Ballot Propositions: Recent Experience, Public Choice Theory and the First Amendment', *UCLS Law Review*, **29**(505): 505–641.

Lupia, A. (1994) 'Shortcuts Versus Encyclopedias: Information and Voting Behavior in California Insurance Reform Elections', *American Political Science Review*, **88**(1): 63–76.

Lydenberg, S. (1983) 'Business Big Spenders Hit the Referenda Votes', *Business & Society Review*, **47**: 54–5.

Magleby, D.B. (1984) *Direct Legislation: Voting on Ballot Propositions in the United States* (Baltimore: Johns Hopkins University Press).

Matsusaka, J. (2004) *For the Many or the Few: The Initiative Process, Public Policy, and American Democracy* (Chicago: University of Chicago Press).

Matsusaka, J. (2005) 'Direct Democracy Works', *Journal of Economic Perspectives*, **19**(2): 185–206.

Matsusaka, J.G. and N.M. McCarty (2001) 'Political Resource Allocation: Benefits and Costs of Voter Initiatives', *Journal of Law Econ and Organization*, **17**: 413–48.

McKelvey, R.D. and P.C. Ordeshook (1987) 'Elections with Limited Information: A Multidimensional Model', *Mathematical Social Science*, **14**: 77–99.

Morton, R.B. (2006) *Analyzing Elections* (New York: W.W. Norton).

Mueller, D.C. and T. Stratmann (1994) 'Informative and Persuasive Campaigning', *Public Choice*, **81**(1–2): 55–77.

Nicholson, Stephen P. (2003) 'The Political Environment and Ballot Proposition Awareness', *American Journal of Political Science*, **47**: 403–10.

Owens J.R. and L.L. Wade (1986) 'Campaign Spending on California Ballot Propositions, Trends and Effects, 1924–1984', *Western Political Quarterly*, **39**: 675–89.

Peltzman, S. (1984) 'Constituent Interest and Congressional Voting', *Journal of Law and Economics*, **27**(1): 181–210.

Price, C. (1988) 'Big Money Initiatives', *California Journal*, **19**(November): 481–6.

Shockley, J.S. (1985) 'Direct Democracy, Campaign Finance, and the Courts: Can Corruption, Undue Influence, and Declining Voter Confidence be Found?', *University of Miami Law Review*, **377**(39): 392–5.

Shockley, J. (1980) *The Initiative Process in Colorado Politics: An Assessment,* Bureau of Governmental Research & Service, University of Colorado.

Smith, D.A. (2000) 'Campaign Financing of Ballot Initiatives in the American States', in Larry J. Sabato, Howard R. Ernst and Bruce A. Larson (eds), *Dangerous Democracy?* (Lanham, MD: Rowman & Littlefield Publishers, Inc.).

Smith, D.A. (2006) *Money Talks: Ballot Initiative Spending in 2004*, Ballot Initiative Strategy Center.

Stratmann, T. (2000) 'Congressional Voting over Legislative Careers: Shifting Positions and Changing Constraints', *The American Political Science Review*, **94**(3): 665–76.

Stratmann, T. (2005) 'The Effectiveness of Money in Ballot Measure Campaigns', **78** *Southern California Law Review*, 1041.

Stratmann, T. (2006) 'Is Spending More Potent For or Against a Proposition? Evidence from Ballot Measures', *American Journal of Political Science*, **50**(3): 788–801.

Tolbert, C. and D. Smith (2005) 'The Educative Effects of Ballot Initiatives on Voter Turnout', *American Politics Research*, **33**(2 March): 283–309.

Zisk, Betty (1987) *Money, Media, and the Grass Roots: State Ballot Issues and the Electoral Process* (Newbury Park, CA: Sage).

3
Regulating Campaign Finance in Canadian Referendums and Initiatives

Richard Johnston

The regulation of money in Canadian referendums is distinguished mainly by its absence. But then, the same might be said of money itself, although it is obviously hard to tell. Although Canada hardly seems like a major player on the world referendum stage, a surprising number have been conducted by senior governments (national and provincial) and hundreds more populate the municipal landscape. As in the USA, direct democracy in Canada has come in waves. Regulators missed the first wave entirely. The second wave, starting in the 1990s, has received some regulatory attention but only in one place, Quebec, is this attention is anything but perfunctory.

This chapter outlines the ebb and flow of referendums and then maps that pattern against the regulatory one. It ventures some thoughts on what difference regulatory laxity makes. It concludes with thoughts about the place of referendums in what is still an elite-controlled Westminster system.

3.1 Referendums in Canadian history

By my count, senior governments in Canada have conducted 74 unique jurisdiction-wide referendums.[1] Table 3.1 indicates that the time path for Canada is rather like that for initiatives in the USA (Magleby, 1994: Table 7.2): a surge early in the twentieth century; a lull that spanned five decades; a further surge in the 1980s and 1990s; and a possible continuation of the 1990s pattern in the new century. It is a reasonable supposition, moreover, that the frequency by decade reflects similar forces to those in the USA. In the early twentieth century, these were mainly agrarian and populist. Of the 36 provincial votes before 1930,

Table 3.1 The frequency of referendums

Decade		Jurisdiction											
	Canada	BC	Alberta	Saskatchewan	Manitoba	Ontario	Quebec	New Brunswick	Nova Scotia	Prince Edward Island	Newfoundland	Territories	All places
1870		1									1			2
1880														0
1890	1				1	1				1	1			5
1900		1			1	1					1			4
1910		2	1	2	1	1	1				1	1		10
1920		2	2	2	3	1		2	2	2				16
1930		1		1										2
1940	1		1							4		1		7
1950		1	1	1	1									4
1960		1							1					2
1970		1	1											2
1980							1			1			1	3
1990	1	2		3			1			1	2	3		13
2000		1						1	1	1				4
All Decades	3	12	7	9	7	4	3	4	4	13	4	4		74

Note: 'Regulated' referendums are shaded.

13 were held in the Prairie Provinces, even though two of these three provinces did not exist before 1905. Whatever the province, the overwhelming majority of the early votes (33 of 36, plus the one national vote) were on a question driven by an agrarian sensibility, regulation (often prohibition) of the sale of alcohol. In the late twentieth century, what seems to have been at work was heightened citizen expectations for involvement as such, almost certainly modelled on the US example. In the latter period, constitutional questions carried special weight. The late-century surge was not quite distinctively agrarian or regional, but certain of the votes carried populist overtones.

3.2 Regulation

Of the 74 votes, only four could be said to fall under any form of financial regulation. This is indicated by the shaded regions of Table 3.1. The shading indicates that Quebec commenced regulation in the 1970s, and that Canada, British Columbia, and Ontario followed suit in the 1990s.[2] Quebec passed its *Referendum Act* in 1978, in anticipation of a vote on secession.[3] The 1992 Canadian *Referendum Act* was part of the run-up to that year's referendum on the Charlottetown Accord. The Act allowed provinces to conduct parallel votes so long as all votes were conducted on the same day and on the same question (Johnston et al., 1996). The 1992 vote in Quebec, although effectively part of the national vote, was conducted under provincial rules. British Columbia passed a *Recall and Initiative Act* in 1996, and regulation pursuant to it has had a peculiarly chequered history. Ontario created both the possibility of referendums and their regulation with the *Taxpayer Protection Act* of 1999.

Quebec represents the high ground, both in going first – arguably serving as the goad for the rest of the country – and in deploying the country's most extensive set of regulatory materials. The whole point of Quebec's legislation was to create a framework for what eventually became the sovereignty referendum of 1980. The referendum was proposed by the Parti Québécois (PQ) so that the larger issue could be decoupled from regular parliamentary elections. The party had deduced that as long as an election could be interpreted as itself a mandate for secession, the party's chance of winning one would remain slim. The decoupling strategy succeeded in that the PQ won the 1976 election. The key features of the legislation are as follows:

- Questions originate, in effect, in divisions in the provincial parliament (the National Assembly). There can be only two organizing committees, one for each side. A five-day window is open for parliamentarians to choose sides, organize a committee for their side, and register it. If no such committee emerges, then the Chief Electoral Officer can solicit interest from outside actors. As a practical matter, the campaign is highly partisan and both the 1980 and 1995 committees were controlled by the government and opposition parties, although the 'No' side was also an area for federal–provincial struggle.[4]

- Each committee may spend up to $1.00 per voter on the province-wide list. In the 1995 referendum, this amounted to just over $5 million. A non-affiliated elector may spend up to $1,000, after obtaining authorization from the Chief Electoral Officer.
- Each committee is given a subsidy of $0.50 per voter. Parties may transfer funds to the committee, to a maximum receipt by each of committee of $0.50 per voter. Individuals may donate to a committee, to a maximum for that committee of $3,000.
- Each committee must report all donations greater than $200. Reports appear to be after the fact.

In 1995, the 'No' (anti-secession) committee spent $4.83 million and the 'Yes' (pro-secession) committee spent $4.71 million.

The *Canadian* government's legislation of 1992 was reactive and improvised. The move was made in the middle of a constitutional crisis occasioned by the 1990 collapse of the elite-negotiated Meech Lake Accord. The two years following the collapse saw Quebec isolate itself from federal–provincial processes and embark on internal soul-searching. Along the way, the Premier of the province, Robert Bourassa, announced that Quebec, after expressing conditions, would entertain an offer from the rest of the country. This offer would be put to a referendum on 26 October 1992; failing an offer, the vote would be on secession. Initially, the federal government discouraged talk of any other form of referendum, for fear of being accused of hijacking Quebec's process. Late in the game it dawned on Ottawa that: (i) other provinces were bound to conduct referendums of their own, possibly on their own timetables and questions; and (ii) it was vital to control the question in Quebec (Johnston et al., 1996). It was easy to imagine that the game could spin out of control, which would probably make secession by Quebec inevitable. To avert these possibilities, the relevant Act was passed in the Spring of 1992. As mentioned, the Act allowed provinces to substitute their own votes for a national one, so long as the date and the question did not differ. The key financial provisions of the Act are:

- A person or a group may apply for registration as an intervener at any time during the referendum campaign.
- Only registered entities can spend more than $5,000, to a ceiling *per committee* of $0.30 per voter in the constituencies in which the committee declares it will be active. There is no formula for coordination or partition among committees on the same side of the question. Unregistered entities may spend up to $5,000.
- There is no limit to the overall amount an elector may donate to one or more committee (although the committee-specific spending ceiling renders donations to a given committee beyond a certain amount pointless).
- Committees must identify donors of $250 or more. Reporting is after the fact.
- Each television network operating in an official language is required to make a total of three hours of free time available during the campaign, divided equally between sides and proportionally within a side. If necessary a Broadcast Arbitrator can make the within-side allocation. The Arbitrator also has the final say on when in the broadcast day and week the time is made available.
- There are no limits on paid advertising.

In August 1992, the senior governments, joined by representatives from Canada's First Nations, reached agreement on a complicated logroll, called the Charlottetown Accord. This was put to a referendum on the date originally set as Quebec's deadline, 26 October. As the act permitted, Ottawa let Quebec conduct the referendum under its own rules, which as described above level the financial playing field between sides. The other provinces that had imposed referendums on themselves also had provisions to subrogate the conduct of their votes to Ottawa, which they all did. In 1992 outside Quebec, 205 committees appeared on the 'Yes' (ratification of the Charlottetown Accord) side and 36 on the 'No' side. Formally, the average ceiling on a 'Yes' committee was about $1.1 million and on the 'No' side, $4.1 million. These were fictions reflecting the geography of declared intent. In fact, spending in support of the Charlottetown Accord totalled $11.25 million, in opposition, $883,000. Notwithstanding the imbalance, the 'No' side won. If the logroll may have made sense to the parties at the table in August, it did not to the electorate at large in October, and the Accord was defeated (Johnston, 1993; Johnston et al., 1996). No national referendum has been conducted since.

The case in *British Columbia* is convoluted. The two BC votes that Table 3.1 indicates for the 1990s referred to 1991 questions asking for approval in principle of recall and initiative. The affirmative results led to the *Recall and Initiative Act* of 1994. Under the terms of the act, both the qualification and the campaign stage for initiatives are subject to spending limits, and the qualification rules seem quite stringent:

- To qualify, a proposal must be signed by 10 per cent or more of the registered voters in *each* parliamentary constituency and the signatures must be collected in a 42-day period. The 10 per cent threshold sits toward the high end of the US distribution (Tolbert et al., 1998: Table 2.1). The geographical breadth of the requirement greatly exceeds that of any US state (ibid.: Table 2.3). And the qualification period is much shorter than in any US state (ibid.: Table 2.2).
- In the qualification phase, the proponent is limited to $0.25 per elector.
- In the campaign phase, each side is limited to $1.25 per voter, with a *pro rata* formula when more than one intervener group appears on a side.
- For both phases, all contributions must be reported, regardless of value. Reports appear to be after the fact.

The rules were almost certainly devised to minimize the likelihood of successful qualification, and so far they seem to have succeeded. Only six petitions are on the record and none qualified. Three were ventured in the first year following the act, one the following year, one each in 2000 and 2002, and none since 2002. Conceivably, the financial limitations have been a major factor in discouragement and lack of success. If so, they may no longer be a factor. Although the website for Elections BC still posts the regulations, a compendium compiled by Elections Canada states that they will no longer be enforced. Provisions in BC's *Election Act* limiting independent (styled 'third-party' in Canadian parlance) advertising expenses were declared to have no force and effect by the Supreme Court of British Columbia (2000) and were consequently repealed. Therefore the advertising expense limits under the *Recall and Initiative Act* are not enforceable (Canada 2003: J.12).[5]

But the financial restraints may be quite incidental. More stringent may be the qualification rules.[6] Tolbert et al. (1998: Table 2.1) indicated that US states with the same statewide signature threshold as in BC see less than one initiative per electoral cycle. When geographical-breadth and qualification-period restrictions are added, the predicted value is presumably close to nil. Thought experiments in the domain are difficult, but Banducci (1998: Table 5.1 *et passim*) provides one way to think about it. She estimates with 1962–90 pooled time series data from 23 states that every additional 2,000 signatures reduces the predicted number measures on a state's ballot by three per cycle, other things equal. The daily rate implied by the number of registered voters in BC, the 10 per cent rate, and the 42-day qualification period is currently about 6,000.

It is of some relevance that the province passed a *Referendum Act* and a *Constitutional Amendment Approval Act* in 1996. In the main, these did little but unpack two elements of a 1990 *Referendum Act*: The first Act simply restates that 50 per cent +1 of votes cast suffices to bind the government and the second, that the legislature would not entertain a motion to amend the Canadian Constitution Acts (1867, 1982) without first referring the amendment to the electorate. Taken together, the acts bind the legislature to the popular will. The *Referendum Act* did carry potential for financial regulation in that it permits (but does not require) the Cabinet to apply or adapt to a referendum elements of the *Elections Act*. As of 1996, that act set ceilings for expenditures on behalf of candidates as well as the ceilings for independent spending mentioned in the preceding paragraph. By implication, no spending limits could be enforced for groups registered to intervene in a referendum. The one referendum since 1996 was governed by reporting rules, read in from the *Elections Act* through a special-purpose executive order, the *Electoral Reform Referendum Regulation* (47/2005). That referendum saw approximately an $80,000 outlay, roughly seven-eighths of the total spent on the winning, 'Yes' side.[7]

Ontario is the final province worthy of discussion. In 1999 a Conservative government, looking for a legacy, enacted the *Taxpayer Protection Act*. The act stipulates that any proposal to raise taxes first be submitted to referendum. Individual contributions are capped at $7,500 across all groups on the same side. Groups' outlays are capped at $0.60 per eligible voter in any constituency where they choose to advertise. These ceilings are subject to indexation for inflation. Reporting of all contributions over $100 is required. As in the other jurisdictions, reporting is after the fact. So far, however, no vote has been conducted.

In other provinces, no stable financial regulatory regime exists. Provisions of the Election Act may be applied, but this is sometimes discretionary, and not all Elections Acts regulate money. The abiding image is of electoral cultures that deny the existence of initiatives and referendums. When provinces resort to referendums, which they do more often than is commonly assumed, they either make up rules for the occasion or apply none at all.

3.3 Impact

Although the situation seems unsatisfactory aesthetically and perhaps even morally, the implications of the general lack of regulation are not clear. Thinking about implications is aided, however, by linking the claim that a 'No' vote is a low-information/uncertainty default to evidence about incidence and impact of spending. Bowler and Donovan (1998) argue that voting 'No' in the absence of clear information about the choices broadly serves voters' interests. Whether or not this is true, ballot failures outnumber successes in the two highest-volume countries, Switzerland and Australia (at least as of 1994, according to Butler and Ranney 1994: Table 1.2), although not in national referendums in the rest of the world. Magleby (1994, Table 7.5) shows that in US states initiatives usually fail, although legislative propositions usually pass. Magleby also argues that spending generally helps opponents more than proponents, such that when spending is balanced, the 'No' side wins 80 per cent of the time. This finding is broadly echoed in Gerber (1999).

What is the pattern in spending? Donovan et al. (1998) suggest that a critical factor is the narrowness of the interest in question: the narrower the protagonist's base, the more it will spend. This yields a crude 2×2 classification:

1. *Both proponent and opponent are narrowly based.* This should produce the highest spending of all. Donovan et al. cite an Oregon battle between upstream and downstream fishing interests as a classic example. Here, money may truly be the key.
2. *The proponent is broadly based but the opponent is narrowly based.* The opponent will spend as much as in case 1, but the proponents will not. Money helps mainly to increase the probability of defeat.
3. *The proponent is narrowly based and the opponent broadly based.* This should yield medium-level spending, but with roles reversed from situation 2. Money may help, but it is climbing a relatively steeper pitch than is true of the other side of the hill.
4. *Both sides are broadly based.* Neither side has much basis for raising money and the decisive consideration is likely to be the underlying distribution of opinion. If one side has money, this seems likely to reflect elite consensus (for example, against demagogic appeals), which facilitates money-raising coordinated by the political class. Classic instances include the California affirmative action and immigration initiatives.

By my estimation, Canadian referendums distribute themselves as indicated in Table 3.2. No votes have pitted two or more narrow interests against each other. This should not be surprising, in that *none* of these are initiatives; the agenda is controlled in some sense by the government of the day.

The largest single category comprises votes apparently serving a broad interest and opposed by a narrowly based one. Most of these concern the regulation of alcohol, and most predate 1930. Without exception they propose to establish or maintain some variant of prohibition. Some propose outright bans on access, although most allow or presuppose alcohol consumption for medical purposes upon prescription. It seems pretty clear that 'temperance' enjoyed broad public support in this period. Only where Catholics were numerous on the ground was there much grassroots resistance, and, significantly, the prohibition vote in Quebec failed. The continued availability of alcohol in Quebec was, in fact, quite important to turning the tide. By 1920, the federal government had essentially vacated the field and province-level control was vulnerable to the logic of extraterritoriality. On the other side in the early period were brewers and distillers, an important economic interest and beyond the regulatory reach of provincial governments; those governments could control (or try to control) only consumers. In the 1990s and 2000s, process votes in BC and Saskatchewan carried strong echoes of the earlier period. BC's votes on Recall and Initiative are obviously like this. As with, for instance, the 1913 Saskatchewan vote on Direct Legislation, these represented elite moves to anticipate what they inferred were – or might become – populist backlashes. Two of Saskatchewan's 1991 votes were similarly structured. British Columbia's 2005 vote on the adoption of the Single Transferable Vote (STV) electoral formula, although complicated in its origins and remarkably deliberative in the setup, ultimately took on this character as well.[8]

The 18 cases in which the breadth distribution is reversed are also mostly about alcohol, and generally about public morality. The shift in balance reflects a changed orientation among provincial governments. In most places by the 1920s, governments realized that prohibition was futile and that alcohol sales could be a source of revenue even as licensing could be a valuable source of patronage and local leverage. Liquor producers were an abiding interest, of course. So questions began to be framed in terms of sale by a provincial agency or private sale under closely regulated circumstances. Electorates were often slow to come around, however.[9] Later votes tend to be for modest extensions of access. In our time, the nearest equivalent to prohibition is the regulation of video

Table 3.2 Breadth of interests

Proponents	Opponents	
	Narrow	**Broad**
Narrow		BC Leg salaries 1873 PEI Autos 1913 Ontario Liquor 1919 Ontario Liquor 1921 NB Liquor 1921 Alta Liquor 1923 Man Liquor 1923 (1) Man Liquor 1923 (2) BC Liquor 1924 Man Liquor 1927 Sask Liquor 1934 PEI Liquor 1948 BC Liquor 1952 Alta Liquor 1957 PEI Gambling 1997 NB Gambling 2001 NS Shopping 2004
Broad	PEI Liquor 1878 Man Liquor 1892 PEI Liquor 1893 Ontario Liquor 1894 NS Liquor 1894 Canada Liquor 1898 PEI Liquor 1901 Man Liquor 1902 Ontario Liquor 1902 BC Liquor 1909 Sask Initiative 1913 Alta Liquor 1915 NF Liquor 1915 BC Liquor 1916 Sask Liquor 1916 Man Liquor 1916 Quebec Liquor 1919 BC Liquor 1920 Alta Liquor 1920 Sask Liquor 1920 NB Liquor 1920 NS Liquor 1920 PEI Liquor 1923 Sask Liquor 1924 NS Liquor 1929 PEI Liquor 1929 BC Health Ins 1937 PEI Liquor 1940 (1) PEI Liquor 1940 (2) PEI Liquor 1940 (3) Alta Utilities 1948 Man Grain Bd 1952 BC Recall 1991 BC Initiative 1991 Sask Budget 1991 Sask Const Am 1991 BC Elections 2005	BC Suffrage 1916 Canada Conscription 1942 NF Confederation 1949 Sask Time 1956 Alta Time 1967 NB Electoral Process 1967 Alta Time 1971 BC Time 1972 Quebec Secession 1980 PEI Fixed Link 1988 Sask Abortion 1991 Canada Constitution 1992 Quebec Secession 1995 NF Schools 1995 NF Schools 1997 PEI Elections 2005

lottery terminals (VLTs). In the abstract, voters tend to oppose them, but publicans, manufacturers and distributors – and revenue-seeking governments themselves – support them.

In the twentieth century, attention also tended to shift towards questions that pitted broad political tendencies against each other. Often, these tendencies cut through the parties' electoral bases and sometimes through their parliamentary elites. The conscription plebiscite of 1942 was like this, for example. Daylight Savings Time has this quality as well, and is bound to be contentious in a country that is physically vast and late to urbanize. Constitutional issues, like conscription, cut to the heart of the identity of a binational and multicultural state. Schools do something of the same, to the extent that the near-even Catholic/Non-Catholic divide remains relevant.[10]

It is difficult to derive coherent predictions from the above analysis. One might argue that to the extent that money buys results, the narrowness of a protagonist's base should, ironically, increase its chance of success or its share of the vote. This argument turns on the incentive to spend and the efficacy of the spending. The difficulty, of course, is that the fact of a narrow base illustrates the protagonists' political problem. The argument only makes sense *ceteris paribus*. Not only is it not entirely clear what should be held equal but deriving indicators for controls is impossible in a context where we cannot always find the proposition's share of the popular vote.

We can at least ask how propositions in each of the populated cells of Table 3.2 fared, on average. That information appears in Table 3.3. The fugitive nature of much of Canadian referendum data is illustrated by the number of observations. I have located shares for only 51 of the 74 votes. For another 13, I have been able to identify the winning side, often by the most indirect of routes.[11] Although the table casts the question in multivariate form, it represents in effect a set of paired comparisons. In the estimation for the 'Yes' share, the actual values for each group can be read from the coefficients, starting with the reference category of broadly based proponent versus a narrowly based opponent. For the estimation of the winning versus losing binary outcome, the probit setup essentially goes to the statistical significance of differences. The bottom line, the percentage of 'Yes' wins, appears in the rightmost column.

The balance of breadth in interests does seem to affect the vote. The effect of breadth is positive, rather than negative. The 'Yes' is most likely to win, and to win most handsomely when the question evokes a broad support base and the 'No', a narrow one. The 'Yes' is least likely to win, or to win by the narrowest margins, when it champions a narrow interest against a broad one. A measure pitting broadly based interests against

Table 3.3   Impact of balance of interests

Balance of interests	Yes share (OLS)	Yes win (Probit)	% wins
Proponent–opponent			
Broad–Broad	-13.79^{**} (4.33)	-0.90^{*} (0.41)	58.3%
Narrow–Broad	-4.87 (6.12)	-40.78^{a} (0.44)	53.3%
Broad–Narrow (constant)	64.86^{***} (2.50)	0.99^{***} (0.25)	83.8%
R^2 (adjusted; pseudo)	0.14	0.08	
F / $-2l_n$(LR)	5.07	6.22	
N	51	64	

a. $p < 0.10$; * $p < 0.05$; ** $p < 0.01$; *** $p < 0.001$
Entries in parentheses are standard errors.

each other is typically an intermediate case.[12] So if money is most likely to be spent by narrowly based groups, it does not buy them an increased chance of victory.

There is, of course, a whiff of tautology about this. Although I tried to avoid looking at the actual voting results in assigning ballot measure to breadth categories, it was impossible from the start to ignore the pattern. It can only be said that my categorization also reflects a reading of party and electoral history. Especially in the early years, that history is full of accounts of liquor money. The industry was one of Canada's first to operate on a global scale. The political parties in turn were quite dependent on money – and donations in kind – from the industry. So it seems reasonable to surmise that the industry did what it could to fend off threats or to expand its market, according to circumstances. The dependence of provincial treasuries on alcohol revenue is also widely remarked upon. Similar patterns hold for video gaming. It is a defensible supposition that the volume of money in play was greater on the narrow protagonist's side. Usually, however, the money does not help, at least not enough.[13]

3.4 Discussion

Perhaps the most important fact about Table 3.3, however, is that the 'Yes' side usually wins. The overall success rate is 72 per cent and the typical 'Yes' share is 60 per cent. The frequency of success suggests a deep endogeneity: measures tend to be proposed because the agenda setter believes that success is likely; in contrary cases, measures are held back. Some measures lose, of course, but many of these are exceptions that prove the rule.

Critically, the identity of the agenda setter is always clear, at least superficially. In the absence of initiatives, the first mover is always a government, more to the point, a party in power in a strongly majoritarian Westminster system. Whatever other interests are in play on the 'Yes' side, one interest will always be the governing party's chances of electoral success. Often that interest aligns the party with a broad mass of opinion; it is the current winner, after all. Under those circumstances, why not just legislate in Parliament? The point may be to make clear to the eventual loser that the weight of opinion against it was truly massive, especially when the target is also vital for the party's finances. Early liquor votes were clearly like this. A related motive might be to split the opposition party or trap it in an unpopular position. The 1991 referrals in BC were like this. The Social Credit government was bruised by its willingness to support the Meech Lake Accord and was struggling for other reasons. It saw in the referendum questions a way to placate populist resentment, to signal that it would not proceed any further on the constitutional front without consulting the people, and – perhaps most importantly – to force the opposition New Democratic Party to confess aloud its traditional hostility to populist devices.[14]

The measures that win by narrow margins or that lose outright often exemplify other partisan objectives. Sometimes the government senses that a strident interest is overreaching. A referendum can call the interest's bluff, so to speak, such that what appears as defeat is in fact a political victory for the government. Transitional alcohol votes tended to be like this. Sometimes, a call for referendum, even where victory is uncertain, can deprive the other side of the political initiative. Sometimes the referendum can externalize conflict *within* the governing party. In this case, the outcome may not matter all; the critical thing is the vote itself.

Money is probably important in the Canadian case. There are certainly some anecdotal claims that money has determined the result. Recent video lottery votes may be a case in point (Belkhodja, no date). For all that, the distinctive thing about Canada is the identity of the agenda setter: it is almost always crystal clear, even if other interests are also suspected to be in play. In one sense, this is reassuring. Gerber and Lupia (1995) argue persuasively that the strongest aid to voters in locating a ballot measure is clarity about the agenda setter. Gerber and Lupia happen to put their argument in the context of initiatives, but it also applies to referendums. So the clarity of the Canadian case is a good thing. On the other hand, Canadian agenda setters have few rivals for that role, and they exercise this particular agenda power in a system that gives them similar power over almost everything else.

Notes

1. The count is based on skimming the sources listed in the references, supplemented by opportunistic trolling of the World Wide Web. Some votes have been arbitrarily excluded or combined. Notably, I treat the 1992 referendum on the Charlottetown Accord as a single vote, although strictly speaking Quebec and the rest of Canada conducted two separate referendums in parallel. I completely discard the multiple-question 2002 vote in British Columbia, as many of the questions were designedly vague – rather like a push poll – and the whole exercise lacked all the usual apparatus of elections: it was a mail-in ballot. This makes it difficult to compare with all other votes, even as it would roughly double the number of ostensible data points for BC. The three 1954 votes in Prince Edward Island are also discarded as they were mail-in votes for farmers only. Similarly excluded are votes conducted by the senior government but only in selected junior jurisdictions. The province of Nova Scotia, for instance, conducts liquor referendums for municipalities. Similarly, Alberta has conducted video gaming votes for many of its towns. Only questions that were guaranteed to yield a majority are included; multiple-option questions, such as Newfoundland's first vote on Confederation, are thus excluded.
2. The two BC referendums actually conducted in the 1990s preceded the enactment of the relevant legislation, hence the lack of shading for that province in that decade.
3. Secession, sort of. The question in each secession referendum, 1980 and 1995 referred to 'Sovereignty-Association', a formula designed to reassure 'soft nationalist' voters who doubted the wisdom of a complete break. Opposition forces, led by the federal government, insisted that voters understand the question as about secession.
4. Quebec's idea for umbrella committees, one for each side, originated, apparently, with the British example in the 1975 referendum on continued adhesion to the European Union (Dunsmuir 1992: 34ff).
5. This comment in the compendium is placed by s. 93(2) of the BC Act, which refers to participants who have not been authorized as interveners on either side, but in effect also guts the restrictions on authorized groups. The ruling was based on the guarantee of political rights in the Canadian Charter of Rights and Freedoms. It might have implications for regulation in other jurisdictions or it could be overturned on appeal. No appeal has been forthcoming, however, so the BC legislation remains voided even as similar rules elsewhere stand.
6. See also Magleby (1994: fn 23: 225).
7. The regulation also made two one-time changes: in the threshold for binding success, from 50 per cent +1 to 60 per cent +1; and required that the vote achieve simple majority status in 60 per cent of the electoral districts. The 'Yes' side captured 57 per cent of the province-wide vote and carried all but two constituencies.
8. STV was the proposal framed by a Citizens' Assembly called by the provincial government and comprising a quite random sample of registered voters. The appeal of STV to the Assembly delegates was that it promised to expand citizens' choice even as it cut through party control of the electoral agenda.

Officially, no party dared oppose the measure publicly but it is pretty clear that political elites were appalled.

9. Even some of the votes necessarily classified as broad in support and narrow in opposition were disingenuous, as the governments posing the question typically wanted to lose the vote. Not all succeeded on the first try.

10. The PEI electoral system referendum is classified differently from the BC one in the same year because the interests engaged in PEI truly were conceptual. The choice was between FPTP (the status quo) and MMP, both systems that are party-controlled. This confined the issue to majoritarianism versus proportionality, for which sociology gives no clues as to interest in PEI. In BC, the presentation of STV as the particular form of proportionality opened up anti-party sentiment as a dimension of choice.

11. The extreme case is the 1913 PEI vote on whether or not automobiles should be permitted on the island. The results of the vote were suppressed, but it is universally assumed that the result was a strong negative and I have coded it accordingly. The government was resolved to bow to the inevitable and permit motor cars on Island roads.

12. Roughly speaking, Canadian ballot measures have migrated upwards in Table 3.3, and it is natural to ask if all that is captured in the table is a positive relationship between electoral censoriousness and time. Entering time into the estimations does not materially affect the coefficients, and so the effect seems intrinsic to the type of question.

13. Another potentially important fact about Canadian financial regulation is that all reporting of donations is after the fact. Thus, the financial backing of each side cannot be used by voters to infer the issues at stake. I do not think that this critical, however, because of the logic outlined in the next section.

14. As it happened, the NDP dodged the bullet, although it did reveal its hand later: when the time came to turn the results of the referendum into law, the now governing NDP wrote the stringent qualification and finance rules described earlier in this chapter.

Sources of referendum data

British Columbia. Elections BC. *Electoral History of British Columbia*. www.elections .bc.ca/elections/electoral_history/part1–23.html.

British Columbia. Elections BC. *Final Referendum Results* Government of BC (2005). Available from www.elections.bc.ca/elections/ge2005/finalrefresults.htm.

British Columbia. Legislative Assembly (1990) *Official Report of Debates (Hansard)*. Tuesday 24 July. http://www.leg.bc.ca/hansard/34th4th/34p_04s_900724p.htm #11394.

Boyce, C.D. (1923) 'Prohibition in Canada', *Annals of the American Academy of Political and Social Science*, **109**: 225–9.

Boyer, P. (1992) *Direct Democracy in Canada: The History and Future of Referendums* (Toronto: Dundurn).

Canada. Elections Canada (1992) *Referendum 92: Official Voting Results* (Ottawa: Office of the Chief Electoral Officer of Canada).

Mayo, H.B. (1949) 'Newfoundland's Entry into the Dominion', *Canadian Journal of Economics and Political Science*, **15**: 505–22.

Mowrey, T. and A. Pelletier (2005) *Referendums in Canada: A Comparative Overview* (Ottawa: Elections Canada).

New Brunswick. Chief Electoral Officer. *2001 Provincial Referendum Unofficial Results*. www.gnb.ca/elections/01mun/01refresult-e.asp.

Prince Edward Island. Elections Prince Edward Island (2001) *History of Prince Edward Island Plebiscites* (Charlottetown: Government of PEI).

Quebec. Directeur général des Élections. *Referendums au Québec* (Québec: Gouvernement du Québec) www.electionsquebec.qc.ca/fr/tableaux/Referendums_Quebec_8484.asp.

Spence, B.H. (1923) 'Prohibitory Legislation in Canada', *Annals of the American Academy of Political and Social Science*, **109**: 230–64.

References

Banducci, S. (1998) 'Direct Legislation: When is it Used and When Does it Pass?', in S. Bowler, S., T. Donovan and C.J. Tolbert (eds), *Citizens as Legislators: Direct Democracy in the United States* (Columbus, OH: Ohio State University Press).

Belkhodja, C. (no date) 'The Referendum Experience in New Brunswick'. Moncton, NB: Université de Moncton, unpublished manuscript.

Canada. Elections Canada (2003) *Compendium of Electoral Administration in Canada* (Ottawa: Queen's Printer).

Donovan, T., S. Bowler, D. McCuan and K. Fernandez (1998) 'Contending Players and Strategies: Opposition Advantages in Initiative Campaigns', in S. Bowler, T. Donovan and C.J. Tolbert (eds), *Citizens as Legislators: Direct Democracy in the United States* (Columbus, OH: Ohio State University Press).

Dunsmuir, M. (1992) *Referendums: The Canadian Experience in an International Context* (Ottawa: Parliamentary Research Branch of Library of Parliament, Law and Government Division).

Gerber, E.R. (1999) *The Populist Paradox: Interest Group Influence and the Promise of Direct Legislation* (Princeton, NJ: Princeton University Press).

Gerber, E.R. and A. Lupia (1995) 'Campaign Competition and Policy Responsiveness in Direct Legislation Elections', *Political Behavior*, **17**: 287–306.

Johnston, R. (1993) 'The Inverted Logroll: The Charlottetown Accord and the Referendum', *PS: Political Science and Politics*, **26**: 43–8.

Johnston, R., A. Blais, E. Gidengil and N. Nevitte (1996) *The Challenge of Direct Democracy: The 1992 Canadian Referendum* (Montreal: McGill-Queen's University Press).

Magleby, D.B. (1994) 'Direct Legislation in the American States', in D. Butler and A. Ranney (eds), *Referendums Around the World: The Growing Use of Direct Democracy* (Washington, DC: The AEI Press).

Quebec. Directeur Général des Élections (2001) *Instruments of Direct Democracy* (Quebec: Gouvernement du Quebec).

Tolbert, C.J., D.H. Lowenstein and T. Donovan (1998) 'Election Laws and Rules for Using Initiatives', in S. Bowler, T. Donovan and C.J. Tolbert (eds), *Citizens as Legislators: Direct Democracy in the United States* (Columbus, Ohio: Ohio State University Press).

4
US States

Daniel A. Smith

Of the three mechanisms of direct democracy – the initiative, the popular referendum, and the recall – the initiative is by far the most widely used form of direct democracy in the American states. Two dozen, mostly western American states currently permit their citizens to serve as Election Day lawmakers. With the initiative process, citizens participate directly in the making of public policy by drafting either statutory or constitutional amendments and collecting a specified number of valid signatures to qualify a measure for the ballot; fellow citizens then adopt or reject the initiative. More so than the popular referendum, which allows citizens to challenge state laws, the initiative is the most important mechanism of direct democracy in the United States, as virtually any public policy or governance issue may be addressed via the plebiscitary process.

This chapter focuses specifically on the campaign financing of ballot initiatives in the American states. Section 4.1 provides a brief historical backdrop covering the adoption and usage of the initiative in the American states. Section 4.2 examines state regulations and the precedent-setting legal decisions that have shaped the campaign financing of ballot initiatives. While some states have tried to regulate the financial contributions and expenditures of groups promoting and opposing initiatives, restrictions on the financing of ballot measures have been sharply curtailed by the federal courts. As a result, the financing of ballot initiatives operates in a relatively *laissez-faire* setting. Finally, in section 4.3, I assess the scholarly literature on the effect that money has on the outcome of ballot initiatives. While campaign financing does influence the success of ballot initiatives in the American states, contingencies abound.

4.1 Background and history of ballot initiatives in the American states

Imported from Switzerland in the late nineteenth century, the idea of direct democracy first became popular in the American states during the Populist movement (Goebel, 2002; Piott, 2003). Although the adoption of the initiative is generally understood as a phenomenon uniquely rooted in the Western region of the United States, inter-party legislative party competition and the relative weakness of state party organizations were two major factors in the initial decision of many state legislatures during the Progressive Era to devolve institutional power to citizens in the form of the initiative (Smith and Fridkin, 2008). In 1898, the citizens of South Dakota were the first in the Union to adopt the initiative, and in 1904 citizens in Oregon were the first to collect signatures and successfully qualify initiatives for the ballot. As Table 4.1 reveals, most of the 24 states that have adopted the initiative did so over a two-decade period (Smith and Tolbert, 2004). Between 1898 and 1918, voters in 20 states – through legislative referendums or the ratification of new constitutions – added the initiative to their constitutions (Smith and Fridkin, 2008). The contagion of adoption, as well as most of the early usage of the initiative, occurred west of the Mississippi River, although the impetus for reform was felt across the country.

In many of those states that make use of the initiative, citizens routinely expect to vote on an array of statutory or constitutional measures that have been petitioned on the ballot. Soon after its adoption in the early 1900s, for example, populists and progressive activists used ballot initiatives to call for numerous social justice reforms, including women's suffrage, the direct primary, the direct election of US Senators, the abolition of the poll tax, home rule for cities and towns, eight-hour working days for women and miners, and the regulation of public utility and railroad monopolies. But the expression of *vox populi* has not always been synonymous with a progressive vision as advanced by the earliest advocates of direct democracy. Even during the Progressive Era many corporate interests – from railroads to public utilities to mining operators to fishermen to ranchers to newspaper owners to morticians – tried to use the initiative to advance their narrow economic agendas (Ellis, 2002; Smith and Lubinski, 2002).

Today, ballot initiatives in the American states continue to reflect a rich mix of progressive and conservative issues. Recently, voters have passed progressive statewide ballot initiatives boosting the minimum wage, requiring utilities to invest in renewable energy, providing public dollars

Table 4.1 Adoption of the initiative in the American states

State	Year adopted
South Dakota	1898
Utah	1900
Oregon	1902
Montana	1906
Oklahoma	1907
Maine	1908
Michigan	1908
Missouri	1908
Arkansas	1910
Colorado	1910
Arizona	1911
California	1911
Idaho	1912
Nebraska	1912
Nevada	1912
Ohio	1912
Washington	1912
North Dakota	1914
Mississippi	1915[a]
Massachusetts	1918
Alaska	1959
Florida	1968
Wyoming	1968
Illinois	1970

[a] Overturned in 1922 by the state Supreme Court; re-adopted in 1992.

Source: Table adapted from Smith and Tolbert (2004).

for embryonic stem cell research, mandating environmental cleanups, financing candidate campaigns with public funds, creating nonpartisan electoral redistricting commissions and fusion voting, providing dedicated revenue streams for public education and class-size reduction, increasing land-use conservation and animal protection, legalizing medical marijuana, allowing euthanasia, and taxing tobacco for health education programmes. Many of these same voters, however, have also supported an array of conservative ballot measures, including bans on same-sex marriage, tax cuts and limits on governmental spending, private school vouchers, caps on medical malpractice lawsuits, prohibitions on affirmative action, the elimination of welfare benefits for illegal immigrants and their children, abortion restrictions, and English-only requirements. Some measures are highly controversial and hotly contested; others are barely noticed by the media and the voting public. Whatever their salience, though, ballot measures know no ideological bounds. And the success of measures depends solely on the majority sentiments of those turning out to vote (Matsusaka, 2004).

Institutionally, substantial procedural differences exist among the states when it comes to qualifying measures on the ballot (Bowler and Donovan, 2004). In practice, the initiative is quite different in California than it is in Massachusetts and all the states in between. State laws regulating the initiative process differ significantly with respect to how the ballot title and ballot language is set, how signature gathering may be conducted and whether petitioners must meet a geographical distribution of signatures, how stringent single-subject laws are enforced by the courts, and how direct the process is (as some states have an indirect initiative process, whereby the state legislature may intervene before the qualified initiative is submitted to citizens for a vote). Several states allow ballot measures to be offered during special, primary, and odd-year elections (Waters, 2003; Tolbert, Lowenstein and Donovan, 1998). Although campaign finance disclosure laws also vary across the states, what is not regulated is the unlimited sum of money that proponents and opponents may raise and spend on ballot issue campaigns.

Since the 1970s, the number of statewide initiatives on ballot has increased dramatically. In 2006, voters in 37 states faced 73 initiatives and five popular referendums on their ballots, 14 more initiatives than were on statewide ballots in 2004. In 2008, voters in the 24 initiative states considered more than 60 initiatives placed on the ballot by issue committees working outside of the traditional legislative process. Coloradoans voted on 14 initiatives in 2008, the most measures on a statewide ballot since 1912, when voters considered 20 initiatives as well as six popular referendums and six legislative referendums (Smith and Lubinski, 2002). In 2006, Arizona and Oregon led the pack, each with 10 initiatives on their November statewide ballots; several states – including California, Colorado, Nevada, and South Dakota – had at least six statewide initiatives on their ballots.

A century ago, as states initially adopted the process, the number of initiatives on statewide ballots increased rapidly during the 1910s, but they tapered off after the First World War. Use of the process regained popularity again in the 1970s, especially with the passage of Proposition 13, California's historic 1978 property tax limitation initiative (Magleby, 1984; Cronin, 1989; Tolbert, 2003; Smith, 1998). During

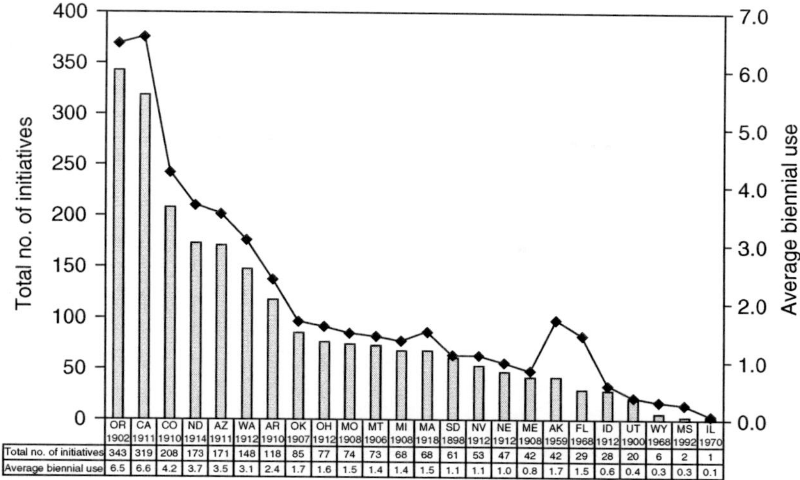

	OR	CA	CO	ND	AZ	WA	AR	OK	OH	MO	MT	MI	MA	SD	NV	NE	ME	AK	FL	ID	UT	WY	MS	IL
	1902	1911	1910	1914	1911	1912	1910	1907	1912	1908	1906	1908	1918	1898	1912	1912	1908	1959	1968	1912	1900	1968	1992	1970
Total no. of initiatives	343	319	208	173	171	148	118	85	77	74	73	68	68	61	53	47	42	42	29	28	20	6	2	1
Average biennial use	6.5	6.6	4.2	3.7	3.5	3.1	2.4	1.7	1.6	1.5	1.4	1.4	1.5	1.1	1.1	1.0	0.8	1.7	1.5	0.6	0.4	0.3	0.3	0.1

Figure 4.1   Historical statewide initiative use, year of adoption through 2008

the 1990s, an average of more than 60 initiatives nationwide appeared on statewide ballots in a given general election. Indeed, the number of statewide initiatives on the ballot across the nation during the 1990s surpassed all other decades, even the previous high which was set during the 1910s. As Figure 4.1 reveals, some states have historically used the process much more than others. Oregon leads the pack, with more than 340 statewide initiatives on the ballot since it adopted the process in 1902, but California is close on its heels with nearly 320 statewide initiatives on the ballot since 1912. Historically, the two states have averaged over six statewide initiatives on the ballot every two years. During the 1990s alone, voters in the two Pacific coast states each cast ballots on more than 60 initiatives.

When reformers advanced the devices of direct democracy in the United States more than a century ago, one of their shared goals – in addition to promoting their educative value – was to limit, if not eliminate altogether, the corrosive effect of corporate money on the legislative process (Smith and Tolbert, 2004). Direct democracy reformers argued that by empowering ordinary citizens to participate in the making of public policy via the initiative, 'the people' would be able to circumvent state legislatures that were controlled by political bosses and entrenched special interests. Acting as election-day legislators, citizens could approve ballot measures and reclaim the right of 'government by the people'. By devolving policy-making decisions directly to the people, the leading proponents of the process thought they could break the political stranglehold on state legislatures by party bosses and vested special interests (Schmidt, 1989; Goebel, 2002; Piott, 2003; Smith and Tolbert, 2004).

Yet far from eliminating money from the political process as early advocates of direct democracy reforms had hoped, money has played a central role in initiative campaigns in the American states for over a century (Allswang, 2000; Crouch, 1950; McCuan et al., 1998; Smith, 1998; Ellis, 2002; Smith and Lubinski, 2002). Critics of direct democracy, especially lawmakers, often argue that the process has spun out of control, with economic interests, rather than ordinary citizens and elected officials, having too much power to shape legislation and tinker with state constitutions (Broder, 2000; Ellis, 2002; Schrag, 1998). As was the case a century ago, ballot measures are susceptible to the same kind of financial pressures present in the legislative process (Goebel, 2002; Smith and Lubinski, 2002). As political scientist John Shockley (1985: 427–8) observed, 'As long as wealth is as unequally distributed as it is in American society, and political interest groups are organized around private rather than public rewards, ballot proposition campaigns, like American politics generally, will reflect the power of the best organized and wealthiest groups in society.' Reflecting on the past century, it becomes fairly clear that the initiative process in the American states has not been any more immune from the influence of money than our representative system of government. As documented in section 4.3, however, this is not to say that money can necessarily 'buy' success at the ballot box. Citizen interests can use the process to advance their causes and successfully triumph over economic interests (Gerber, 1999). Nevertheless, economic interests are able to set the agenda of initiative campaigns and often use the process to (re)assert their privileged position (Smith, 1998; Garrett, 1999; Garrett and Gerber, 2001; Smith, 2004).

Unlike federal and many state candidate elections in the United States, statewide ballot measures have virtually no campaign finance limitations. As such, there is a tremendous amount of unregulated money flowing in and out of many ballot issue committees. In 1998, ballot issue committees in 44 states spent nearly $400 million promoting and opposing initiatives and legislative referendums (Smith, 2001a). In comparison, the national Republican and Democratic parties raised *only* $193 million in 'soft money' during the 1997–98 election cycle, with congressional committees raising another $92 million in soft money contributions. Spending on ballot measures by economic interests is much more significant than what is annually spent lobbying state legislatures. In California, for example, in 1976 interest groups lobbying the state legislature spent $20 million, double the amount spent on ballot measures. Just twelve years later, ballot issue committees expended nearly $130 million on ballot measures, a third more than the total amount spent on lobbying in the state in 1988 (California Commission, 1992: 264).

The amount of money spent on ballot initiative campaigns continues to increase. In the 2004 general election, more than $398 million was spent on 59 initiatives on the ballots of 18 states. The total set a new national record for the most ever spent on initiatives in a single election. The most expensive initiative in 2004 was California's Proposition 68, which was placed on the ballot by a coalition of 14 casino and racetrack owners trying to expand their operations in the state and force American Indian tribes to renegotiate their tribal gaming compact with the state. Proponents of Proposition 68 spent $25.4 million to qualify and promote the measure; 99 per cent of the total contributions came from 14 gaming-related interests. A coalition of Indian tribes opposed the constitutional amendment, spending $47.4 million to defeat the measure (Smith, 2006b). But in 2006, issue committees once again broke the record for expenditures on statewide ballot measures. Proponents and opponents in 18 states spent over $524 million on 73 initiatives on the November ballot. The $524 million easily surpassed the previous high-water mark set in 2004. Expenditures in California accounted for nearly 60 per cent of total spending in 2006; issue committees spent more than $300 million on eight initiatives in the November election, which was six times more than that spent in the next highest state.

Vast expenditures on ballot initiatives are not limited to general elections. In 2005, ballot issue committees in California spent more than $200 million on ballot initiatives in a special election called by Governor Arnold Schwarzenegger. PhARMA, the national association of pharmaceutical corporations, spent nearly $80 million to defeat a single ballot initiative (Proposition 79), which was backed by labour unions and consumer organizations and would have required companies to provide steep discounts on prescription drugs or not be allowed to participate in the state's Medicaid programme. In a blatant effort to confuse the voters, PhARMA advanced its own counter-initiative, Proposition 78. Pharmaceutical companies spent over $50 million on television ads alone. Four firms (Pfizer, Johnson and Johnson, Merck and GlaxoSmithKline) each contributed nearly $10 million in the effort, with several other companies anteing nearly $5 million apiece. The consumer groups and union-backed proponents of Proposition 79 spent less than $1 million in advancing their failed effort. As we shall see in the final section, big money has always been part of the initiative process in the American states.

4.2 Financial regulations

Decisions by the US Supreme Court have shaped the terrain of state campaign finance laws not only for candidate elections, but also for ballot measure campaigns. Both federal and state courts in the United States have been generally unsympathetic towards the notion that money can have a corrosive effect on the initiative process. As with the financing of candidate elections, the courts have played a major role in defining the parameters of the campaign finance regulation of ballot measures. While many states have made significant inroads in campaign finance reform with regard to candidates, the same cannot be said for the regulation of campaign contributions and expenditures on ballot measures.

With the exception of disclosure (Garrett and Smith, 2005), the federal courts have struck down a series of state campaign finance regulations of ballot measure campaign contributions or expenditures. In general, the courts have found there to be a fundamental conflict between First Amendment rights and restrictions on the contributions and expenditures of ballot measures, as the courts have essentially equated the campaign financing of ballot measures with 'speech', rather than 'conduct'. In its 1976 landmark decision *Buckley* v. *Valeo*, the US Supreme Court extended substantial First Amendment protections to spending in candidate campaigns, reasoning that this form of 'speech' should be afforded the highest level of protection. In *Buckley*, the Court outlined its views on campaign finance reform legislation in the context of candidate campaigns, striking down as unconstitutional portions of the 1974 Federal Election Campaign Act (FECA) that limited expenditures by candidates and independent campaign expenditures on behalf of candidates. The court argued that limits on expenditures could not be justified as a method of preventing 'corruption or the appearance of corruption'. The Court found no danger of *quid pro quo* corruption when individuals made independent expenditures on behalf of candidates because the absence of pre-arrangement or coordination with the candidate's campaign reduced the value of such expenditures to the candidate and the danger that such expenditures would be given for improper commitments from the candidate. The Court also found that limiting expenditures by the candidate could not be justified by the danger of corruption because such concerns were adequately addressed by the contribution limitations (Smith, 2001a).

Two years after *Buckley*, in its decision *First National Bank of Boston* v. *Bellotti*, the Court ruled specifically against campaign finance restrictions in ballot measure campaigns. In *Bellotti*, the Court considered a Massachusetts state statute banning contributions and expenditures by corporations in initiative or referendum campaigns unless the issue materially affected the corporation's business. The statute further specified that no question concerning an income tax could be deemed to materially affect the business of a corporation. Corporate plaintiffs challenged the statute as a violation of their First Amendment right to make expenditures to defeat a ballot measure. The Court struck down the statute by extending First Amendment protection for the expenditure of funds by a corporation and by rejecting the state's assertion of legitimate interests in preventing corruption and protecting the interests of shareholders (Smith, 2001a).

Although the high court found expenditure limitations in ballot campaigns to be unconstitutional in *Bellotti*, it did not address the question of whether limits on contributions to ballot campaigns might also be unconstitutional. The court addressed this question in 1981 in its ruling, *Citizens Against Rent Control* v. *City of Berkeley (CARC)*. The Court found that a local ordinance limiting contributions to ballot campaigns was unconstitutional. Relying on *Bellotti*, the Court in *CARC* concluded that the state had no interest in preventing corruption in a ballot campaign since no danger of corruption existed in the setting of an initiative or referendum campaign. Winkler (1998) argues that the *Bellotti* Court may not have been serious when it claimed that evidence of corporate influence might justify a state's contribution limitation for ballot measures and that the findings of studies analyzing the effects of spending may not support restrictions on spending. In any event, the possibility of sustaining campaign finance reform legislation in the ballot measure context appeared bleak after *Bellotti*.

The series of decisions by the high court clearly separated candidate campaigns from ballot measure campaigns with regard to the regulation of campaign finance (Lowenstein, 1992; Briffault, 1996). In *Bellotti*, the Court had removed other possible justifications for regulations of ballot measures, such as a state's interest in equality and protecting shareholders (Tolbert et al., 1998). In *CARC*, the Court made the further distinction that contribution limitations could be allowed in the context of candidate campaigns, but not allowed in ballot measure campaigns, as the perceived danger of potential or actual *quid pro quo* corruption could occur in candidate campaigns, but not in ballot measure campaigns. As such, *quid pro quo* corruption has seemed to be the only state interest 'compelling' enough to justify a limitation on campaign finances in ballot campaigns (Garrison, 1989). Yet a few legal scholars have argued that the *Bellotti* and *CARC* decisions may have left open the slight possibility that contribution and expenditure limitations could be regulated by a state interest (Winkler, 1998). In particular, four recent Supreme Court decisions dealing with the financing of candidate elections – what Hasen (2004, 2005) calls the 'New Deference Quartet' – have seemingly reduced the amount of evidence needed to defend campaign finance laws, accepted an equality rationale, and limited the level of corporate and union involvement in campaigns.

Despite this tempered optimism, at present no state has placed limits on campaign contributions or expenditures for ballot initiative campaigns. This was not always the case. At one time in the not too distant past, roughly half of the 24 states that permit the process had some regulations on ballot campaign finances (Shockley, 1980). Indeed, citizens have been more than willing when given the opportunity to impose campaign finance regulations on the initiative process. Following the Watergate crisis, for instance, voters in California overwhelmingly approved Proposition 9 in 1974, the Political Reform Act. The ballot initiative called for strict spending limits to be placed on ballot initiatives. Proponents and opponents were each limited to $1.2 million in spending per ballot measure, and they were also prohibited from spending $500,000 more than the other side. The act was short-lived, however. Following the lead of the United States Supreme Court's *Buckley* decision, the California Supreme Court struck down the PRA as unconstitutional (California Commission, 1992). Voters in November 2006 were afforded yet another chance to regulate ballot measures when they cast their lot on Proposition 89. The measure, which ended up receiving only 26 per cent of the vote, would have placed restrictions on contributions to statewide ballot measures if a statewide candidate was involved with a committee supporting or opposing a ballot measure; individuals, corporations, and other select groups would have been restricted to donating no more than $10,000 to that committee. In addition, the measure would have prohibited corporations from donating to a ballot issue committee or spending more than $10,000 in support or opposition of a ballot measure, although some non-profit corporations would have been exempt from the restriction (Moran, 2006).

California is not the only state that has made recent attempts to reintroduce regulations on the campaign financing of ballot measures. In 1996 Montana voters passed a statutory initiative banning corporate contributions to ballot measure campaigns. The measure, Initiative 125, was not the state's first ban on corporate spending on ballot initiatives in Montana. In 1975, the legislature had amended a statute that had been on the books since 1912 prohibiting corporate spending in candidate elections, and extended the ban to state ballot campaigns (Winkler, 1998). The 1975 statute, however, was found to be unconstitutional the following year in the Federal District Court. The 1996 ballot measure, sponsored by the Montana Public Interest Research Group, called for the strictest statewide campaign finance laws concerning ballot measures in the country. The measure stipulated that corporations could not make contributions or expenditures in connection with ballot measures, but included a provision exempting nonprofit corporations formed for the purpose of promoting political ideas that did not engage in business, did not have shareholders, and did not accept a substantial amount of contributions from business corporations. The statute added a provision allowing corporations to fund political speech through a segregated fund consisting only of voluntary contributions. Immediately following the passage of I-125, the Montana Chamber of Commerce, the Montana Mining Association, and several other business associations successfully challenged the measure in the Federal District Court. The lower court's decision, *Montana Chamber of Commerce* v. *Argenbright*, was upheld by the 9th Circuit Court of Appeals. As with the effort in Montana, state laws trying to rein in campaign financing of ballot measures have been struck down as unconstitutional by the federal courts.

In terms of regulations on the campaign financing of ballot measures, then, disclosure is virtually all that remains, although the standards vary considerably across the states. Despite numerous legal challenges, the federal courts have consistently found state statutes requiring the disclosure of contributions and expenditures in ballot campaigns to be a compelling state interest (Garrett and Smith, 2005). In *Bellotti*, as part of its dictum, the Court noted that states could require public disclosure of ballot issue financing to allow citizens to better assess the arguments for and against the measures. In *CARC*, the Court similarly reasoned that the integrity of the political system would be sufficiently protected through the public filing of campaign contributions. Following the court's lead – that disclosure is permissible, perhaps even necessary – all states that permit the initiative require the mandatory disclosure of ballot measure contributions and expenditures. The detail, immediacy, and public availability of these disclosure regimes, however, vary considerably across the states. Several states, including Colorado, Florida, Oregon, and Washington, require regular reporting of financial activities by ballot issue committees; other states (including Michigan, Nevada,

North Dakota, Ohio, and South Dakota), however, do not require proponents and opponents of ballot measures to file disclosure reports until just prior to an election, making it nearly impossible for their campaign finance activities to be disseminated to the public. Although a handful of states (most notably Arizona, California, Massachusetts, and Washington) require electronic filing of campaign finance activities, several states (including Arkansas, Montana, Oklahoma, and Wyoming) do not require issue committees to electronically file their disclosure forms, slowing both the timeliness and accessibility of campaign finance information. As a result of the patchwork of disclosure requirements, 'Veiled Political Actors' are often able to obfuscate their contributions and expenditures in ballot measure campaigns (Garrett and Smith, 2005).

4.3 Effects of money and financial regulations

While there is undeniably a great deal of money involved in the initiative process, the empirical evidence amassed by scholars assessing whether or not campaign contributions and expenditures in ballot initiative campaigns affect their outcomes is mixed. Much of the research suggests that disproportionate campaign spending by opponents is effective in defeating ballot measures, but that it is not as effective in passing them. As such, money is a necessary, if not sufficient condition in ballot measure contests. Other scholars, though, suggest that ballot measure contributions and expenditures may have a more symmetric impact on the outcomes of ballot measures.

Few scholars have tried to assess the impact of campaign finance on ballot measure outcomes in early initiative campaigns. There is good reason for this, as public records of campaign contributions and expenditures made by ballot committees are either incomplete or never existed in the first place. In most states, no formal records were kept by state agencies on campaign contributions and expenditures until the second half of the twentieth century. In California, although full disclosure of campaign receipts and expenditures for every candidate and ballot committee were required after the passage of the Purity of Elections Act in 1907, the 'financial statement [was] only partly enforced' by the Secretary of State, making the California campaign disclosure law 'hopelessly inadequate' and 'wholly incomplete' (Crouch and McHenry, 1949: 63–4). In 1923, the state tightened its disclosure law by requiring any group receiving or spending more than $1,000 on a ballot measure to file with the Secretary of State, but frequently no reports were filled out, even though ads on billboards and newspapers were ubiquitous (Crouch and McHenry, 1949).

Research on initiative campaign contributions and expenditures conducted contemporaneously by scholars during the first decades of the twentieth century is scant, but it does reveal that campaign financing of some ballot measures may have had an impact on whether measures passed or failed. In South Dakota in 1910, for example, 11 out of 12 ballot propositions were rejected by the voters. The defeat of the measures – which included a popular referendum invoked by the railroads to overturn a law requiring electric headlights for locomotives and a referendum regulating embalmers – was directly attributable to the 'activity of certain parties, especially interested in the defeat of one or two propositions, who filled the newspapers with advertisements and plastered the fences with billboards advising the electors to "Vote No"' (Beard and Schultz 1912: 49). Additionally, substantial expenditures were made by rival fishing interests in Oregon during the months leading up to the June 1908 election. Upstream and downstream fisherman each placed initiatives on the ballot to eradicate the other's right to fish for salmon on the Columbia River; voters passed both measures (Cushman, 1916; Eaton, 1912; Bowler and Donovan, 1998). In Colorado, as in other states, official records of early ballot campaigns are in short supply. The City Club of Denver (1927), which assessed the initiative and referendum process, reported that the cost to groups submitting initiatives was 'impossible to ascertain'. During the 1920s, legal talent was employed to draft petitions, solicitors were being paid to circulate petitions, and 'substantial' campaign funds were collected and disbursed for and against measures. In 1926, for example, proponents paid circulators upwards of 3 cents per name, and a 'flat sum of $1,000' was paid to one circulator by a group of proponents to secure their petition on the ballot. During the 1920s, $15,000 was spent by 'friends' of a ballot measure, and $9,000 by those who opposed it; the measure passed (Smith, 2001a).

From the very first statewide initiative placed on the ballot in those states permitting the process, economic interests used the initiative to advance their vested interests (Beard and Schultz, 1912; Barnett, 1915). A California state Senate committee in the 1920s unearthed the 'startlingly large expenditures in [ballot initiative] campaigns' (McCuan et al., 1998: 57), reporting that more than $1 million was spent on seven measures on the 1922 ballot. In one ballot campaign alone – the Pacific Gas and Electric Company's successful effort to defeat the Water and Power Act – proponents and opponents combined to spend over $660,000. The initiative became more centralized and capital-intensive in the 1930s in California (Key, 1936; Crouch and McHenry, 1949; Kelley, 1956; McCuan et al., 1998). At the forefront of the industrialization of the initiative process was the husband and wife team, Clem Whitaker and Leone Baxter. This savvy public relations couple joined forces in 1933 to promote candidates as well as ballot initiatives. They pioneered numerous campaign techniques in California, including direct mail solicitation, television ads, 'building public attitudes', and the use of 'gimmicks', all of which drove up the costs of ballot campaigns (Kelley, 1956; Smith, 1999). It was even common for Whitaker & Baxter's Campaigns, Inc. to run five or six ballot campaigns every election (McCuan et al., 1998). By 1936, over $1.2 million was spent by proponents and opponents who were fighting over a ballot measure taxing chain stores, and nearly $1 million was spent by groups battling for and against an initiative on a retirement life payment proposal (Crouch, 1950). During the 1940s and 1950s, the campaign financing of initiative and referenda campaigns would often cost millions of dollars (Heard, 1960), with the payment of circulators to qualify an initiative costing close to $65,000 (Crouch, 1950). In 1956, Whitaker and Baxter represented four of the wealthiest corporations in California – Pacific Telegraph and Telephone, Standard Oil, Pacific Gas and Electric, and Southern Pacific Railroad – all of whom joined together to fight an oil conservation initiative, Proposition Four. Despite a war chest of $3.45 million, which was more than double the $1.42 million spent by the proponents, Whitaker and Baxter suffered a rare defeat (Pritchell, 1958). Typically, though, during the first half of the century in California, scholars typically found 'the old adage of politics that "the side that spends the most wins" has been proven true' (Crouch 1950: 32).

Scholars, however, have failed to reach a consensus about whether spending on ballot measure campaigns has a definitive effect upon outcomes. One reason for the lack of scholarly consensus on this question is due to the tremendous variation among the 24 states that permit the initiative. It seems unrealistic, perhaps, to expect that ballot issue campaign contributions and expenditures to have the same impact on such dissimilar ballot measures across such disparate states. Much of the quantitative research examining the outcomes of ballot measures either ignores or fails to control for an array of variables affecting ballot campaigns.

In the late 1970s, scholars began to more systematically accumulate and analyze data on the effects of ballot issue expenditures (Lee, 1979; Lowenstein, 1982; Shockley, 1980, 1983, 1985). Their studies generally concluded that one-sided spending had little impact when done in support of a measure, but was almost always successful in defeating a ballot measure. Support for the asymmetric finding – that campaign expenditures are more effective in shaping ballot outcomes when it is spent by groups *opposing* ballot measures – has been supported by several other scholars (Magleby, 1984; Zisk, 1987; Ji, 1998). Magleby (1984: 146–8) examined 51 ballot measures in California between 1954 and 1982, finding that 16 of the measures (31 per cent) were adopted by the voters. Not all of the propositions had the same likelihood of success, though. Following Lowenstein (1982), Magleby separated the measures into three categories: (1) those in which the proponents had a two-to-one spending advantage; (2) those in which the opponents had a two-to-one spending advantage; and (3) those in which neither side had a two-to-one spending advantage. Magleby found that proponents with at least a two-to-one spending advantage over their opponents won on less than half of the occasions (48 per cent). In contrast, opposition groups with a two-to-one spending advantage could 'virtually guarantee the defeat of an initiative', winning 87 per cent of the time.

In her multi-state study of 50 ballot campaigns between 1976 and 1982 in four diverse states – California, Massachusetts, Michigan, and Oregon – Zisk (1987) shows that money matters, regardless of which side spends it. In 40 of the cases (80 per cent), the high-spending side prevailed on Election Day, regardless of the amount spent by the other side, the source of the money, or the type of issue (Zisk, 1987: 92–8). With few exceptions, she also finds that public opinion may change drastically when one side outspends the other by a substantial margin. Controlling for media and elite endorsements of the measures, Zisk (1987: 98–103) demonstrates that in 17 of the 32 campaigns for which polling data were available, the initial preferences of voters shifted toward the direction of the side spending more money.

Despite these findings, a few scholars contend that campaign expenditures have little impact on ballot measure outcomes (Price, 1975; Owens and Wade, 1986; Schmidt, 1989). Owens and Wade (1986) present the most compelling argument that higher campaign expenditures do not lead to ballot success. Surveying the initiative process in California, they examine a total of 708 referendums and initiatives placed on the ballot between 1924 and 1984. Using Lowenstein's (1982) criteria for one-sided spending and a minimum $250,000 spending threshold, they analyze the success rate of 85 one-sided ballot measures (68 initiatives; 17 legislative referendums) over the 60-year period. Like Lowenstein (1982), they find that one-sided negative spending is very successful, with the opponents winning 29 out of 32 times (91 per cent). But they also report that even when opponents had less than a two-to-one spending advantage, they were able to defeat ballot measures 89 per cent of the time (17 out of the 19 measures). Owens and Wade (1986: 684–5) conclude that 'the emphasis on one-sidedness found in the leading scholarly studies ... may simply be superfluous spending in terms of electoral outcomes', as 'money has simply been overemphasized as a determinant of voting on direct legislation'.

All of these studies examining campaign expenditures and ballot measure outcomes use aggregate spending levels of the groups proposing and opposing initiatives. While convenient to analyze the total amount of money spent by initiative groups, it might not be the best measure of whether money really is a decisive factor in ballot outcomes. Aggregate spending levels do not always reflect the underlying mechanics of the initiative process. There are at least four limitations with using aggregate expenditures when explaining initiative outcomes. First, aggregate campaign expenditures fail to 'disaggregate media spending from spending on petition efforts' (Bowler and Donovan, 1998: 154). The costs to proponents in ensuring that their measures qualify for the ballot – most notably paying petitioners to collect signatures – can be substantial. Donovan et al. (1998: 97) call the difference in spending between proponents and opponents an 'asymmetry of resource deployment', since opponents do not have to bear any qualification costs. Procedurally, it costs opponents much less to 'move second'. At least 65 per cent of total expenditures by proponents can go towards qualification costs (Bowler and Donovan, 1998; Berg and Holman, 1989; Price, 1988; Smith, 2004). Secondly, an examination of aggregate expenditures tends to overlook the importance of the timing of campaign expenditures. Voters in ballot campaigns tend to 'make their decisions during the last few days of the election – precisely when media blitzes take place' (Cronin, 1989: 117). Smith and Herrington (2000) find that the timing (as well as the content) of the paid advertising by the opponents of the Parental Rights Amendment in Colorado in 1996 was crucial to the defeat of the measure. Finally, the reliance on aggregate spending data disregards non-monetary sources that may influence ballot outcomes. Cronin (1989: 113–16) notes that when the low-spending side wins it is usually because the victorious side has put together a well-organized, grassroots coalition with skillful campaign leadership who knows how to obtain free publicity. Gaining earned media coverage and elite endorsements can help to legitimate the arguments made by backers or detractors of ballot measures and provide citizens with voting cues (Cronin, 1989; Karp,1998; Smith and Herrington, 2000; Zisk, 1987; Smith, 2004). Lupia (1994) cites this phenomenon with regard to the auto insurance industry's massive campaign expenditures on five ballot measures in 1988, which may have 'signalled' to those going to the polls to vote against the industry's preferences.

Stratmann (2006) uses much more sophisticated data and statistical methods than previous research examining the effects of spending on ballot measure outcomes. Concerned about problems of endogeneity, Stratmann uses campaign finance data from 18 ballot measures in California to isolate the spending on television ads in five major media markets by proponents and opponents. Through disaggregating the total spending by proponents and opponents, he is able to omit expenditures by proponents (and opponents) during the pre-qualification phase. What he finds by looking solely at media buys is that as the level of spending by proponents on television ads increases, the likelihood of the ballot measure succeeding also increases. He also finds, consistent with his earlier research, that campaign spending both for and against ballot measures affects their outcomes (Stratmann, 2005) and that the more money spent on television by opponents' ads depresses support for ballot initiatives. The substantive magnitude of the findings, however, is fairly negligible.

Instead of examining the effects of campaign expenditures on initiative campaigns, a few scholars (Gerber, 1999; Braunstein, 2004) have examined the effect that campaign contributions may have on ballot measure outcomes. Since information costs for voters can often be high for ballot measures (Lupia, 1994; Bowler and Donovan, 1998; Magleby, 1994), knowing what interests support a measure can serve as an important cue to those voters who are looking for informational shortcuts (Garrett and Smith, 2005). Knowing which groups financially support or oppose ballot measures through their contributions to issue committees may be an important source of information to voters (Bowler and Donovan, 1998; Lupia, 1994). Campaign contributions may be a very important source of information for voters. In particular, voters might have the perception that measures receiving large amounts of out-of-state money might not reflect the sentiments of the voters in the state (Cronin, 1989: 115–16; Smith and Herrington, 2000; Garrett and Smith, 2005). Of course, the question of who is behind a measure is often a tricky one to answer (Smith, 1998, 2004). Frequently, the names of the groups sponsoring or opposing an initiative can be misleading, intentionally so or otherwise.

In her study of how campaign contributions might impact upon ballot measure outcomes, Gerber (1999) offers a bifurcated typology ('citizen' and 'economic') to classify ballot measure committees depending on whether the committee obtains a majority of its funding from 'economic interests' or 'citizen interests'. She finds that ballot measures supported by citizen interests have higher passage rates, whereas those measures financed largely by economic interests have lower levels of success, although those backed by economic interests are able to block ballot initiatives. Gerber's binary typology is not without its limitations. First, measuring contributions made to ballot issue committees ignores independent expenditures made for and against ballot measures (Garrett and Smith, 2005). Second, and more problematic, the category of 'citizen' does not distinguish among contributions given by individuals, citizens' groups, and labour unions. By collapsing discrete actors under a broad classification, individual contributors – from those who contribute small amounts to millionaires – are all treated equivalently (Smith, 2004). As Gerber (1999: 93) herself acknowledges, a large portion of contributions to initiative campaigns flows from wealthy individuals who can be 'motivated as either autonomous individuals or as quasi-economic actors making contributions on behalf of their economic/ professional/ business interests'. Finally, the placement of organized labour within this category raises some concerns about the utility of the typology. Unions might just as easily be considered economic interests, as individual union members have little opportunity to voice how their dues will be spent on ballot campaigns. Furthermore, unions tend to become engaged in ballot measure campaigns either to promote their own economic well-being or to fend off threats to their economic strength.

4.4 Conclusion

Big money in ballot initiative campaigns in the American states is here to stay. For strategic reasons, ballot measures are increasingly being tied to candidate elections (Smith and Tolbert, 2004; Nicholson, 2005; Smith, 2006a; Smith, DeSantis, and Kassel, 2006; Donovan, Tolbert, and Smith, 2008). Yet it is unlikely that the United States Supreme Court will reverse course and start to uphold campaign finance regulations on either ballot measure contributions or expenditures. Because there are no limits on what groups sponsoring and opposing ballot measures can raise or spend, direct democracy will continue to attract large sums of money.

The scholarly debate over the consequences of money in ballot initiative campaigns is also not likely to be over. While the study of the impact of money on ballot measure outcomes is not conclusive, it is safe to say that ballot initiative campaigns in the American states are a far cry from what early twentieth-century social reformers had originally envisioned. Contrary to the expectations of the Populists and Progressives who saw direct democracy as a means to eradicate the dominance of interest groups in state legislatures, vested economic interests and wealthy 'populist entrepreneurs' (Smith, 1998) have embraced the initiative to advance their goals as well as protect their turf (Smith and Tolbert, 2004). Citizen groups, of course, have not been wholly displaced from the process, but without adequate financing, most ballot measures do not stand a chance of prevailing on Election Day.

Unfortunately, innovative research strategies, such as isolating ballot measure expenditures on media buys (Stratmann, 2006), mask the sizeable sums spent by proponents and opponents prior to a measure's qualification. Much of this spending is not a matter of public record, as backers of ballot initiatives can shield their efforts by channelling money through nonprofit groups that do not have to report their pre-qualification involvement. From hiring lawyers to write and consultants to run focus groups to test the language of a ballot measure, wealthy proponents are able to carefully craft ballot measures well before they begin circulating their petitions. Similarly, opponents of potential ballot measures do not have to report their expenditures when figuring out how to frame and attack issues in focus groups and public opinion surveys. Opponents are also not required to report pre-election single-subject challenges regarding the language and summary of a potential initiative, their public education efforts to dissuade citizens from signing petitions, or their efforts to challenge the validity of signatures submitted by petitioners. All of these expenditures, which can amount to millions of dollars every election cycle but are not reported, fall well below the radar screen of most political scientists studying the campaign financing of ballot measures. Yet all of these activities can have a major impact on which measures actually qualify for the ballot and how they are eventually perceived by the public.

In the future, scholars should continue to devise new research designs to examine the role of money in initiative campaigns. At a minimum, more comparative state analyses are needed. Initiative campaigns in California are over-studied and they are not necessarily representative of how ballot issue campaigns in other states are conducted. Launching new research designs, of course, is no easy task, even if campaign finance data in some states are becoming considerably easier to compile due to electronic filing. As Cronin (1989: 110) wisely cautioned, '[e]xplaining outcomes over a broad range of issues and in diverse states is a challenge that defies tidy causal analysis'. Difficulties with causal analysis remain true today. Scholars interested in the campaign financing of ballot initiatives in the American states, though, should nevertheless continue to try new approaches to the study of money in ballot measure campaigns.

References

Allswang, J. (2000) *The Initiative and Referendum in California, 1898–1998* (Stanford: Stanford University Press).

Barnett, J. (1915) *The Operation of the Initiative, Referendum, and Recall in Oregon* (New York: The Macmillan Company).

Beard, C. and B. Schultz (eds) (1912) *Documents on the State-Wide Initiative, Referendum and Recall* (New York: The Macmillan Company).

Berg, L. and C. Holman (1989) 'The Initiative Process and its Declining Agenda Setting Value', *Law and Policy*, **11**: 451–69.

Bowler, S. and T. Donovan (1998) *Demanding Choices: Opinion and Voting in Direct Democracy* (Ann Arbor: University of Michigan Press).

Bowler, S. and T. Donovan (2004) 'Measuring the Effects of Direct Democracy on State Policy', *State Politics and Policy Quarterly*, **4**(3): 345–63.

Braunstein, R. (2004) *Initiative and Referendum Voting: Governing Through Direct Democracy in the United States* (New York: LFB Scholarly Publishing).

Briffault, R. (1996) 'Ballot Propositions and Campaign Finance Reform', *Annual Survey of American Law*, **102**: 413–40.

Broder, D. (2000) *Democracy Derailed: Initiative Campaigns and the Power of Money* (New York: Harcourt Brace Publishers).

Butler, D. and A. Ranney (eds) (1994) *Referendums Around the World: The Growing Use of Direct Democracy* (Washington, DC: The AEI Press).

California Commission on Campaign Financing (1992) *Democracy By Initiative* (Los Angeles: Center for Responsive Government).

City Club of Denver (1927) *Direct Legislation in Colorado* (Denver: Eames Brothers).

Cronin, T. (1989) *Direct Democracy: The Politics of Initiative, Referendum, and Recall* (Cambridge: Harvard University Press).

Crouch, W. (1950) *The Initiative and Referendum in California* (Los Angeles: The Haynes Foundation).

Crouch, W. and D. McHenry (1949) *California Government* (Berkeley: University of California Press).

Cushman, R. (1916) 'Recent Experience with the Initiative and Referendum', *American Political Science Review*, **10**: 532–9.

Donovan, T., S. Bowler and D. McCuan (2001) 'Political Consultants and the Initiative Industrial Complex', in L. Sabato, B. Larson, and H. Ernst (eds), *Dangerous Democracy? The Battle Over Ballot Initiatives in America* (Lanham, MD: Rowman and Littlefield).

Donovan, T. et al. (1998) 'Contending Players and Strategies: Opposition Advantages in Initiative Elections', in S. Bowler, T. Donovan and C. Tolbert (eds), *Citizens as Legislators: Direct Democracy in the United States* (Columbus: Ohio State University Press).

Donovan, T., C. Tolbert and D.A. Smith (2008) 'Direct Democracy, Agendas, and Presidential Vote: Gay Marriage and the 2004 Election', *Journal of Politics*, **102**: 1217–31.

Eaton, A. (1912) *The Oregon System* (Chicago: McClurg and Co.).

Ellis, R. (2002) *Democratic Delusions: The Initiative Process in America* (Lawrence: University Press of Kansas).

Garrett, E. (1999) 'Money, Agenda Setting, and Direct Democracy', *Texas Law Review*, **77**: 1845.

Garrett, E. and D. Smith (2005) 'Veiled Political Actors and Campaign Disclosure Laws in Direct Democracy', *Election Law Journal*, **4**: 295–328.

Garrett, E. and E. Gerber (2001) 'Money in the Initiative and Referendum Process: Evidence of its Effects and Prospects for Reform', in M. D. Waters (ed.), *The Battle Over Citizen Lawmaking* (Durham, NC: Carolina Academic Press).

Garrison, M. (1989) 'Corporate Political Speech, Campaign Spending, and First Amendment Doctrine', *American Business Law Journal*, **27**: 163–213.

Gerber, E. (1999) *The Populist Paradox: Interest Group Influence and the Promise of Direct Legislation* (Princeton: Princeton University Press).

Goebel, T. (2002) *A Government by the People: Direct Democracy in America, 1890–1940* (Chapel Hill: University of North Carolina Press).

Hasen, R. (2004) 'Buckley is Dead, Long Live Buckley: The New Campaign Finance Incoherence of *McConnell v. Federal Election Commission*', *University of Pennsylvania Law Review*, **31**: 152.

Hasen, R. (2005) 'Rethinking the Unconstitutionality of Contribution and Expenditure Limits in Ballot Measure Campaigns', *Southern California Law Review*, **78**: 885.

Heard, A. (1960) *The Costs of Democracy* (Chapel Hill: University of North Carolina Press).

Ji, C. (1998) 'California's Direct Democracy 1976–1998: Predictors, Outcomes, and Issues', paper prepared for presentation at the 1999 *Western Political Science Association Meeting*, Seattle, Washington (March).

Karp, J. (1998) 'The Influence of Elite Endorsements in Initiative Campaigns', in S. Bowler, T. Donovan and C. Tolbert (eds), *Citizens as Legislators* (Columbus: Ohio State University Press).

Kelley, S. (1956) *Professional Public Relations and Political Power* (Baltimore: The Johns Hopkins University Press).

Key, V.O. (1936) 'Publicity of Campaign Expenditures on Issues in California', *American Political Science Review*, **4**: 713–23.

Lee, E. (1978) 'California', in D. Butler and A. Ranney (eds), *Referendums: A Comparative Study of Practice and Theory* (Washington, DC: AEI Press).

Lowenstein, D. (1982) 'Campaign Spending and Ballot Propositions: Recent Experience, Public Choice Theory, and the First Amendment', *UCLA Law Review*, **86**: 505–641.

Lowenstein, D. (1992) 'A Patternless Mosaic: Campaign Finance and the First Amendment after Austin', *Capital University Law Review*, **21**: 381–427.

Lupia, A. (1994) 'Shortcuts versus Encyclopedias: Information and Voting Behavior in California Insurance Reform Elections', *American Political Science Review*, **88**: 63–76; **77**: 1845–90.

Magleby, D. (1984) *Direct Legislation: Voting on Ballot Propositions in the United States* (Baltimore: Johns Hopkins University Press).

Magleby, D. (1994) 'Direct Legislation in the American States', in D. Butler and A. Ranney (eds), *Referendums Around the World* (Washington, DC: American Enterprise Institute).

Matsusaka, J. (2004) *For the Many or the Few: The Initiative, Public Policy, and American Democracy* (Chicago: University of Chicago Press).

McCuan, D. et al. (1998) 'California's Political Warriors: Campaign Professionals and the Initiative Process', in S. Bowler, T. Donovan and C. Tolbert (eds), *Citizens as Legislators: Direct Democracy in the United States* (Columbus: Ohio State University Press).

Moran, D. (2006) 'Taking Aim at California Election Funding', *Los Angeles Times*, 26 September.

Nicholson, S. (2005) *Voting the Agenda: Candidates, Elections and Ballot Propositions* (Princeton, NJ: Princeton University Press).

Owens, J. and L. Wade (1986) 'Campaign Spending on California Ballot Propositions, Trends and Effects, 1924–1984', *Western Political Quarterly*, **39**: 675–89.

Piott, S. (2003) *Giving Voters a Voice: The Origins of the Initiative and Referendum in America* (Columbia: University of Missouri Press).

Price, C. (1975) 'The Initiative: A Comparative State Analysis and the Reassessment of a Western Phenomenon', *Political Research Quarterly*, **28**: 243–62.

Price, C. (1988) 'Big Money Initiatives', *California Journal*, **19**: 481–8.

Pritchell, R. (1958) 'The Influence of Professional Campaign Management Firms in Partisan Elections in California', *Western Political Quarterly*, **11**: 278–300.

Schmidt, D. (1989) *Citizen Lawmakers: The Ballot Initiative Revolution* (Philadelphia: Temple University Press).

Schrag, P. (1998) *Paradise Lost: California's Experience, America's Future* (New York: New Press).

Shockley, J. (1980) *The Initiative Process in Colorado Politics: An Assessment* (Boulder: Bureau of Governmental Research and Service, University of Colorado).

Shockley, J. (1983) 'Money in Politics: Judicial Roadblocks to Campaign Finance Reform', *Hastings Constitutional Law Quarterly*, **10**: 679–92.

Shockley, J. (1985) 'Direct Democracy, Campaign Finance and the Courts: Can Corruption, Undue Influence, and Declining Voter Confidence be Found?', *University of Miami Law Review*, **39**: 377–428.

Smith, D.A. (1998) *Tax Crusaders and the Politics of Direct Democracy* (New York: Routledge).

Smith, D.A. (1999) 'Reevaluating the Causes of Proposition 13', *Social Science History*, **23**: 173–210.

Smith, D.A. (2001a) 'Campaign Financing of Ballot Initiatives in the American States', in L. Sabato, B. Larson and H. Ernst (eds), *Dangerous Democracy? The Battle Over Ballot Initiatives in America* (Lanham, MD: Rowman & Littlefield).

Smith, D.A. (2001b) 'Special Interests and Direct Democracy: An Historical Glance', in M.D. Waters (ed.), *The Battle Over Citizen Lawmaking* (Durham, NC: Carolina Academic Press).

Smith, D.A. (2004) 'Peeling Away the Populist Rhetoric: Toward a Taxonomy of Anti-Tax Ballot Initiatives', *Public Budgeting and Finance*, **24**: 88–110.

Smith, D.A. (2006a) 'Initiatives and Referendums: The Effects of Direct Democracy on Candidate Elections', in S. Craig (ed.), *The Electoral Challenge: Theory Meets Practice* (Washington, DC: CQ Press).

Smith, D.A. (2006b) 'Money Talks: Ballot Initiative Spending in 2004', *Ballot Initiative Strategy Center*, June. Available online at http://ballot.org.

Smith, D.A. and Dustin Fridkin (2008) 'Delegating Direct Democracy: Interparty Legislative Competition and the Adoption of the Initiative in the American States', *American Political Science Review*, **102**: 333–50.

Smith, D.A. and R. Herrington (2000) 'The Process of Direct Democracy: Colorado's 1996 Parental Rights Amendment', *Social Science Journal*, **37**: 179–94.

Smith, D.A. and J. Lubinski (2002) 'Direct Democracy during the Progressive Era: A Crack in the Populist Veneer?', *Journal of Policy History*, **14**: 349–83.

Smith, D., M. DeSantis and J. Kassel (2006) 'Same-Sex Marriage Ballot Measures and the 2004 Presidential Election', *State and Local Government Review*, **38**: 78–91.

Smith, D.A. and C. J. Tolbert (2004) *Educated by Initiative: The Effects of Direct Democracy on Citizens and Political Organizations in the American States* (Ann Arbor: University of Michigan Press).

Stratmann, T. (2005) 'The Effectiveness of Money in Ballot Measure Campaigns', *Southern California Law Review*, **78**: 1041–64.

Stratmann, T. (2006) 'Is Spending More Potent For or Against a Proposition? Evidence from Ballot Measures', *American Journal of Political Science,* **50**: 788–801.

Tolbert, C. (2003) 'Cycles of Democracy: Direct Democracy and Institutional Realignment in the American States', *Political Science Quarterly*, **118**: 467–89.

Tolbert, C., D. Lowenstein and T. Donovan (1998) 'Election Law and Rules for Using Initiatives', in S. Bowler, T. Donovan, and C. Tolbert (eds), *Citizens as Legislators: Direct Democracy in the United States* (Columbus, OH: Ohio State University Press).

Waters, M.D. (ed.) (2003) *The Initiative and Referendum Almanac: A Comprehensive Reference Guide to the Initiative and Referendum Process* (Durham: Carolina Academic Press).

Winkler, A. (1998) 'Beyond Bellotti', *Loyola of Los Angeles Law Review*, **32**: 133–220.

Zisk, B. (1987) *Money, Media, and the Grass Roots: State Ballot Issues and the Electoral Process* (Newbury Park, CA: Sage).

5
Campaign Financing in Danish Referendums

*Sara Binzer Hobolt**

Direct democracy has been an important component of Danish democracy since the 1953 Constitution expanded the use of referendums. In particular, direct democracy has shaped Denmark's relations with the European Union (EU), as all Danish referendums since 1978 have concerned aspects of European integration. The Danish electorate notably rejected both the Maastricht Treaty in 1992 and full membership of the EMU in 2000, despite broad elite support for these proposals. This apparent disconnect between a largely pro-European political elite and an electorate, which is more evenly divided on issues of European integration, has raised the question of how public funding should be allocated in referendums on EU questions. Public funding constitutes the bulk of financing for referendum campaigns, yet there are no constitutional provisions or legal framework for determining its allocation. Instead, the distribution of funds is based on a political compromise in parliament prior to each referendum. Funding purely on the basis of seats in the national parliament would give the 'Yes' side a considerable financial advantage. We know from the literature on campaign spending in (mainly US) elections and referendums that campaign spending provides important information to voters, by reducing uncertainty, transmitting signals about the quality of the proposal, and in turn, influences outcomes. Yet, we have limited knowledge of the nature and effects of campaign financing in Danish referendums. Whereas existing studies of voting behaviour in Danish referendums have placed great emphasis on campaign and media effects (Siune et al., 1992, 1994; de Vreese, 2004; Hobolt 2007, 2009), no studies have looked at the potential importance of campaign funding and spending. To fill this gap, this chapter examines the rules and practice of campaign financing in Denmark and considers which effect, if any, campaign financing may have on referendum outcomes.

The chapter proceeds as follows. First, it presents a brief overview of the history and constitutional provisions for referendums in Denmark. Thereafter, it discusses campaign financing in Danish referendums, both in terms of public allocation of funds and spending by individual parties and organizations. Finally, the chapter considers the effect that variation in campaign funding and expenditure has on referendum outcomes, focusing in particular on the two Danish referendums on the Maastricht Treaty.

5.1   Background and history of Danish referendums

To date, Denmark has held 20 national referendums; six of these related to the European Union, five to changes in the voting age and four to amendments of the constitution, whereas the remaining five concerned the sale of the Danish West Indies (1916) and land laws (four ballot questions in 1963). The frequency of referendums is increasing: 17 of the 20 referendums have been held in the period since 1953.

The legal basis of referendums was first introduced in the 1915 Danish Constitution as a part of the procedure for constitutional amendments. Under these constitutional rules, any amendments to the Constitution required the approval by at least 45 per cent of all eligible voters in a referendum (Svensson, 2003). In the 1953 Constitution, this was reduced to 40 per cent of eligible voters. The 1953 Constitution also introduced the optional (facultative) rejective referendum. Under Article 42 of the Constitution, one-third of the members of the Danish Parliament, *Folketinget*, can demand that a bill is submitted to the voters for either approval or rejection. In other words, Danish citizens can vote on a proposal that has been passed in Parliament, but has not yet been enacted. In addition, the 1953 Constitution introduced an obligatory referendum on voting age and on the delegation of Danish sovereignty to international authorities if a bill on the subject is not accepted with a majority of five-sixths of the members of Parliament. Both of these forms of referendums apply a qualified principle of rejection which means that there must be a negative majority comprising at least 30 per cent of the electorate in order to reject a passed bill.

As a consequence, the present-day Danish Constitution mentions five possibilities for holding referendums: (1) a mandatory referendum on constitutional amendments (Article 88); (2) an optional rejective law referendum (Article 42); (3) a mandatory law referendum on the voting age (Article 29); (4) a mandatory law referendum on the delegation of constitutional powers to international authorities (Article 20); and, finally, (5) a voluntary and binding referendum on treaties (Article 42.6). In addition to these constitutional provisions, it is also possible by law to call ad hoc referendums that legally have only an advisory status (Svensson, 2003). The Danish constitution does not, however, contain any provisions for the abrogative referendum, used in Italy, in which citizens can force a vote on existing legislation, nor for popular initiatives, which is a referendum on any subject brought about by petition of citizens, frequently used in Switzerland (Setälä, 1999).

It is noteworthy that Danish political leaders have held more referendums than required by the constitution, specifically on the issue of European integration. The Social Democrats initiated this development in 1971 when they announced that a referendum on Danish entry to the European Community would take place regardless of Parliamentary approval for the proposal with a five-sixths majority in favour of membership. The use of referendums further evolved in 1986 when the minority centre-right government was defeated in Parliament on the issue of the Single European Act (SEA). Instead of calling a new election after this defeat, the government decided to hold a referendum on the SEA, which was subsequently passed.

The fact that all of the recent referendums on the EU – from the Maastricht Treaty referendum in 1992 to the Euro referendum in 2000 – have been very close races suggests that the campaign could potentially have made a considerable difference. The next section of this chapter looks at the regulation and sources of campaign financing in Danish referendums.

5.2   Financial regulations and public funding

Campaigning in referendums fulfils a multiplicity of functions. Ideally, it should inform the electorate about the ballot proposal, the consequences of voting in favour and against, and enable voters to make enlightened decisions. In practice, campaigning is also used by parties and other organizations to get their specific 'messages' across to the electorate and to sway voters to vote in a particular way. There are reasons to believe that campaigns may matter more in referendums than in elections, since voters are asked to decide on often relatively unfamiliar topics with no partisan labels or candidate names on the ballot to guide them (Owens and Wade, 1986; LeDuc, 2002; Hobolt, 2009). But just as in elections, voters rely on cues and heuristics to overcome their information short-falls (Lupia and McCubbins, 1998). As Lau and Redlawsk (2001: 953) have pointed out, elite endorsements have an obvious heuristic value as 'all that is necessary is to learn the candidate endorsed by a group and one's own attitude toward the group, and an obvious cognitively-efficient inference can be made'. Kriesi (2005: 139) has referred to the partisan heuristic as 'the quintessential shortcut in direct democratic votes', and the endorsements of political parties are arguably the most visible elite cues in Danish referendum campaigns (Hobolt, 2006). However, the dissemination of information in campaigns – through advertisement, posters, billboards and mailings – costs money. Political parties are there-fore not only the key actors, but also the primary spenders in Danish referendum campaigns. In EU-related referendums, however, traditional political parties are not the only key players, since popular Euroscep-tic movements – notably the 'People's Movement against the EU' and the 'June Movement' represented in the European but not the national parliament[1] – have also played a pivotal role in the campaign. Dan-ish EU referendum campaigns have been amongst the most intense in Europe, with very high levels of turnout, high levels of spending and intense media coverage (Hobolt, 2007, 2009). But how do political par-ties fund the campaigns leading up to referendums, and what are the rules regulating their campaign activities?

There are no constitutional provisions concerning the financing or funding of referendum campaigns in Denmark. Nor are there specific legal provisions that limit the spending of parties or other organizations in referendum campaigns or the sources of their funding. There are, how-ever, general legal provisions concerning party finances, which state that parties are required to make their sources of funding public (if contribu-tions exceed 20,000 Danish kroner (DKK) or approximately US$4,000) in their annual accounts.[2] Since these annual party accounts include spe-cific items on campaign expenditure, such as referendum campaigns, we have fairly good knowledge about both the sources of party campaign income as well as the size of their campaign spending.

The main source of income for Danish parties is state funding. Danish parties receive generous funding from the state on the basis of their share of seats in the national parliament. In addition, parties, movements and organizations also receive funding specifically assigned for the purpose of information on the EU (which includes campaigning). Table 5.1 shows the main sources of party funding in 2000, which was the year of the most recent Danish EU referendum on joining the Single European Currency, the euro.

Table 5.1 Sources of Danish party funding, 2000

Parties	Seats in Parliament (1998–2001)	Total income in 2000	Public party funding		Membership fees		Private sponsorship	
	%	*DKK (thousands)*	*DKK (thousands)*	*% of total income*	*DKK (thousands)*	*%*	*DKK (thousands)*	*%*
Social Democrats	35.9	48,809	26,614	55	5,112	10	16,456	34
Liberals	24.0	33,026	17,789	54	5,205	16	7,360	22
Conservatives	8.9	14,940	7,894	53	1,089	7	1,089	7
Socialist People's Party	7.6	7,906	5,598	71	1,739	22	564	7
Danish People's Party	7.4	6,706	5,490	82	951	14	98	1
Centre Democrats	4.3	3,788	3,192	84	175	5	4,201	11
Social Liberals	3.9	4,066	2,854	70	672	17	240	6
Red-Green Alliance	2.7	4,542	2,872	63	1,096	24	396	9
Christian Democrats	2.5	4,419	2,701	61	1,555	35	140	3
Progress Party	2.3	2,007	1,793	89	54	3	58	3
June Movement	n/a	6,511	5,243	81	202	3	450	7
People's Movement against the EU	n/a	4,444	3,019	68	376	8	746	17

Source: The accounts of the political parties 2000; *Finansudvalgets Aktstykke 284*, 2000.

Table 5.1 illustrates clearly that public funding is the largest source of income for all parties, ranging from between just over half to four-fifths of their income. Party membership fees are another important source of income, as are private contributions. The latter mainly consists of contributions from trade unions (primarily the Social Democrats), industry (primarily centre-right parties) and tax on the incomes of party MPs and MEPs (primarily the socialist parties and the Eurosceptical movements). Yet Danish parties are heavily dependent on public subsidies. Included in the public funding in the 2000 budget was 6.75 million DKK (~US$1.3 million) for EU information activities. In addition to these subsidies, the Ministry of Education granted an extra 30 million DKK (~US$5 million) to information and campaign activities related to the Euro referendum.[3] Of these 30 million, 11.5 million were allocated to the parties and movements, as shown in Table 5.1. This extra funding constitutes a substantial part of overall income, especially for the two Eurosceptic movements and the smaller parties. In total, the funding that was targeted specifically at EU information activities (and, hence, campaigning on EU issues) constituted more than 20 per cent of the overall funding for parties in 2000. Hence, the allocation of these subsidies can make a substantial difference to the campaign spending of individual parties and the resource balance between the two opposing sides in a referendum campaign.

Allocation of public funding in referendums

The size of funding allocated to individual parties is based on their proportion of seats in the parliament. Hence, as is shown in Table 5.1, the Social Democrats as the largest party after the 1998 election received the largest share of public funding in 2000, in terms of both general and referendum-specific funding. The two single-issue Eurosceptic movements, the June Movement (established in August 1992) and the People's Movement against the EU (established in 1972), also received public funding. Their key source of income is public funding assigned for 'EU information'. In 2000, EU-specific funding was allocated on the basis of two-thirds to the parties represented in the national Parliament (based on the size of their mandate) and one-third to the two Eurosceptic and pro-EU movements.

The allocation of these funds is based on a political compromise in Parliament and in recent years it has been distributed by an independent body. In the Autumn of 1992, Parliament established *Europanævnet* (in their own translation: *the Board of EU Enlightenment*) for the purpose of ensuring and widening general debate and information about the EU. Since 1972 the Ministry of Education had been regularly subsidizing the

EU debate, but after the 'No' vote in the Maastricht referendum in 1992, it was decided that a separate board should be set up, consisting of a number of impartial persons, to distribute the allocated funds to the advancement of information about the EU (Board of EU Enlightenment, 2004).

Some controversy has surrounded the allocation of these 'EU information' funds, given that the parties represented in Parliament (and the members of the Board of EU Enlightenment) are overwhelmingly pro-European, whereas voting behaviour in referendums and European Parliament elections suggest that the Danish electorate is far more Eurosceptic. In the Danish Parliament today, only the far-right Danish People's Party (which split from the Progress Party) and the far-left Red–Green Alliance are openly Eurosceptic. Broadly speaking, the allocated funds have normally been divided into two portions – one political and one popular. The first portion has been allotted to the political parties in Parliament and to the two movements. The resources allocated to elected representatives have been apportioned via political agreements. The other portion has been awarded in grants to independent popular projects and to popular organizations whose main objective has been the furtherance of discussion about Denmark in the European Union. As an example, the 2002–04 allocation of EU information funding consisted of three funding pools. First, the Political Party Pool (US$4.2 million), which was given to parties and Eurosceptic movements on the basis of their seat share (one half was equally allocated and the other half was allocated with one-third to the two movements and two-thirds on the basis of national party share). Second was an Organization Pool (US$1 million), where the bulk of the money was given to two pro-European movements, the European Movement (*Europabevægelsen*) and New Europe (*Nyt Europa*). Finally, the largest fund, the Activities Pool (US$5.7 million), distributed money to various ad hoc informational activities. The Board of EU Enlightenment considered these applications on their merits and not necessarily with a view to achieving absolute equality in the allocation to the 'two sides'.

Representatives of the Eurosceptic parties have often complained about the allegedly unfair allocation of EU information funding and have argued that the allocation of open funding is biased towards pro-European activities. In particular, they have complained that organizations such as the Europhile European Movement, which is not represented in any parliament and has a very small membership, receives a large share of public funding. The MEP for the People's Movement against the EU, Ole Krarup, has complained that 'pro-Europeans received

13 times more funding than anti-Europeans'. Speaking about the composition of the Board of EU Enlightenment, Krarup has further argued that 'it is a democratic parody when a majority of active pro-Europeans are responsible for allocating the public subsidies. The composition of the Board is unreasonable given that all EU referendums have shown that about half of the Danish population is Eurosceptical'.[4]

These controversies are even greater when it comes to specific allocation of funding for EU information and campaign activities in referendums. In general, the Danish Parliament allocates extra funds for such activities, in addition to the support for EU information detailed above (see Table 5.1 for details on funding in 2000). The details vary from campaign to campaign, but in general quite substantial sums have been allocated on the basis of a political compromise in Parliament. While quite large funds are allocated to the Eurosceptical movements, the funds are not equally allocated between the 'Yes' and 'No' sides, which may be unsurprising given large parliamentary majorities in favour of the ballot proposals in recent referendums (the last time the Danish Parliament was close to evenly split on a referendum proposal was in 1986, when the Single European Act was opposed by all centre-left parties including the Social Democrats). The question is whether the allocation of funding should be allocated equally to each side of the argument or whether the allocation should closely reflect the distribution of seats in parliament. The actual allocation has most often been a compromise between these two positions. The Eurosceptic movements have, unsurprisingly, argued in favour of an equal distribution between the 'Yes' and the 'No' sides. They came close to achieving this aim in the recent allocation of funds prior to the planned referendum on the European Constitution. According to this agreement, the 'party fund' would be equally divided between the 'Yes' and the 'No' side. This agreement was quite unprecedented, but never came into force, since the European Constitution fell at the hands of the French and the Dutch voters in 2005.

As a consequence of the predominantly pro-European consensus among most mainstream Danish political parties and the allocation formula for public funding, the Yes' side has tended to outspend the 'No' side by a factor of 3 to 1 in EU referendums. The annual party accounts provide us with valuable insight into the spending by parties and movements in referendum campaigns. Unfortunately, it is not possible to get perfectly comparable figures, given that parties do not necessarily include exactly the same expenses under the heading of 'referendum expenditure', but we can nevertheless obtain a fairly good estimate of their campaign spending. On the basis of these figures, Table 5.2 shows the campaign spending of individual parties (in absolute figures and as a proportion of their overall income) in the past four Danish referendums.

The figures in Table 5.2 are revealing in many ways. They show that parties on average spend quite a substantial proportion of their income (around 20 per cent) on their campaigning in EU referendums and other EU information activities. This corresponds roughly to the funding normally provided by the state to fund EU information activities and referendum campaigning. This suggests that the allocation of public funding is one of the most important determinants of how much money is spent by parties in referendum campaigns, since the parties appear to rely primarily on the subsidies provided by the state for their campaign activities. Private contributions play a relatively limited role in the funding of party activities in Danish referendums. But campaign financing also varies across referendums and parties. Notably, much less was spent on the campaign leading up to the 1998 referendum on the Amsterdam Treaty. The relatively limited financial engagement of parties on this occasion (even though an extra 25 million DKK was allocated for information on the Amsterdam Treaty) might have been due to the relatively low salience of the Treaty and, more importantly, the fact that a parliamentary election was also taking place in 1998 and parties prioritized their resources accordingly. Of the parties represented in *Folketinget,* only the far-right Eurosceptical Danish People's Party spent more resources on their referendum campaign than their election campaign.

In all of these four referendums, the outcome was very close. The 1992 referendum was rejected by a very narrow margin (50.7 per cent), and in 1993 the Maastricht Treaty as amended by the Edinburgh agreement was accepted by a small majority (57.7 per cent), as was the Amsterdam Treaty (55.1 per cent). In 2000, 53.2 per cent of voters rejected the proposal to join the eurozone. Hence, the electorate has been almost equally divided in each of these referendums but, as is shown by Table 5.2, parties in favour of the proposal have spent far more money on the campaign than parties arguing against. Despite the large budgets of the People's Movement against the EU, and after 1992, the June Movement, the overall expenditure of the organized 'No' side amounts to less than a third of overall spending by the parties. It is very difficult to establish empirically whether the financial advantage of the 'Yes' side has had an effect on the outcome. First of all, we have too few cases to examine the question systematically (even if we had access to spending data from all of the 20 Danish referendums this would not allow for statistical analysis). Secondly, the 'balance' of spending has remained very similar across recent referendums, so we have only limited variation in our key independent

Table 5.2 Expenditure on campaigns and EU information in Danish referendums, 1992–2000

	1992 Maastricht		1993 Edinburgh		1998 Amsterdam		2000 Euro	
	DKK (thousands)	*% of total party spending*	*DKK (thousands)*	*% of total party spending*	*DKK (thousands)*	*% of total party spending*	*DKK (thousands)*	*% of total party spending*
Yes side	13,043	**70**	12,581	**89**	8,277	**74**	25,680	**79**
No side	5,475	**30**	1,536	**11**	2,942	**26**	7,003	**21**
	DKK (thousands)	*% of party income*	*DKK (thousands)*	*% of party income*	*DKK (thousands)*	*% of party income*	*DKK (thousands)*	*% of party income*
Social Democrats	2,533	**11**	3,324	**12**	2,431	**4**	9,012	27
Liberals	4,611	**30**	4,505	**28**	2,600	**8**	8,322	25
Conservatives	5,482	**36**	3,581	**25**	1,965	**10**	5,907	40
Socialist People's Party	1,265	**24**	1,078	**21**	223	**3**	634	8
Danish People's Party	n/a		n/a		1,221	**27**	1,882	28
Centre Democrats	264	**28**	*not specified*		630	**17**	872	23
Social Liberals	153	**8**	93	**5**	651	**16**	645	16
Red-Green Alliance	120	**24**	114	**24**	605	**16**	895	20
Christian Democrats	*not specified*		*not specified*		*not specified*		922	21
Progress Party	466	**29**	741	**32**	*not specified*		200	10
June Movement	n/a		*not specified*		246	**26**	1,962	30
People's Movement against the EU	3,624	**56**	681	**18**	1,252	**25**	2,064	46

Source: The accounts of the political parties 1992, 1993, 1998 and 2000.

Note: Not all accounts include a budget item referring specifically and exclusively to expenditure on EU referendums and EU information activity, and hence in certain instances other figures have been included in the table (assuming that they at least partially cover referendum campaign activities). The expenditure item in the Conservative Party's budget (1992, 1993, 2000) is general 'Referendum and Election expenses'. The Centre Democrats' budget item in 2000 is 'general information activity'; the Progress Party's budget item (1992, 1993, 2000) is 'advertisements'; the June Movement's budget item in 2000 is 'information and campaign activity'.

variable. Finally, other factors are likely to confound the specific effect of spending. Hence, we cannot say with any certainty whether campaign expenditure has any effect on the outcomes in Danish referendums, but the next section discusses the potential effects and evidence in more detail.

5.3   The effect of campaign spending and funding in referendums

Whilst the literature on the effect of campaign spending in the United States is extensive (see Jacobson, 1990; Abramowitz, 1991; Gerber, 1998), less has attention has been paid to campaign spending outside the USA, and even fewer studies have focused on referendums. The studies which have examined campaign spending in the context of referendums and initiatives in the USA (mainly California), present mixed findings. The earliest studies, such as Lowenstein (1982) and Magleby (1984), have compared passage rates for small samples of initiatives in which one side heavily outspent the other to success rates where the levels of spending were approximately equal. The general finding was that heavy spending against a measure tended to lead to the measure's defeat, while heavy spending in favour of a measure had a minimal effect. But in a later study, Owens and Wade (1986) found a much smaller effect of campaign spending on referendum outcomes, arguing that 'it is clear that voting on direct legislation can eventually be explained only by factors other than campaign spending' (1986: 688). More recent studies, however, have found that whereas money may be ineffective in passing a ballot proposal, it may have an impact on defeating a proposal. For example, Gerber (1999) has shown that spending against a measure had a large and significant negative effect on the probability of success, while spending in favour had a small and insignificant effect (see also Garrett and Gerber, 2001). Stratmann (2006) has gone even further and argued that spending (advertisements) of both the supporting and the opposing sides in US initiative campaigns has a significant effect on outcomes, and that previous studies have failed to discover this because their estimation techniques do not take into account that spending decisions may be endogenous to the likelihood of success.

The evidence concerning the effect of campaign spending is thus very mixed. But the arguments concerning the imbalanced effects of campaign spending on outcomes might help to explain why the much higher spending by the 'Yes' side in Danish EU referendums has not ensured an easy passage of proposals. One could argue that this suggests that campaign spending in general matters little in Danish EU referendums. But it could also be that whereas spending *in favour* of a proposal has little effect, increases in spending *against* would have a greater effect. There could be several reasons for these potentially imbalanced effects of campaign spending. It may be that different groups have different resources available to influence voters – for example, citizens' groups, such as the Eurosceptic movements, often have a larger number of volunteers and a larger membership, and their efforts have different productivities – for example, citizens' groups may find it easier to persuade voters if their motives are honest and genuine than established politicians and business groups. As a result, campaign spending by some groups is likely to be more effective than spending by other groups (Gerber, 1999). The marginal impact of campaign spending in referendums may also vary across specific policy areas. Since Denmark has held several referendums on the EU, a large proportion of the population has an 'established' view in favour or against most propositions concerning the EU. The marginal return of spending may therefore be smaller than in referendums on issues that are largely unfamiliar to voters.

However, in very close races, such as the Danish EU referendums, even a small 'campaign spending effect' could make an important difference to the outcome. In the next section, we look at whether there is a relationship between the spending of individual parties, and their ability to 'get the message across' in the two Danish Maastricht referendums.

Effects of campaign spending in the two Maastricht referendums

The marginal Danish 'No' in the Maastricht Treaty referendum of 1992 came as a shock to the European political establishment. Even though the Treaty was ratified in a second referendum a year later by 57 per cent of voters, many commentators see this popular rejection as marking the end of the 'permissive consensus' on Europe. The Maastricht Treaty proposal was backed by a broad spectrum of parties in the Danish Parliament, nearly all interest organizations and every major newspaper, yet Article 20 of the Danish Constitution made its ratification subject to popular approval, since the parliamentary majority ratifying the Maastricht Treaty fell just short of the required five-sixths. In contrast to the strong and resourceful 'Yes' side, the 'No' side was small and lacking in funds. In Parliament, only the small Socialist People's Party and the far-right Progress Party voted against the Maastricht Treaty. In addition to these political parties, there were several extra-parliamentary groups advocating a 'No' vote. Most important of these was the People's Movement

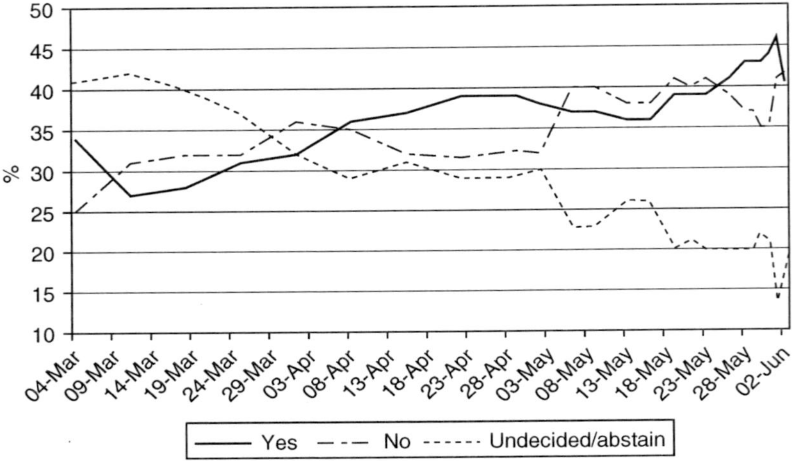

Figure 5.1   Voting intentions during the 1992 Maastricht Referendum campaign
Source: Berlingske Tidende/Gallup and Politiken/Vilstrup.

against the EC, which launched a very vigorous and well-resourced campaign against the Union. However, Table 5.2 also shows that the supporters of the Maastricht Treaty spent almost 2.5 times more on the campaign. In spite of the apparent position of strength, the referendum campaign became an uphill struggle for the 'Yes' side, not least because of the level of public scepticism towards the elements of further economic and political integration contained in the Treaty. Figure 5.1 shows the development in vote intentions during the 1992 Maastricht campaign.

Figure 5.1 shows that at the beginning of the campaign there were a large number of undecided voters, who could potentially be swayed by the cues and messages disseminated over the course of the campaign. However, despite the larger amount of cash spent by the 'Yes' side, they appear to have been no more successful at getting their message through than the 'No' side.

To examine whether spending had any effect on the visibility of messages and candidates during the campaign, we can look at whether the spending is in any way related to the visibility of parties in the media. A systematic media study by Siune, Svensson and Tonsgaard (1992, 1994) allows us to compare the spending of individual parties and movements (Table 5.2) with the visibility of parties in the newspapers. This content analysis includes a measure of the number of articles, contributions

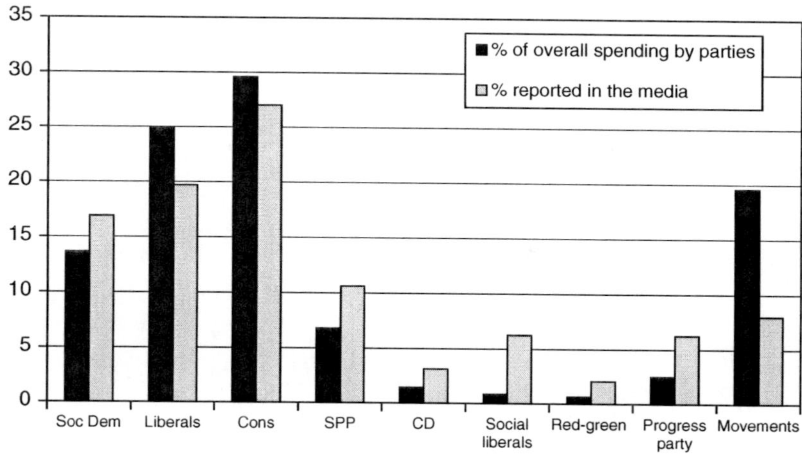

Figure 5.2   Campaign spending and media visibility in 1992

and comments published in national newspapers by representatives of political parties and movements (Siune et al., 1994: 57–8). This is, of course, not a perfect measure of the visibility of parties, but gives some indication of how much access politicians had to citizens during the campaign, via the media.

The close correlation between the visibility of parties and their visibility in the media shown in Figures 5.2 and 5.3 implies that money can in fact buy access to the media. A more plausible explanation for this close correlation is that whilst larger parties are likely to spend more money in a campaign, they are also more likely to be given access to the media, but that spending itself does not necessarily cause media access. The other interesting thing to note about both Figures 5.2 and 5.3 is the much larger access given to pro-European parties compared with the Eurosceptic parties and movements. On this basis alone, we would expect that the 'Yes' side could easily have convinced the undecided voters. But one reason why this did not happen might have been that whilst the 'Yes' side had greater access to the media, they did not succeed in setting the agenda. In 1992, the 'Yes' side emphasized the economic advantages of the European Union and the danger of isolation if the Danes were to reject the Treaty. The 'No' side, on the other hand, emphasized issues concerning the political aspects of integration, such as loss of sovereignty and the development of the United States of Europe (Hobolt, 2006). However, the content analysis of the media coverage clearly shows that issues related to political integration and national sovereignty dominated the agenda (see Siune et al., 1992; Hobolt, 2006). Hence, the 'No' side to a large extent managed to set the agenda, and given that the Danes were particularly negatively disposed towards the political aspects of the integration process, this may have contributed to the majority of no votes.

Given the failure of the government to secure a ratification of the Treaty in 1992, a 'National Compromise' was agreed by all parties except the Progress Party, which laid down four exemptions from full Danish participation in the EU in the areas of defence policy, the single currency, union citizenship and justice and police affairs. This was adopted as a 'decision' by the other EU member states at the Edinburgh Summit in December 1992, and thus became known as the 'Edinburgh Agreement'. The crucial question was whether the mainstream political parties could frame this proposal in a way that would be acceptable to a majority of voters in a second referendum to be held on 18 May 1993. The campaign leading up to the second Maastricht referendum was headed by a new minority government, consisting of the Social Democrats and the Social Liberals. The 'Yes' side was strengthened in the second referendum by the support of the Socialist People's Party and the small Christian People's Party. The strategy of the 'Yes' side was to argue that the Edinburgh Agreement differed substantially from the proposal presented in 1992, and the shift in position of the Socialist People's Party lent credibility to this strategy. Furthermore, the 'Yes' side clearly emphasized that a second 'No' would have serious consequences for Denmark, since it was unrealistic to expect that the other EC members would offer any further concessions. The main argument put forward by the 'No' side was that the electorate was essentially being asked to vote on the same thing twice. In addition to the far-right Progress Party, the 'No' campaign was run by the People's Movement against the EC, and a splinter group, the June Movement. But the 'Yes' side was far ahead in the opinion polls from the outset. On 18 May 1993, 56.7 per cent of the Danish electorate gave their 'Yes' to the Maastricht Treaty. Turnout had increased from 83 per cent in the first Maastricht referendum to 87 per cent.

Table 5.2 shows that the financial advantage of the 'Yes' side was even greater in the 1993 referendum than it had been in the 1992 referendum,[5] although overall spending was similar in the two referendums. This increased imbalance between the two sides was caused by the dramatic drop in spending by the People's Movement against the EU[6] and the fact that the Socialist People's Party had gone to the other side.

Figure 5.3 shows that the 'Yes' side had much better access to the media than the 'No' side, although compared with 1992 it also reveals a

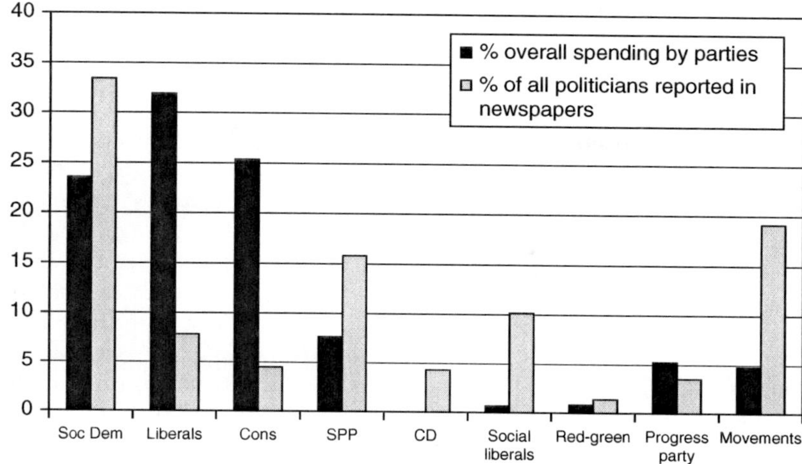

Figure 5.3   Campaign spending and media coverage in 1993

weaker correlation between spending and access to the media, largely because the parties who established the National Compromise – the Social Democrats, the Socialist People's Party and the Social Liberals – were given disproportionately generous access to the media. Whether the further imbalance in campaign spending by the 'Yes' and the 'No' sides in the 1993 campaign had any effect on the outcome is impossible to establish empirically, given that so many other factors played a role. The more interesting and perhaps surprising observation is that the Maastricht Treaty was rejected in the first place, despite the spending differentials between the supporting and opposing sides. But although the supporting side clearly outspent the opposing side in both campaigns, the 'No' side nevertheless had sufficient funds to be able to provide clear cues to voters during the campaign, and thus avoid the 'mainstream effect' associated with an entirely one-sided campaign (Zaller, 1992).

5.4   Conclusion

In recent decades, Denmark has held several intense and divisive referendums on aspects of European integration. But despite the salience of these campaigns, we know very little about how campaign activity is funded, how much money is spent during campaigns, and whether this matters to the outcome.

This chapter has sought to address these questions. It has shown that whilst there are few legal restrictions on the spending of parties and organizations in Danish referendum campaigns, the state nevertheless exerts considerable influence over campaign spending through its ability to allocate funding to parties and organizations. Danish parties are heavily dependent on public subsidies, and the allocation of public funding thus influences the balance of spending in campaigns. Given that a large majority of parliamentary parties have been in favour of recent ballot proposals on the EU, allocation of public funding purely on the basis of parliamentary mandates would create highly imbalanced campaign expenditure in referendums. In practice, the political consensus has been to allocate substantial, but not equal, subsidies to the Eurosceptic movements. This has resulted in imbalanced, but not entirely one-sided, campaign spending in recent referendums in favour of the ballot. Nevertheless, the electorate has been fairly evenly split in these referendums, suggesting that 'money can't buy you votes' in Danish EU referendums. Possibly the Danish case displays similar characteristics to the pattern found in US initiatives, where research has shown that campaign spending in favour of a proposal has a very limited impact, whereas campaign spending against has a much greater effect. Campaign effects are difficult to examine empirically with only a small number of cases. Yet the Danish case raises an interesting question about whether future Danish Parliaments will risk losing votes by providing substantial public funding for citizen movements and organizations that oppose their ballot proposals on European integration. In other words, how far are political elites willing to support their opponents in the name of democracy and fairness?

Notes

* I am grateful to the editors of this volume, Karin Gilland Lutz and Simon Hug, for their valuable input. Several people and institutions have kindly provided me with information and data for this chapter. In particular, I would like to thank Lars Bille, Naja Binzer, Peter Egemose Grib (*Folketingets Bibliotek*), Martin Jørgensen (*Folketingets EU-Oplysning*), Anna de Klauman (*Folketingets EU-Oplysning*), Ib Roslund (*Folkebevægelsen mod EU*), Marcus Schmidt (*Europanævnet*) and Palle Svensson.

1. In the 2004 election, the June Movement and the People's Movement against the EU each won one of the 14 Danish seats in the European Parliament. In the previous election in 1999, they gained 4 out of 16 seats.

2. Law no. 404 of 13 June 1990 as amended by law no. 394 of 14 June 1995 and law no. 464 of 7 June 2001.

3. See 'Aktstykke 284', approved by the parliamentary Finance Committee, 17 May 2000.
4. Ole Krarup in a press statement issues by the Popular Movement against the EU, 27 May 2005.
5. However, note that it has not been possible to obtain any estimates of the spending of the June Movement, which split from the People's Movement against the EU in August 1992.
6. Ib Roslund from the People's Movement against the EU explains that the Movement spent all of its resources in 1992 and took extra loans to fund their campaign in order to match the expenditure by the yes-side, and hence they were not in a position to fund an expensive campaign in 1993. Moreover, the split in 1992 further worsened the movement's finances.

References

Abramowitz, Alan I. (1991) 'Incumbency, Campaign Spending, and the Decline of Competition in US House Elections', *The Journal of Politics*, **53**(1): 34–56.

Board of EU Enlightenment (2004) *The Triennial Allocation Period 2002–2004 Report*.

de Vreese, Claes H. (2004) 'Primed by the Euro: The Impact of a Referendum Campaign on Public Opinion and Evaluations of Government and Political Leaders', *Scandinavian Political Studies*, **27**(1): 45–65.

Garrett, Elizabeth and Elizabeth R. Gerber (2001) 'Money in the Initiative and Referendum Process: Evidence of Its Effects and Prospects for Reform', in M.D. Waters (ed.), *The Battle over Citizen Lawmaking* (Durham, NC: Carolina Academic Press), pp. 73–96.

Gerber, Alan (1998) 'Estimating the Effect of Campaign Spending on Senate Election Outcomes Using Instrumental Variables', *American Political Science Review*, **92**(2): 401–11.

Gerber, Elizabeth R. (1999) *The Populist Paradox: Interest Group Influence and the Promise of Direct Legislation* (Princeton, NJ: Princeton University Press).

Hobolt, Sara B. (2006) 'How Parties Affect Vote Choice in European Integration Referendums', *Party Politics*, **12**(5): 623–47.

Hobolt, Sara B. (2007) 'Campaign Information and Voting Behaviour', in Claes H. de Vreese (ed.), *The Dynamics of Referendum Campaigns* (Basingstoke: Palgrave Macmillan).

Hobolt, Sara B. (2009) *Europe in Question: Referendums on European Integration* (Oxford: Oxford University Press).

Jacobson, Gary (1990) 'The Effect of Campaign Spending in House Elections: New Evidence for Old Arguments', *American Journal of Political Science*, **34**(2): 334–62.

Kriesi, Hanspeter (2005) *Direct Democratic Choice: The Swiss Experience* (Lanham: Lexington Books).

Lau, Richard R. and David P. Redlawsk (2001) 'Advantages and Disadvantages of Cognitive Heuristics in Political Decision Making', *American Journal of Political Science*, **45**(4): 951–71.

LeDuc, Lawrence (2002) 'Referendums and Elections: How Do Campaigns Differ?', in David M. Farrell and Rüdiger Schmitt-Beck (eds), *Do Political Campaigns*

Matter? Campaign Effects in Elections and Referendums (London: Routledge), pp. 145–62.

Lowenstein, Daniel (1982) 'Campaign Spending and Ballot Propositions: Recent Experience, Public Choice Theory and the First Amendment', *UCLA Law Review*, **29**(3): 505–641.

Lupia, Arthur and Mathew D. McCubbins (1998). *The Democratic Dilemma: Can Citizens Learn What They Need to Know?* (Cambridge: Cambridge University Press).

Magleby, David B. (1984) *Direct Legislation: Voting on Ballot Propositions in the United States* (Baltimore: The Johns Hopkins University Press).

Owens, John R. and Larry L. Wade (1986) 'Campaign Spending on California Ballot Propositions, 1924–1984: Trends and Voting Effects', *Western Political Quarterly*, **39**(4): 675–89.

Setälä, Maija (1999) 'Referendums in Western Europe – A Wave of Direct Democracy?', *Scandinavian Political Studies*, **22**(4): 327–40.

Siune, Karen, Palle Svensson and Ole Tonsgaard (1994) – *fra et nej til et ja* (Aarhus: Politica).

Siune, Karen, Palle Svensson and Ole Tonsgaard (1992) – *det blev et nej* (Aarhus: Politica).

Stratmann, Thomas (2006) 'Is Spending More Potent For or Against a Proposition? Evidence from Ballot Measures', *American Journal of Political Science*, **50**(3): 788–801.

Svensson, Palle (2003) *Folkets Røst, Demokrati og Folkeafstemninger i Danmark og andre europæiske lande* (Aarhus: Aarhus Universitetsforlag).

Zaller, John R. (1992) *The Nature and Origins of Mass Opinion* (Cambridge: Cambridge University Press).

6
Financing Referendums and Initiatives in the Baltic States

Daunis Auers, Jüri Ruus and Algis Krupavicius

6.1 Introduction

Having gained independence following the collapse of the Russian Empire, at the end of the First World War, the three Baltic States of Estonia, Latvia, and Lithuania set about constructing their states. In writing their constitutions in the early 1920s, all three states chose parliamentary models with clauses for the use of direct democracy. However, by 1934 all three had abandoned their inter-war constitutions and were in the thrall of benign authoritarian dictatorships. The Second World War saw Baltic independence swept away by foreign invasion. The Baltic States were incorporated into the Soviet Union at the end of the war, only re-emerging on the international stage in 1991, following the collapse of the Soviet Union.

Latvia and Estonia were heavily russified during the Soviet era, and by 1991 barely half of the Latvian population was ethnically Latvian, while one-third of the Estonian population was Russian-speaking. Fearing for their statehood, and seeking to establish historical continuity with the independent states of the inter-war era, Latvia and Estonia renewed their inter-war constitutions. Lithuania, in contrast, wrote a new constitution. Despite the differences, all three constitutions have proven to be rigorous, with the Baltic States emerging as durable multi-party democracies and joining both the European Union and NATO in 2004.

This chapter focuses on the financing and use of referendums and initiatives in the Baltic States since 1991. Although the three Baltic States had a similar starting point in 1991 and all three held parallel referendums on independence in 1990, their use of initiatives and referendums has diverged sharply. This chapter begins with a discussion of the historical use of initiatives and referendums in the inter-war era, and focuses

81

in particular on their significance in the independence movements of the late 1980s. The following section focuses on the financial regulations governing referendums and initiatives in the Baltic States, and then considers the effects of these rules and regulations.

6.2 Background and history

Referendums are one of the few instruments available for society to reach decisions in a collective fashion. Citizen participation in direct decision making is a key element in the understanding and practice of contemporary democracy. In new democracies, such as the Baltic States, conventional forms of political participation are neither well established from a legal point of view, nor deeply rooted in national political culture, resulting in low levels of conventional and unconventional participation. Nevertheless, referendums played a significant role in the process of restoring Baltic statehood and the establishment of democratic regimes in the Baltic States in 1990 and 1991. Referendums have continued to be used frequently in Latvia and Lithuania, if not Estonia, since then.

Estonia

Article 31 of the first Estonian constitution (adopted in 1920) allowed for popular initiatives. 25,000 votes were required to initiate or change any laws passed by the Estonian Parliament (Riigikogu). In practice, this happened only once – a law on restoring religious instruction in secondary schools came into force after popular adoption in 1923.

Between 1919 and 1933, the average term of office of national governments was just eight months. Political instability was greatly aggravated by the social effects of the great depression. Pressure for political reform mounted, particularly from the right-wing conservative 'League of Freedom Fighters', an association of veterans of the war of independence. In 1933, their proposal for constitutional reform won 72.7 per cent of the votes in a referendum. A new constitution was adopted and the following March, the acting president Konstantin Päts made use of the new authoritarian Constitution to declare a state of emergency, close parliament and disband the League of Freedom Fighters. A referendum on a new Constituent Assembly formally legalized his caretaker regime in 1936, and he ruled by presidential decrees until 1938.

In the post-Soviet transition to democracy, referendums bestowed legitimacy on independence movements by allowing them to counter claims that their desire for independence was merely an extremist or minority opinion. In the best circumstances, elites took them seriously

Table 6.1   Referendums in Estonia since 1990

Year	Purpose	Turnout (%)	For (%)	Against (%)	Spoiled (%)
1991	Estonian independence	82.9	77.8	21.4	0.74
1992	Constitution	66.8	91.3	8.1	0.60
2003	EU	64.0	66.8	33.1	0.49

Source: Estonian Central Election Commission (2008).

and tried to find a peaceful path to independence. In the worst circumstances, they countered with force. In the USSR, for example, the referendums in the Baltic States in February and March 1991 caused Gorbachev to rethink his strategy for the union treaty, but also contributed to the reactionary coup attempt of August 1991. The failure of this coup then made it possible for the restoration of state sovereignty and Baltic independence.

The question put to the March 1991 consultative referendum asked: 'Do you want the restoration of state sovereignty and the independence of the Republic of Estonia?' A 'Yes' vote was cast by 77.8 per cent and a 'No' by 21.4 per cent of those answering the question. The high percentage of 'No' votes reveals the importance of the active group of pro-union forces among the adult population of Estonia (Auer and Bützer, 2001: 52).

The next referendum, on the draft constitution, was held in June 1992 following Estonian independence. This new draft constitution was approved by 91.3 per cent of those who went to the polls. A sub-question asked if Russian-speakers that had applied for Estonian citizenship should be allowed to participate in the election. 53 per cent of voters voted against allowing them to vote in the upcoming election. The prevailing viewpoint was that only ethnic Estonian citizens should have the right to make decisions concerning the Estonian state. Moreover, the majority of non-citizens had voted against independence in the referendum on independence.

The new constitution provides provisions for the kind of direct democracy represented by referendums, although only two nationwide referendums (in 1992 and 2003) have been held. Referendums are obligatory in cases where the law proposed includes changes in the first (general provisions) or in the last (changing the constitution, Article 15) chapter of the main law. There are also some restrictions on the range of issues that may be referred to the citizens. Thus the constitution does not allow referendums on issues related to budget, taxation, state finances, a ratification or rejection of foreign agreements, effecting and calling off a state emergency, and issues of state defence (Article 106). Other laws can be adopted or amended only by a majority of the full house of Parliament. These include the law on citizenship, law on parliamentary elections, law on electing the president of the republic, and referendum law (Article 104).

Article 161 of the constitution states that the right to initiate amendments to the constitution rests with a minimum of one-fifth of the members of Parliament and the President. The constitution may be amended by a law which has been adopted by referendum or two successive parliamentary callings. A draft law to amend the constitution shall be debated in three readings in parliament, whereby the interval between the first and second readings shall be at least three months, and the interval between the second and third readings shall be at least one month. The manner in which the constitution is to be amended is decided at the third reading. However, the Constitution Implementation Act states that 'the right to initiate amendment of the Constitution during the three years following the adoption of the Constitution by a referendum also rests, by way of public initiative, with no less than ten thousand citizens with the right to vote. A proposal to amend the constitution made by public initiative shall be entered onto the agenda of the Riigikogu as a matter of urgency and shall be resolved pursuant to the procedure provided by paragraph one of this section' (Article 8).

Putting a proposed amendment of the constitution to a referendum requires the approval of a three-fifths majority of the full membership of parliament. The referendum cannot be held earlier than three months from the time that the resolution is adopted by parliament (Article 164). The law to amend the constitution shall be proclaimed by the President of the republic and it shall enter into force on the date determined by the same law, but not earlier than three months after its proclamation (Article 167). An amendment to the constitution dealing with the same issue may not be re-introduced within one year of the rejection of the respective draft by referendum or by parliament (Article 168).

The referendum is regulated by a special law on referendums (1994, 2002), and according to this law the Estonian Parliament decides whether a referendum will be held or not at all, the timing of such a referendum, as well as the questions to be posed. Thus, the Parliament can put draft legislation or other national issues to a referendum.

Local governments derive their powers largely through representative democracy. Every four years people elect the council and the council makes decisions on behalf of the people. To bring the local government closer to the interests of the people, it has been necessary to introduce additional elements of participatory democracy. Thus, in certain circumstances, people have the right to initiate the adoption, repeal and amendment of council legislation. According to the amended law of local municipalities, a public initiative is possible, if 1 per cent of the local population living in the municipalities raise issues, but not less than five of the local residents (the initiative is non-binding). Furthermore, the council is empowered to hold opinion polls on important issues.

Latvia

In 1922 the Latvian Constitutional Convention adopted a constitution based largely on the parliamentary Weimar model. A number of key Latvian Social Democratic Party representatives at the convention had spent many happy years of exile in Switzerland and been much taken with its tradition of referendums and initiatives (Šilde, 1976: 355). They ensured that the newly crafted constitution contained several provisions for popular initiatives and referendums. Following the collapse of the Soviet Union in 1991, and the end of 50 years of occupation, newly independent Latvia readopted its inter-war constitution. Thus the modern Latvian state inherited several constitutional vehicles of popular democracy.

The constitution contains five referendum mechanisms. The first three trigger mandatory referendums. A referendum is called if parliament changes key articles of the constitution (Article 77), or if the president calls for the dissolution of parliament (Article 48). In both cases, half the total electorate must vote for the changes for them to come into effect.[1] The latter case is a zero-sum game in that new elections must be called within two months of the referendum if the electorate sides with the president, but the president steps down and parliament elects a new head of state if voters support parliament. Thirdly, amendments to the constitution in May 2003, made prior to accession to the European Union, state that 'membership of Latvia in the European Union shall be decided by a national referendum, which is proposed by the *Saeima* [parliament]. Substantial changes in the terms regarding the membership of Latvia in the European Union shall be decided by a national referendum if such a referendum is requested by at least one-half of the members of the *Saeima*' (Article 68).

The two other mechanisms are facultative. First, a referendum is triggered if the president (acting independently, or at the request of at least one-third of parliamentary deputies) has suspended the proclamation of a law for up to two months, and at least 10 per cent of the electorate have petitioned for a referendum on the issue within this two-month period. The law is then repealed if at least half of the voters in the previous parliamentary election participate, and more than half this turnout votes in favour of annulling the law.[2] Secondly, if at least one-tenth of the electorate has petitioned parliament with a 'fully elaborated draft of an amendment to the Constitution or of a law to the President, who shall present it to the *Saeima*. If the *Saeima* does not adopt it without change as to its content, it shall then be submitted to national referendum' (Article 78). A constitutional amendment is accepted if at least half the electorate has voted for it. In other cases, at least half of the number of voters in the previous parliamentary election will suffice. Minimum turnout must be at least half of the electorate.

At the same time, however, the constitution strictly lays out the limits of popular democracy. Article 75 states that 'should the *Saeima*, by not less than a two thirds majority vote, determine a law to be urgent, the President may not request reconsideration of such law, it may not be submitted to national referendum, and the adopted law shall be proclaimed no later than the third day after the President has received it'. The constitution also details the legislative areas that cannot be subjected to a referendum (Article 73).[3] Finally, the 1994 'Law on Referendums and Popular Initiatives' details the organizational aspects of the process.

Latvia has seen several referendums and initiatives in both the inter-war and the modern eras. The inter-war era saw six popular initiatives gather the signatures of 10 per cent of the electorate necessary to trigger a referendum. In two cases the parliament adopted the law, while in the other four cases the referendums failed to attract the minimum turnout. Modern Latvia has seen eight referendums – two called by parliament, two by the president and four resulting from popular initiatives (three other popular initiatives have failed to garner the 10 per cent of signatures needed to lead to a referendum) (Latvian Central Election Commission, 2008).

The two initiatives adopted by the inter-war parliament were connected to a key issue of the inter-war era – the dispersal of land. The first concerned the granting of compensation to former landowners whose properties had been nationalized, and the second cancelled Baltic-German *landeswehr* privileges in privatizing nationalized land (Šilde, 1976). The four initiatives that failed to attract enough voters were a mixed bag. Two dealt with national-religious issues. A 1923 initiative attempted to prevent the transfer of the *Jekaba* church from the Latvian Lutheran evangelical church to the Catholic church, while

Table 6.2 Referendums in Latvia since 1990

Year	Purpose	Turnout (%)	For (%)	Against (%)	Spoiled (%)
1991	Latvian independence	1,666,128 (87.6)	73.7	24.79	1.6
1998	Citizenship	928,040 (69.2)	45.0	52.5	2.5
1999	Pensions Law	339,879 (24.1)	94.2	5.3	0.5
2003	EU membership	1,010,467 (72.5)	67.0	32.3	0.8
2007	National Security Law A	338,764 (23)	96.5	3.0	0.5
2007	National Security Law B	338,747 (23)	96.4	3.1	0.5
2008	Constitutional Amendments	629,119 (42)	96.8	3.0	0.2
2008	Pensions Law	347,182 (22.9)	96.4	3.3	0.3

Source: Latvian Central Election Commission (2008).

a 1931 initiative aimed to confiscate the *Doma* church from its Baltic-German tenants, and pass it over to the Latvian Lutheran evangelical church. Indeed, this was an overtly nationalist campaign, organized by the Latvian Social-Democratic Worker's Party, with the slogan '*Maras baznica – Latvju Tautai!*' (Mara's Church for the Latvia Nation!). A 1927 initiative attempting to cancel the easing of naturalization restrictions (popularly nicknamed the Jewish law) also failed to garner a sufficient turnout. The final referendum of this era, held at the end of 1933, aimed to introduce extensive social security legislation guaranteeing pensions, unemployment benefits and other payments. Despite an impressive turnout of 414,897 (of whom 385,258 voted in favour of the legislation), the turnout did not quite reach the minimum required.

The first referendum of the modern era was called while Latvia was still a constituent part of the Soviet Union.[4] As a result, the poll was symbolic rather than binding in nature. Indeed, the lack of a legal base for referendums in the Soviet constitution meant that the Latvian Supreme Soviet (which was dominated by the pro-independence Latvian Popular Front) passed laws on organization and financing less than a month before the poll, on 12 February 1991 (Latvian Central Election Commission, 2008). The referendum question asked: 'Are you in favor of a democratic and independent Latvia?' In contrast to subsequent referendums, the 1991 poll on Latvian independence was voted on by all permanent inhabitants in Latvia over the age of 18, and had a high participation of 1,666,128 voters. Later referendums were limited to citizenship holders, thus excluding the one-third of the Latvian population that had been denied automatic citizenship in 1994 (Dreifelds, 1996).

The first referendum in post-Soviet Latvia was held in October 1998 (the same day as a parliamentary election), and concerned the repeal of the law on amendments to the citizenship law. Following severe external pressure from the Organization for Security and Cooperation in Europe (OSCE), the European Union (EU) and NATO, the Latvian parliament passed significant changes to the citizenship law lifting the 'window' system of naturalization on 22 June 1998. However, the nationalist For Fatherland and Freedom/Latvian national Independence Movement party succeeded in gaining the support of one-third of parliamentary deputies, suspending enactment of the legislation while holding a petition drive to force a referendum on the issue. Indeed, well over 10 per cent of citizens signed the resulting petition.[5] Liberal commentators and politicians described the referendum as a pivotal moment in Latvia's democratization, arguing that the amendments had to be adopted if Latvia was to join the European Union and NATO. The 'No' vote garnered 52.5 per cent of the ballots cast.

The 1999 poll was called after more than one-third of parliamentary deputies had requested that the president delay enacting a new law on state pensions. The organizers of the petitioning process, the organizing left-wing parties, were successful in collecting the signatures of over 10 per cent of the electorate.[6] However, when it actually came to the vote, a low turnout meant that the result was ruled invalid – 339,879 voters cast their ballot, but 482,334 were needed to give the referendum legal force (Latvian Central Election Commission, 2008). Indeed, the government coalition parties had urged people to boycott the poll. However, the low-key nature of the referendum campaign meant that a low turnout was, in any case, the likely result.

The turnout of 72.5 per cent for the 2003 referendum on European Union accession actually exceeded the turnout at the previous parliamentary election, and was the second highest among the ten EU referendums held in the candidate countries in 2003. Moreover, the 'Yes' vote of 67 per cent came as a surprise, as opinion polls had predicted a much closer race. Panicked government ministers had spent the week before the poll frantically racing around Latvia pushing for a 'Yes' vote.

2007 and 2008 saw a sharp acceleration in the use of referendums. Referendums were effectively seen as a way of challenging an unpopular incumbent government. First, the hugely popular then president, Vaira Vīķe Freiberga, opposed government-coalition sponsored changes in two national security laws that she believed would undermine Latvia's defence. She blocked the laws and triggered a referendum that was ultimately unnecessary as the government coalition caved in to her demands and dropped the changes to the law (although for legal reasons the referendums went ahead anyway and consequently failed to gather the necessary turnout). Then in 2008 two separate legal initiatives managed to attract the 10 per cent of signatures needed to trigger a referendum, but failed to garner the minimum turnout for the laws to go onto the statute book. The first vote was on a constitutional amendment that would give the public the power to dissolve a sitting parliament through referendum (Archdeacon, 2008a). The second was a vote on raising the size of the state pension (Archdeacon, 2008b). While they may have failed, the overwhelming number of people voting for the referendum proposals (over 96 per cent in all four cases) reveals the extent of their popular support.

Lithuania

There were no provisions for either initiatives or referendums in Lithuania in the Soviet era, or even during the first period of independence in 1918–40. The Supreme Soviet of the Lithuanian Soviet Socialist Republic passed the first law on referendums on 3 November 1989. Article 1 of the 1989 referendum law stated that 'the most urgent issues relating to the life of the State and the Nation shall be resolved and the provisions of laws of the Republic of Lithuania may be adopted by a referendum'. The 1989 law on referendums was amended by the Lithuanian parliament (*seimas*) several times in 1990, 1992, 1994, 1995, 1996, 1997, 1999 and 2000. Because the initial Lithuanian referendum law was passed in the last days of the communist regime, during a period of political upheaval, it was designed only for decisions on nationwide issues. A new referendum law was passed by the Lithuanian parliament in June 2002. It is evident that within this law, the manner in which to implement direct democracy was afforded a high level of attention.

The legal regulation of national referendums can be found in two legislative acts. First, in Articles 9, 69, 71, 148, 151–4 of the Lithuanian constitution. Article 9 of the Lithuanian constitution states that 'the most significant issues concerning the life of the State and the nation shall be decided by referendum. In the cases established by law, the Seimas shall announce a referendum.' Second, in the Law on referendums (2002) which established two different types of referendum – obligatory and consultative.

The obligatory referendum requires a participation quorum – one half of the citizens having the right to vote and having been registered on voter lists, or 50 per cent + 1. An approval quorum is also required. This entails a 'Yes' from more than one half of the citizens who took part in the referendum, but at least one-third of the citizens having the right to vote and having been registered on voter lists, or one-third of the electorate, except on issues of national independence, i.e. Article 1 of the Constitution, plus rules to amend the Constitution, and non-alignment to the post-Soviet alliances. Until 2002, obligatory referendums also required a high approval quorum (50 per cent of the electorate in order to pass the subject). This led to most referendums being declared invalid (seven of eleven). The 2002 referendum law partially lowered the approval quorums.

The obligatory referendum was designed to deal primarily with constitutional issues, including Lithuania's membership in international organizations, if such membership requires the delegation of certain functions of the Lithuanian state to supranational bodies of these international organizations (for example, the European Union). A new referendum law partially removed the approval quorums, i.e. for referendums on accession to international organizations where there is a transfer of sovereignty.

Consultative referendums can be held on all other issues on which it is not necessary to hold an obligatory referendum. The consultative (facultative) referendum has a participation quorum of one half of the citizens who are eligible to take part, or 50 per cent +1, and an approval quorum – 'Yes' from one half of those voters who have participated or 25 per cent of the total electorate.

High participation and decision approval thresholds were the main weaknesses in the procedure but were reduced after adoption of the new referendum law in 2002. However, particularly in the case of consultative referendums, participation and approval quorums remain inadequately high.

Both obligatory and consultative referendums can be called under identical rules, i.e. on all major issues in the life of the state and society as a result of a citizens' or parliamentary initiative. The lack of distinction in the rules between obligatory and consultative referendums substantially decreases the use of this direct democratic device in the Lithuanian political arena. Since 1991 all referendums held in Lithuania have been obligatory and national, except a consultative referendum on the extension of the Ignalina power plant held in 2008.

Initiatives must have the support of no less than one-quarter of the members of Parliament, or at least 300,000 citizens of voting age. The high number of signatures (300,000 or 12 per cent of the total electorate) that must be collected in order to initiate a referendum is an additional and serious obstacle to the use of referendums as an instrument of political decision making in Lithuania. Such a high quota of signatures has a certain rationale. Initially, fears existed that the referendum would be used too frequently for populist tasks. This was based on the idea that in new democracies, where both citizens and politicians lack democratic habits and behavior, direct democratic means were often chosen to mobilize protest votes. Even in this context the same high signature quota applied to both obligatory and consultative referendums is a political misunderstanding.

Before the 1996 amendments, the proposal of a referendum required the support of more than half of the members of parliament. After 1996, the procedure was made easier for members of parliament in that a minimum of only one-third of parliamentary deputies was required to initiate a referendum. The 2002 referendum law further decreased the threshold for members of the *Seimas* to one-quarter of the deputies of the legislative assembly. The President and the government have no right to initiate a referendum. Parliament decides on the organization of referendums.

Referendums in Lithuania are organized by the Central Electoral Commission (CEC), the city and regional referendum commissions and the polling district commissions. The CEC is a permanent supreme state institution for organizing and conducting elections and referendums. According to the Law on the Central Electoral Commission, it is an independent institution and when organizing and conducting elections or referendums, interference into CEC activities by other state institutions, members of parliament, political parties, nongovernmental organizations or citizens is prohibited. The CEC is responsible for managing state funds allocated for the organization of referendums, the dissemination of official information on the referendum issue, and vote counting.

The results of a referendum can be binding or indicative (consultative). Obligatory referendums are binding. In the case of consultative referendums, all decisions are indicative. However, if the referendum is valid, the Parliament must hold a debate on the issue (or issues) within one month of the announcement of the referendum results. If participation is less than 50 per cent of the total electorate, the binding referendum is deemed invalid. When constitutional decisions have been adopted by referendum, they can only be amended or repealed by referendum.

Lithuania is a unitary state and thus most decisions are taken at the national level. As a result, the referendum law of 2002 still has no provisions on local referendums and initiatives. Moreover, municipalities have also made no attempt to introduce their own referendum bylaws or to allow the popular initiative. In theory, it is possible to use the right of legislative initiative at regional and local levels, but it has not been employed since 1998, i.e. since the adoption of the law on the legislative initiative. However, since 2002 the law on local self-government has a special chapter (13) on the right of local government to organize local public opinion polls in local communities and cities. Civic groups have the right to initiate local public opinion polls, if they manage to collect the signatures of 10 per cent of local inhabitants, or one-quarter of local councilors in a certain area.

Referendums played a significant role in the process of the restoration of Lithuania's statehood in 1990 and 1992. On the one hand, the referendum was an instrument for expression of political protest against the Soviet regime, and, on the other, it was a means to legitimize democratic institutions in Lithuania. The first general poll, scheduled by Lithuania's government for 9 February 1991, included the question 'Do you favor [the idea] that the Lithuanian state should be an independent democratic republic?' This poll was a reaction of resistance against the 'parade of referendums' on sovereignty which Gorbachev planned to hold in March 1997. These referendums were viewed as a way out of a real decision on independence, because the act on the restoration of the Lithuanian state had already been adopted on 11 March 1990 by the Supreme Council – Re-constituent Seimas. The referendum in June 1992 on a complete withdrawal of the former Soviet troops from Lithuania served the same function of popular resistance and reaffirmed the political position already taken.

After 1992, referendums were used as expressions of political opposition, rather than instruments of law. Decision making in the domestic political framework, i.e. national referendums became an instrument of party politics. If the right-wing political parties, especially the Homeland Union (Lithuanian Conservatives), initiated various referendums and were gradually able to mobilize a relatively stable and broad electorate, the moderate and left-wing parties usually argued for opposition to the majority of referendum issues.

Among the 11 referendums and one plebiscite held in Lithuania between 1991 and 2008, eight may be classified as constitutional, because their subject matter was related to the country's independence and/or the building of democratic institutions. Another four dealt with economic issues: privatization, restoration of bank deposits lost during the period of hyperinflation in 1991–92, the free sale of agricultural land and on the extension of operation of the Ignalina Nuclear Power Plant. Referendum efficiency from the perspective of decision-making was low. Out of 12 issues only four decisions were passed, including the 2003 referendum on EU membership. These referendums revealed the weaknesses in the design of the procedures: the high turnout quorum (50 per cent of the electorate) led to many referendums being declared invalid.

Table 6.3 Referendums in Lithuania since 1990

Year	Subject, or question	Turnout (%)	For (%)	Against (%)
1991	On Lithuania's independence (plebiscite)	2,247,810 (84.74)	90.24	6.54
1992	On restoration of Presidential Institution in Lithuania	1,525,985 (59.18)	69.27	25.57
1992	On an immediate and non-conditional withdrawal of military troops of the former Soviet Union from the territory of the Lithuanian Republic in 1992, and compensation of material damage to Lithuania	1,931,278 (76.05)	90.67	7.25
1992	On the adoption of new Constitution	1,919,073 (75.26)	75.42	20.98
1994	On illegal privatization, compensation of banking savings and distorted justice	895,778 (36.89)	83.63	10.34
1996	Constitutional amendment: The Seimas consists of 111 Members, and the Seimas is considered as acting body if no less than three-fifths of its members are elected in the elections	1,353,448 (52.11)	65.00	17.63
1996	Constitutional amendment: A regular election to the Seimas is held every four years on the second Sunday of April	1,353,448 (52.11)	74.31	19.10
1996	Constitutional amendment: No less than a half of national budget expenditures are devoted to the needs of social welfare, health care, education, and science	1,353,448 (52.11)	43.41	40.05
1996	On a compensation of banking savings through a just privatization of state property	1,362,573 (52.46)	89.95	8.82
1996	On free sale of agricultural land in Lithuania	1,031,623 (39.73)	90.24	6.54
2003	On Lithuania's membership in the European Union	1,672,317 (63.37)	69.27	25.57
2008	On the extension of operation of the Ignalina Nuclear Power Plant	1,305,825 (48.43)	88.58	8.33

Source: Lithuanian Central Electoral Commission (2008).

Altogether, the plethora of referendums between 1992 and 1996, rather than encouraging a participatory culture, stimulated protest behaviour in Lithuania's politics, in which citizens became politically active only in order to oppose something rather than to support a position or discuss various political alternatives. Though it is a conventional form of political behaviour and participation, albeit inefficient for reaching practical and desirable political decisions, the referendum, was frequently used to solve domestic political deadlock and fostered an increase in protest culture. Many issues presented for referendums in the autumn of 1996 lacked political logic and consistency, as well as being essentially populist.[7] The direct and real goal of the referendums was the political mobilization of the supporters of one party or another.

In all referendums and plebiscites held in Lithuania since 1991, turnout has averaged 57.7 per cent, compared to the 60.9 per cent voter turnout in parliamentary elections between 1990 and 2004. The mean turnout rates in referendums declined significantly after 1992. Relatively low voter turnout in referendums in Lithuania was related to several country-specific factors, i.e. the high threshold of 'Yes' votes necessary to win a referendum issue and the high frequency of unsuccessful referendum initiatives. This has also caused citizens to lose interest in participatory politics in recent years.

6.3   Financial regulations

None of the three Baltic States has specific legislation covering the financing of referendum campaigns. While the state is responsible for the organizational costs of holding the referendum, participating actors have to provide private resources in order to engage the public in debate. This has resulted in the use of initiatives and referendums as tools of party competition in Latvia and Lithuania, while Estonia has seen only two referendums since 1991. The only exceptions to this rule were the referendums on accession to the European Union in 2003, which saw a broad coalition of the state (which also provided extensive resources for the 'Yes' vote campaign), parliamentary parties, and mainstream non-governmental organizations successfully campaign in favour of accession. This financial and political commitment reflects a high level of elite cohesion on the importance of 'rejoining the West'.

Estonia

There is no legislation governing the general financial aspects of referendum campaigns in Estonia. The state is the leading provider of funds in referendum campaigns, keeping in mind the political aims elaborated by major governing political parties. To this end various institutions and commissions are usually arranged. The state also resolves possible misunderstandings, conflicts and problems. For instance, the Estonian EU referendum campaign was to a large extent typical of those seen elsewhere in the post-communist accession states. The 'No' camp was relatively weak while the 'Yes' movement benefited considerably from government and EU support. The 'Yes' side was heavily propagated by political elites: The President, Parliament, government, parliamentary parties, entrepreneurs and interest groups (e.g. Chambers of Commerce), the EU Commission, and foreign diplomatic missions. A special parliamentary decision in 2003 determined an additional state budget for EU referendum costs exceeding a total of 30,767,400 EEK (approximately two million euros). The State Electoral Commission was in charge of budget spending.

In addition, the electoral commission received 400,000 EEK (25,809 EUR) allocated for lectures and the introduction of new voting arrangements and procedures. In addition, the EU Representation in Estonia, together with the EU Information Secretariat, received 10 million EEK to carry out the political campaign. The campaign itself was a good example of innovative advertising and PR as well as good value for money, since a large amount of coverage was achieved at relatively little cost. This was done by using private–public partnerships, third sector involvement, grassroots level mobilization, and pretty extensive news coverage of the campaign. The Government EU Information Secretariat also contributed 1.1 million EEK to a larger (2.1 million EEK) project designed to help NGOs organize public debate on EU related topics. The other main partner was the Soros-based Open Estonia Foundation (Past and Palk, 2005: 71–5).

Like most contemporary European countries, Estonia has an established tradition of financing political parties from the state budget. The principle of direct public financing of parties was introduced into Estonian legislation in 1994. Since then, the amount of subsidies has increased more than tenfold. Until 2004 public financing was targeted only towards parliamentary parties. Now, according to new law, marginal subsidies are allocated for parties receiving at least one per cent of the votes in nationwide elections. This support for extra-parliamentary parties is stated in the Law on Political Parties and is therefore not automatically subject to the annual review that takes place when the state budget is set and the total amount of financing for parliamentary parties is determined. Regular annual declarations on all the financial activities

Table 6.4 State expenditures in 2003 EU Referendum Campaign (In Estonian EEK and euros)

Personal costs	Republican electoral commission	County electoral commissions	Polling stations	Ministry of foreign affairs	Total
	900,000	2,492,946	12,147,500	200,000	15,740,446
	(58,064.5EUR)	(160835.2EUR)	(783,709.6EUR)	(12,903.2EUR)	(1,015,512.6 EUR)
Administrative	2,284,000EEK	701,458	1,741,500	300,000	5,026,954
costs	(147,354.8EUR)	(45,255.3EUR)	(112,354.8EUR)	(18,522.3 EUR)	(324,319.6EUR)
Total	3,184,000EEK	3,194,400	13,889,000	500,000	20,767,400
	(205,419.3EUR)	(206,090.3 EUR)	(8,960,645.5 EUR)	(32,258.0EUR)	(1,339,832.2EUR)

Source: Vabariigi valimisskomisjon http://www.vvk.ee/.

of political parties, with the exception of campaign declarations and campaign spending, have been required from the year 2000.

However, there have been no limits on campaign expenditures. Parties have been free to buy media time, restricted only by general advertising law. Before the 2003 nationwide parliamentary elections, commercial advertising was banned on public television, but remained on two nationwide and popular private channels. Limits on campaign expenditures are still debated among political elites, the proposed benchmark has been estimated at US$2.5 million per party, however, this has yet to be implemented in practice (Sikk, 2006: 72–3).

Latvia

In both the inter-war and modern post-Soviet era, the organization of referendums and initiatives has been financed by the state (Article 26 'Law on referendums and popular initiatives'). However, this is the full extent of state support and regulation pertaining to the financial aspects of the process. There is no legal basis for the financing and regulation of debates or pro and contra actors. Indeed, there is no legislation governing the general financial aspects of campaigning in a referendum.

While the initial stage of collecting 10,000 signatures, and then later persuading 10 per cent of the electorate to support the initiative over the month in which the Central Election Commission structures the signature gathering, calls for a certain sophisticated level of organization and financing, there is no financial state support available. In the actual run up to a referendum, pro and contra campaigning is also privately financed and largely unregulated. There is no financial or organized state financial support for parties in general, or for parties or other organizations wishing to take part in a referendum campaign.

The only indirect form of financial regulation is the annual audit of political party accounts. Latvian party financing law limits annual personal and corporate donations to 10,000 Lats (approximately 15,000 euros). However, until recently political parties have tended to play a marginal role in referendums. In the 1990s the most explicit party involvement came in the campaign over the 1998 citizenship law. The polarized Latvian nationalist and Russian-speaking parties adopted differing positions, and campaigned actively. However, there is no data on the extent of party spending on the referendum campaign. This is because the latter coincided with the election campaign (and these parties combined their referendum campaigns with their parliamentary campaigns), and party campaign financing regulations did not draw a distinction between these two types of campaign. Indeed, there was no limit on party expenditure in 1998, which meant that parties were not constrained in their campaigning for the referendum. Finally, to complicate matters further, in 1998 political party accounts were not made public (changes to the law to make this possible were only made in the run-up to the 2002 parliamentary election).

More recently, the major actors in referendum campaigns have been opposition parties and third-person organizations. Opposition parties have begun to treat referendums as opportunities to criticize governments and to build up their own support. The 2007 and 2008 referendum campaigns also witnessed a rise in the use of third-party advertising (which remains unregulated in Latvia). Indeed, much of the campaigning in the four referendums held in 2007 and 2008 was done by third parties that, as NGOs, do not have to publicly declare their income and expenditure. Moreover, government-coalition parties (typically the wealthiest in Latvia, attracting the largest private donations) have not taken part in referendum campaigns, preferring to have the referendums fizzle out by dint of low turnout and then legislate through parliament. As a result, referendum campaigns tend to be unbalanced, with a strong anti-government rhetoric, but little qualitative debate on the substance of the issue.

The only campaign to have received state financing was the referendum on accession to the European Union. Not only did the Latvian state stump up 1 million Lats (1.4 million euros) for the campaign (only 5 per cent of which went to activities organized by the loose coalition in the 'No' campaign), but the Latvian political elite also united in order to create a favourable environment for a 'Yes' vote. Latvia was the last accession country to organize a referendum, hoping to benefit from the wave of public *europhoria* as applicant country after country voted 'yes' to EU accession. Indeed, the question was also framed in a slightly disingenuous way in order to gain greater public support. It asked: 'Are you for Latvia's participation in the European Union,' avoiding more correct phrases such as 'membership' (Auers, 2003). The campaign was essentially organized as a vote on the future direction of Latvia – would it become a 'boring' Nordic state, or sink into the grey zone that Belarus and pre-Yushenko Ukraine occupied. Unsurprisingly, perhaps, there was a solid 'Yes' vote.

Lithuania

Since 1989 the Lithuanian law on referendums has stated that all organizational costs must be covered by the state. The financial regulation of referendum campaigns is the same as that for all other political campaigns, including electoral campaigning. This is because, from 1997 onwards, Lithuania has had a single law on the control of financing of all political campaigns.

Referendum actors are substantially different compared to those involved in an election campaign. While electoral campaigns are dominated by relatively well-organized and permanently functioning political parties, referendum campaigning is dominated by weakly organized ad hoc citizens' groups. The only exceptions have been those referendums initiated by political parties. Since 1995, none of the 12 failed referendum initiatives were initiated by an influential political party. Rather, all these initiatives were presented by groups of citizens or marginal parties.

A standard political campaign in Lithuania has three phases: (i) the initial phase after the declaration of the election date (including the registration of candidates); (ii) the agitation or campaigning period (30 days); and (iii) the declaration of voting results and disclosure of campaign funding. The first phase of the political campaign applies only partly to referendums. The referendum campaign period starts from the day when the initiative referendum group was registered by the Central Election Commission. This means that, formally, a referendum campaign is substantially longer than the official 30-day electoral campaign in presidential, parliamentary, local or European elections. Still however, referendum campaigns may be regarded as following the standard rules of an election campaign.

The main provisions of referendum financing are focused on the referendum agitation phase. Only political parties, candidates, expected candidates, initiators and opponents of the referendum and their representatives, who are responsible for the finances of a political campaign, have the right to collect and receive financial support during the campaign process. All monetary donations are accumulated in special bank accounts. All donations exceeding 1,000 Litas cannot be kept or accumulated in cash. Further, all donations need to be registered on special lists of donors. The main sources of political campaign funding are individual and corporate donations during the campaign, bank loans, and funds owned by political parties (the funds of civic organizations or NGOs are not mentioned at all).

Certain types and amounts of contributions are banned and individual and corporate contributions are limited to an annual 37,500 Litas or 10,689 euros. Indeed, all contributions above 100 Litas or 28.9 euros need to be registered, and all contributions over 1,000 Litas or 289 euros must be transferred via bank account; donations may be made only by citizens of Lithuania and private corporations, except those with shares in central or local government, which are registered in Lithuania; political parties with no less than 3 per cent of the total vote after elections have the right to receive compensation for up to 25 per cent of campaign expenditures, but in the case of referendum campaigns there are no such provisions.

The most recent rules regarding public funding for referendum campaigns were established in the 2004 Law on the financing and control of financing of political parties and political campaigns. However, these rules prioritize campaigns initiated by political parties against those initiated by civic groups. The most expensive referendum in Lithuania was a government-led referendum on Lithuania's membership in the EU with expenditures equal to 11.4 million Litas (3.3 million euros), but including costs of voting administration. Nonetheless, public funds went mainly to the government's information campaign, but were not distributed among political and civic campaigners representing the 'No' and the 'Yes' supporters. Indeed, the 'No' campaign was represented by only three members of parliament and two small non-parliamentary parties, i.e. National Progress and Republican parties.

If we compare referendum costs to election campaign expenditures, the referendum on Lithuania's membership in the EU was an exception from the rule, as the average electoral campaign is several times more expensive than the average referendum campaign. From 1996 to 2007 the average costs generated by electoral campaigns were equal to

Table 6.5 Campaigning expenditures in Lithuania, 1996–2008 (in million Litas)

	Campaign expenditures
1996 Seimas elections	between 4.0 and 5.0
1997–1998 Presidential elections	6.2
2000 Local elections	3.5
2000 Seimas elections	5.1
2002 Local elections	4.9
2002–2003 Presidential elections	9.7
2003 Referendum on Lithuania's membership in the European Union	11.4*
2004 Euro elections	4.4
2004 Presidential elections	6.9
2004 Seimas elections	19.6
2007 Local elections	19.4
2008 Consultative referendum on the extension of operation of the Ignalina Nuclear Power Plant	0.5

*Expenditures also include voting administration costs.

more than 8 million Litas, excluding voting administration expenditure. Nonetheless, an especially extreme increase in the cost of electoral campaigns has been observed since the 2004 Seimas elections, when the campaign expenditures of seven political parties and coalitions receiving more than 3 per cent of the total vote reached 19.6 million Litas (5.7 million euros).

The data on referendum funding in Lithuania are fragmented and incomplete. However, the total spending on campaigns during the consultative referendum on the extension of the operation of the Ignalina Nuclear Power Plant held in October 2008 was equal to only 0.5 million Litas. This means that this expenditure was far less than for the parallel 2008 parliamentary election campaign, the estimated agitation costs of which will be close to 30 million Litas. This highly unequal funding meant that the 2008 election campaign wholly overshadowed consultative referendum agitation. This is despite the fact that all major parties and the government formally supported the draft referendum proposal. The reason for their passive approach to the campaign is because they did not see dividends, which would strengthen their political positions in the election.

All referendum initiatives have an equal right to be successfully communicated to the citizens. Free and equal airtime on radio and television is granted to government members, parties, public organizations and citizens. However, the Central Electoral Commission has a duty to define differences between referendum agitation and referendum information. Along legal lines referendum information needs to be comprehensive, and needs to be informative regarding the negative and positive outcomes of passing a referendum issue. Information can encourage the participation of voters in a referendum, but voters cannot be asked to vote for or against an issue. State institutions responsible for referendum information need to provide expert analysis to both supporters and opponents of the issue. The only full-scale informational campaign in Lithuania came during the EU membership referendum in 2003. In general, the information campaign was evaluated positively by voters. In a poll on the information campaign, 76.6 per cent of the respondents said they had received enough information during the campaign, 6.9 per cent said they had received too much information, and 11.5 per cent said they had received too little. 47.6 per cent approved the information on Lithuanian–EU relations provided by Committee of European Affairs to the Lithuanian government, and only 8.0 per cent disapproved. The way the issue was advertised in the mass media was seen positively by 60.5 per cent of the respondents, and negatively by only 21.8 per cent.

The divide between referendum agitation and referendum information opens the gates to the potential for manipulation of power resources, especially, if the referendum is initiated by ruling parties.

As some sort of compensation for the unclear rules pertaining to referendum funding, Lithuania has provisions allowing the initiators of the direct vote to free use of public media. The initiative referendum group, the President, the Prime Minister, ministers, parties, nongovernmental organizations, and citizens all have the right to use public media free of charge. The Central Electoral Commission coordinates with National Radio and Television in order to approve regulations regarding the preparation of broadcasts intended for referendum agitation and the actual duration and time of the National Radio and Television of Lithuania broadcasts. The broadcast time is distributed in such a way that secures the equal rights of both the initiative referendum group and its opponents. Representatives of the initiative referendum group and the opposition are accorded at least seven hours each of national radio and television time for staging debates.

In contrast, the use of private media is dependent on the financial resources of the campaigning organizations. According to the law, campaigning organizations may be compensated even for private media expenses, but no clear provisions exist on the matter of how this might be done. The Central Electoral Commission is obliged to resolve all disputes arising of referendum agitation.

6.4   Effects of financing in the Baltic States

The lack of financing instruments available for referendum and initiative campaigns has resulted in party-centred campaigning in Latvia and Lithuania. There have been only two referendums in post-1991 Estonia, and both have been on major constitutional issues (adopting a new constitution and accession to the European Union). In Latvia, opposition parties use the initiative mechanism as a way of garnering support for populist measures that they hope to convert to party support at the following election. In contrast, major Lithuanian government parties use the referendum and initiative devices to make policy.

The evidence for Estonia indicates that there is no correlation between money spent on referendum campaigning and electoral results. Despite heavy spending in the 2003 accession referendum, the result was only a modest success for the 'Yes' vote. Eurosceptic campaigners claimed that the 'No' vote in the referendum was probably 50 times less expensive the 'Yes' vote when the funding of the two sides was compared. The anti-EU activists could not afford any public relations experts, expensive advertising or media professionals.

It should be stressed that Estonian political parties were not particularly active in the EU accession referendum campaign, partly because the nationwide elections took place in Spring 2003. The government coalition came to power in April 2003. Party finances were exhausted. Moreover, party spending reports do not specify exactly how much money was spent in nationwide elections to the Estonian Parliament, nor in the EU referendum.

The governing *Respublica* party spent a total of 2.3 million EEK on various pro-EU activities, including a special campaign directed towards young voters. The party activists distributed 10,000 buttons supporting the European Union and 100,000 stickers on products ranging from groceries to agricultural machinery to plane tickets. The neoliberal Reform party propagated a pro-EU referendum campaign; however, unlike *Respublica*, the party focused mainly on rallying the support of its own supporters rather than society as a whole. This was not unproblematic for the Reform party, since according to one campaign official 86 per cent of its supporters also supported the EU. The party relied heavily on cost-effective electronic resources whereas other channels of communication were used only as needed.

In Latvia referendums and initiatives have been used by government opposition movements and parties to protest against government policies, as well as to promote their own esteem and recognition through support for populist policies such as higher pensions and nationalist-restrictive citizenship laws. These opposition movements have generally been able to organize only limited campaigns due to financial restrictions. Moreover, the campaigns have been rather low-key, as government parties do not engage in the debate, hoping that referendums fail through low turnouts. Only the EU accession referendum campaign was well funded with 95 per cent of the 1 million Lat budget (1.5 million euros) being spent on pro-accession advertising that acted to overwhelm the opponents to enlargement, who were hardly heard. The debate on accession rumbled on for months in advance of the poll, and turnout was high. But the impact of the campaign, and financing in general, is hard to measure.

A major feature of the Lithuanian political context is the high degree of party control over referendum initiatives. There are several important aspects here: because of the high level of citizen support necessary to initiate a referendum, only large political parties have been able to campaign successfully for a particular issue or, alternatively, to put a particular question to referendum directly through parliament. The agenda of referendum issues has also been under the full control of political parties. Ten referendums and one plebiscite since 1991 have each been held upon the initiative of one or a few political parties, and no single successful referendum initiative has been implemented without the active role of political parties.

The Lithuanian party-centred referendum allows political parties to use direct democratic means, first of all, to mobilize the party electorate, but also to increase the legitimacy of party policy (rather than to reach political decisions on which politicians disagree), and of party decisions (which are brought to the political stage independent of the wishes of government). Civic groups, non-governmental organizations, and local communities in the referendum initiative and campaign are often in a disadvantageous position compared to political parties.

These facts refute the conventional notion that the referendum is an instrument of policy making which offers citizens the opportunity to take political decisions directly and over the heads of political parties. Moreover, national referendums are relatively expensive instruments of decision making. While electronic communication might decrease the costs of referendums substantially, these issues do not feature in contemporary Lithuanian discourse.

6.5 Conclusions

The three Baltic States diverge with regard to the frequency and purposes of initiatives and referendums in their contemporary democracies. Estonia makes only occasional use of referendums, to resolve contentious constitutional issues, largely because the constitution sets limits on the use of direct democracy and emphasizes the representative component. Referendums are more frequent in Latvia and Lithuania, but the lack of state financing means that referendums have become tools of party politics rather than structured expressions of popular opinion. Moreover, the lack of structured financing instruments means that referendums and initiative measures must be supported by groups with access to extensive private financial resources in order to have any hope of success.

Notes

1. These key articles state that: 1. Latvia is an independent democratic republic. 2. The sovereign power of the State of Latvia is vested in the people

of Latvia. 3. The territory of the State of Latvia, within the borders established by international agreements, consists of Vidzeme, Latgale, Kurzeme and Zemgale. 4. The Latvian language is the official language in the Republic of Latvia. The national flag of Latvia shall be red with a band of white. 6. The parliament shall be elected in general, equal and direct elections, and by secret ballot based on proportional representation. 77. If the parliament has amended the first, second, third, fourth, sixth or seventy-seventh Article of the Constitution, such amendments, in order to come into force as law, shall be submitted to a national referendum (Latvian Constitution).

2. However, there is a mechanism that allows parliament to prevent a referendum: 'A national referendum shall not take place, if the *Saeima* again votes on the law, and not less than three-quarters of all members of the *Saeima* vote for the adoption of the law' (Article 72).

3. 'The budget and laws concerning loans, taxes, customs duties, railroad tariffs, military conscription, declaration and commencement of war, peace treaties, declaration of a state of emergency and its termination, mobilization and demobilization, as well as agreements with other nations may not be submitted to national referendum' (Article 73).

4. The referendum was called to counter a Moscow-mandated union-wide referendum on the future of the Soviet Union. On 17th March, the Latvian government announced that it would not formally participate in the all-union referendum on preserving the Soviet Union. Thus the Gorbachev referendum, held two weeks after the independence poll, had a very low turnout in Latvia (Dreifelds, 1996).

5. 226,548 signatures were collected – about 17 per cent of the electorate (Central Election Commission, 2006).

6. 184,383 signatures were collected – some 13.7 per cent of the electorate.

7. For instance, the Lithuanian Democratic Labour Party proposed three different themes for referendums just before the Seimas elections of 1996: on a decrease in the number of members of Seimas; on establishing a fixed date for parliamentary elections; and on the allocation of no less than half of the national budget to social welfare. At the same time the HU(LC) proposed a referendum on compensation for the population's savings which were lost in the hyperinflation of 1991–92. HU(LC) lost a similar referendum in 1994.

References

Archdeacon, T.S. (2008a) 'People Power Vote Shot Down', *The Baltic Times*, 6 August.

Archdeacon, T.S. (2008b) 'Voter Turnout Too Low for Pension Increase', *The Baltic Times*, 27 August.

Auers, D. (2003) 'How Democratic was the 2003 Latvian Referendum?', www.policy.lv. Accessed 17 August 2008.

Butler, H. and S. Kaplan (1997) 'Eastern Europe and the former Soviet Union', in D. Butler and A. Ranney (eds), *Referendums Around the World: The Growing Use of Direct Democracy* (London: Palgrave Macmillan).

Constitution of the Republic of Latvia (with amendments up to 23rd September 2004), http://www.ttc.lv. Accessed 16 August 2008.

Constitution of the Republic of Lithuania (Approved by the citizens of the Republic of Lithuania in the Referendum on 25 October 1992). Available online at: http://www3.lrs.lt/home/Konstitucija/Constitution.htm.

Constitution of the Republic of Estonia. Available online at: http://www.president.ee/en/estonia/constitution.php (accessed 29 August 2008).

Dreifelds, Juris (1996) *Transition in Latvia* (New York: Cambridge University Press).

Estonian Central Electoral Commission, http://www.vvk.ee/. Accessed 29 August 2008.

Ehin, P. and P. Vello (eds) (2005) *Deciding on Europe: The EU Referendum in Estonia* (Tartu: Tartu University Press).

Krupavičius, Algis and Giedrius Žvaliauskas (2001) 'Lithuania', in A. Auer and M. Butzer (eds), *Direct Democracy: The Eastern and Central European Experience* (Aldershot: Ashgate), pp. 109–28.

Krupavičius, Algis (2004) 'Lithuania', in B. Kaufmann and M.D. Waters (eds), *Direct Democracy in Europe: A Comprehensive Reference Guide to the Initiative and Referendum Process in Europe* (Durham: Carolina Academic Press), pp. 86–9.

Latvian Central Election Commission (2008). www.cvk.lv Accessed 4 August 2008.

Law on Referendums and Popular Initiatives (with amendments up to 6th April 2006), http://www.cvk.lv. Accessed 11 September 2008.

Law on Referendum, 4 June 2002. Available online at: http://www3.lrs.lt/pls/inter3/dokpaieska.showdoc_l?p_id=206332.

Lithuanian Central Electoral Commission – www.vrk.lt. Accessed 18 September 2008.

Past, Liisa and Palk Paavo (2005) 'The Referendum Campaign', in P. Ehin and V. Pettai (eds), *Deciding on Europe: The EU Referendum in Estonia* (Tartu University Press).

Politinių partijų ir politinių kampanijų finansavimo bei finansavimo kontrolės įstatymas (Law on financing and control of financing of political parties and political campaigns), 23 August 2004. Available online at: http://www3.lrs.lt/pls/inter3/dokpaieska.showdoc_l?p_id=323445.

Ruus, J. (2001) 'Estonia', in A. Auer and M. Bützer (eds), *Direct Democracy: The Eastern and Central European Experience* (London: Ashgate).

Šilde, Adolfs (1976) *Latvijas Vēsture: 1914–1940* (A History of Latvia 1914–1940). (Stockholm: Daugava).

Sikk, A. (2006) *Highways to Power: New Party Success in Three Young Democracies* (Tartu: Tartu University Press).

7
The Financing of Referendum Campaigns in France

Francis Hamon

7.1 Background and history

Before addressing the financing of referendum campaigns it is useful to summarize the French experience in the matter of direct democracy. It is a well-known fact that, more than two centuries ago, in 1793, France was the first modern state to implement direct democracy at the national level by holding a referendum on the draft of its new Constitution.

Despite this early breakthrough, France has made only limited use of direct democracy, from both a quantitative and a qualitative point of view. Throughout the period from 1793 to 2006, France held only 24 referendums at the national level: while this is a much larger number than in Belgium or the United Kingdom, compared to Switzerland or even Italy, it is relatively few. Further, it is important to bear in mind that these 24 referendums have been of the same type: each was planned by the executive, triggered by the executive, and their purpose was at least as much to confirm or strengthen the legitimacy of this power as to adopt a new statute or a new constitution. Two of the most influential French political philosophers of the eighteenth century, Rousseau and Condorcet, favoured more democratic forms of referendum, such as the Initiative or the people's veto. However, their ideas were never put into practice within their own country.

In the nineteenth century, the referendum acquired a bad reputation in French public opinion: it was seen as a tool of dictatorship, owing to the use made of it by the emperors Napoleon I, from 1799 to 1815, and Napoleon III, from 1851 to 1870. It was largely admitted within republican circles that parliamentary democracy was the best safeguard against the temptations of personal power and this is why the referendum almost disappeared from French institutions, from the beginning of the Third

Republic (1870) until the end of the Fourth (1958). But for General De Gaulle, the founder of the Fifth Republic, the Head of State had to be the true leader of the nation and, in that regard, it was essential that he could make a direct appeal to the people whenever he thought it necessary. This is why, in our present Constitution, the referendum has been reintroduced: according to Article three, 'National sovereignty belongs to the people who shall exercise it through their representatives and by means of referendum.' As was already the case in the nineteenth century, the ultimate decision to trigger the referendum device lies within the realm of the Head of State; according to Article 11, 'The President of the Republic may, on a proposal from the Government [...] or on a joint motion of the two assemblies [...] submit to referendum any Government bill which deals with the organization of public authorities, or with reforms relating to the economic or social policy of the nation and to the public services contributing thereto, or which provides for the authorization to ratify a treaty that, though not contrary to the Constitution, would affect the functioning of the institutions.'

Following up on one of the themes in his presidential campaign of 2007, namely that the balance of power under the Fifth Republic was tilted too far in favour of the President, Nicolas Sarkozy proposed introducing additional elements of both parliamentary and direct democracy into the French Constitution. To fulfill this promise, in July 2008, a Constitutional Act was adopted by Parliament and no less than 37 articles of the Constitution were modified, Article 11 among them. The purpose of the amendment of this article was to provide a new way of starting the referendum process, without requiring the President. In the French media, and among the commentaries of some political leaders, this new way was often referred to as 'a right of popular initiative'. If this were indeed true, the change would be profound. This is because in France up to the present, only the President has been able to put a referendum on the agenda. In my view, this is a misleading denomination. Rather, the new procedure enshrined in Article 11 is a double-triggered one, in which the first move has to be made by members of Parliament, and not by the people themselves. This formulation is so difficult to implement that its workability looks very doubtful.

First, the bill which is the issue of the potential referendum must be put forward by one-fifth of all members of Parliament, the National Assembly and Senate included. As most members of the French Parliament are elected on a majority basis, the support of one of the two main parties

(Socialist on the left, Union for a popular majority on the right) will be required at this first stage, although there are relatively few partisans of direct democracy in their ranks.

At the second stage, this bill must receive the support of 10 per cent of all of France's registered electors, which, in the present circumstances, amounts to more or less 4.5 million signatures, that is to say nine times as many as in Italy, where the number of signatures required to start an abrogative referendum is only 500,000. Collecting such a high number of signatures in a limited time will be next to impossible, save perhaps for some very powerful pressure groups ready to invest a good deal of money in the process. If these two stages are successfully completed the bill will be submitted to a referendum. However, the referendum will not occur if the two assemblies of Parliament examine the bill before a time limit determined by an institutional Act. This means that if the Government and its majority in Parliament do not want the referendum to take place, they only have to bring the bill up for discussion and the initiative process will be cancelled, whatever the result of the parliamentary debate.

The manner in which the new provisions of Article 11 are to be implemented shall be determined by an institutional Act, which is still in preparation. Therefore, the new procedure is not yet applicable. However, it is my opinion that, even when applicable, there will be very few occasions to make use of it, and perhaps none at all. It looks likely that, despite the change in Article 11, the referendum will remain basically what it was before 2008: a presidential prerogative.

Of the nine referendums on which the French people have voted since the beginning of the Fifth Republic, eight were organized on the basis of Article 11. There are two other provisions related to referendums in the French Constitution: Article 88–5 and Article 89. However, the former, Article 88–5, has only limited scope, due to its exclusive concern with treaties pertaining to the accession of a State to the European Union or the European Communities. As for the latter, Article 89, this deals with amendments to the Constitution already voted on by the two assemblies of Parliament and it enables the President of the Republic to choose between a referendum and a joint meeting of the two assemblies to achieve the passing of the amendment. It has been implemented only once, in 2000, to replace the seven-year Presidential term with a five-year term of office.

To sum up this constitutional analysis, there cannot be a referendum in France at the national level, without the direct involvement of the President of the Republic. As far as the financing of referendum campaigns is concerned, we can infer three important points from this situation:

First, the referendum campaign does not involve the collection of signatures. Consequently, expenses related to the referendum process are not as important as is often the case, in countries or states like Switzerland, Italy, or California, where the people themselves can take the initiative.

Secondly, whatever the subject of the referendum, the prestige of the President is always at stake and the media can be expected to provide wide coverage without anybody having to pay for political advertisements.

Thirdly, since the referendum has been conceived primarily as one of the President's prerogatives, it is not surprising that the regulation of the entire campaign, including all financial matters, has been planned to coax a presidentially desired response from the people.

7.2   Financial regulations

In France, a political actor's ability to take part in a referendum campaign depends less upon the money the actor can spend, than on two particular points. First, the share the actor is able to acquire of the means to provide propaganda given freely by the state. Secondly, the attention the actor is able to draw from the mass media. Let us admit that, for the purpose of this report, the scope of 'financial regulation' includes the rules pertaining to the use not only of actual financial resources but of all material facilities that can be employed in a referendum campaign: access to the radio and television channels controlled by the State, free disposal of billboards or lecture halls, and so on.

It is worth noting that, while the rules pertaining to all electoral campaigns (presidential, parliamentary, European or local) are entrenched into a statute or organic law, and sometimes even in the Constitution itself, inasmuch as referendum campaigns are concerned, there are no standing provisions. For each referendum, the regulation of the campaign is a matter of ad hoc provisions, set by the executive power in the form of an Order in Council. This situation has been heavily criticized, particularly by the Constitutional Council and the Council of State: it can even be held as unconstitutional because the regulation of referendum campaigns pertains to the implementation of civic rights, a matter which, according to the French Constitution, comes within the competence of Parliament. But let us not forget that, according to the spirit of the French Constitution, the referendum is a presidential prerogative: the absence of statute law, as far as referendum campaigns are concerned, has the advantage of giving the President more room for manoeuvre.

The general pattern of regulation, however, does not vary much from one referendum to another. In order to be allowed to participate in the official campaign, a party must satisfy an alternative criterion: either to have five seats in Parliament without any distinction between members of the National Assembly and members of the Senate; or to have received 5 per cent of the votes in the latest political election held at the national level, whatever the nature of this election (according to the calendar, it can be a national parliamentary election, an election of the French representatives in the European Parliament, or the election of the town councils).[1]

Every party which meets one of these two alternative conditions is entitled to three advantages:

First, the party can advertise on public noticeboards without having to pay any stamp duty.

Secondly, the party has at its disposal free broadcasting time on the public channels of both television and radio. In 2005, the total time allotted for the referendum campaign was 140 minutes on television and 140 minutes on radio. Eight parties had been retained to participate in the campaign; each of them had ten minutes on both television and radio, and the remaining time was divided up between the parties for one half according to the number of seats they have in Parliament and for the other half according to the number of votes they got at the latest national election.

Thirdly, in 2005, for the first time, each party on the list was able to receive, within the limit of €800,000, reimbursement from the State for some of its campaign expenses: those relating to the printing of posters, the production and distribution of handouts and leaflets, and the holding of public meetings.[2] But expenses not included on this list (for instance, those relating to an opinion poll or to a propaganda website) were non-refundable. There are two possible explanations for this innovation: a rational one and a more political one. The rational explanation is that the parties had to deal with a difficult issue, in which both the length of the treaty and the complexity of the matter were exceptional. The more political reason is that the government, afraid of losing the referendum, allocated money as a means to pressure the most influential parties to expand their campaigns in favour of the 'Yes' side.

If we turn now to the regulations concerning election campaigns, we can say that they are both similar and different.

They are similar with regard to the facilities given to the political parties. This is because, at least in the parliamentary election, the criterion to participate in the official campaign on the radio and on television is roughly the same. They are different, however, in as far as the balance of information given to the electors is concerned.

In parliamentary and presidential elections, the main objective of regulation is to place all of the candidates on the same footing, so that the electors can get a balanced view of the options open to them. The principle of equality between the candidates entails not only that each candidate is entitled to the same facilities from the State, but also that means of propaganda not provided by the State are severely regulated. Disclosure requirements exist for all resources and expenses related to the campaign, and the total amount of expenses must not exceed a maximum fixed by the regulations.[3]

On the contrary, as far as referendums are concerned, regulation does not guarantee that the electors will receive a balanced view of both sides of the argument throughout the campaign.

On the one hand, expenses are unlimited and there is no disclosure requirement with the exception of those expenses which can be repaid by the State. Commercial advertising is forbidden but only during the three weeks prior to the election, while, for electoral campaigns, this prohibition reaches back three months before the election.

On the other hand, since the departure of General De Gaulle, in 1969, the government bills submitted to referendums have always dealt with subjects on which there is an agreement between the presidential majority and the leaders of the main parties of the parliamentary opposition. Consequently, all of the big parties taking part in the official campaign are usually on the 'Yes' side. It does not follow from this that the subject is necessarily consensual. On Europe, particularly, there have always been big divides, not only in public opinion but also inside each party. For instance, in 2005, Laurent Fabius, former French Prime Minister and number two in the internal hierarchy of the Socialist Party, was an active campaigner for the 'No', while his party officially sustained the 'Yes' side. However, since Fabius was in the minority inside his own party, he was excluded from the official campaign.

On the whole, it can be said that while referendum campaigns are always politically pluralist,[4] they are often one-sided inasmuch as the subject of the referendum is concerned.[5]

7.3   Effects of money and financial regulations

The imbalance of the referendum campaign, which is due partly to the inadequacy of financial regulations, may affect both the electoral turnout and the result of the ballot. However, these effects vary according to the subject matter of the referendum and they are sometimes paradoxical.

By way of illustration, let us consider the two most recent French national referendums, which took place in 2000 and 2005.

The former dealt with the duration of the presidential mandate proposing replacement of the seven-year presidential term with a five-year term of office. As the subject was technical and removed from the concerns of everyday life, a high level of non-voting could be expected, unless the campaign succeeded in convincing the mass of the electors that something important was at stake. Owing to its imbalance, however (more than 90 per cent of the broadcasting time for the 'Yes' side), the official campaign was repetitive and boring. Many people were given the impression that it was not worth going to the polls because the decision was already made. A livelier and more balanced campaign would most probably not have changed the result (the 'Yes' side won by 73 per cent), but it would perhaps have increased the turnout (which was only 30 per cent).

The latter referendum dealt with the authorization to ratify the European Constitutional Treaty. When the announcement of the referendum was made by President Chirac, in September 2004, the 'Yes' side was leading in the opinion polls (with 69 per cent against 31 per cent), but 60 per cent of the people had not yet made up their minds how to vote. Therefore, the stakes of the referendum campaign were high as it looked very likely that the final result would depend on the evolution of this mass of undecided electors.

There is no doubt that, on the whole, the referendum campaign was rather imbalanced in favour of the 'Yes' side:

Among the advocates of the treaty were not only the leaders of the two main parties (UMP and PS), but also most of the key figures of the French establishment (politicians, journalists, managers and civil servants) and their views were given wide coverage in the media.

Of the 140 minutes of broadcasting time in the official campaign, parties supporting the 'Yes' got 90, while parties supporting the 'No' got only 50. Moreover, in his capacity as Head of State, President Chirac who was, of course, an advocate of the treaty, was allowed to intervene in the campaign, without the time of his intervention being taken into account for the repartition between the two sides.

According to the statistics published by the National Commission of Campaign Accounts and Political Financing (CNCCFP): the campaign expenses of the four parties supporting the 'Yes' amounted to €4,792,239 (of which €3,137,468 were reimbursed by the State). The campaign expenses of the four parties on the 'No' side amounted to only €3,022,441 (of which €2,612,302 were reimbursed by the state).[6]

This disproportion in the means of propaganda did not, however, prevent the bulk of undecided electors from shifting to the 'No' side, as shown by successive opinion polls and by the final result of the ballot (more than 55 per cent voted 'No'). The opponents of the treaty, who had only limited access to the mass media, made substantial use of the Internet.[7] When all is said and done, it is even possible to suggest that the imbalance of the campaign did more harm than good to the 'Yes' side.

Valéry Giscard d'Estaing, former President of the French Republic, used to say that, when they are called to vote on a referendum, French electors tend to answer 'the author of the question, and not the question itself'. The greater the imbalance of a referendum campaign, the more this formula gets closer to the truth. In 2005, overfed with propaganda in favour of the treaty, and irritated by the massive involvement of their leaders on the 'Yes' side, the people tended to forget the treaty and to focus on their grievances about the social and economical situation. The result of the 29 May poll was as much a rebuff directed at the French establishment as a rejection of the treaty.

The lesson to be learnt from these two examples is that more balanced referendum campaigns, with approximately equal means for both sides, would better serve democracy, by increasing interest the subject and encouraging people to focus on the question itself.

In particular, so far as financial regulation is concerned, I think it is important to focus attention on three points.

First and foremost, money and broadcasting time should be distributed not only according to the weight of the parties on the political scene, but also with a view to getting a proper balance between the two sides.

Secondly, public financing of the campaign could be more generous than in 2005: a limit of €800,000 for the reimbursement of expenses seems rather low for a campaign at the national level, the more so since, for the presidential campaign, each candidate is able to claim expenses within a maximum limit of €6,850,000.

Finally, the parties should be entitled not only to be repaid their expenses; they should also receive an advance when they need it. In 2005, one of the parties on the 'No' side (the 'Rassemblement pour la

France' of Charles Pasqua), was unable to invest more than €247,858 in its campaign owing to cash problems.

Notes

1. When the subject dealt with in the referendum pertains to a specific territory, as was the case in 1988 (New Caledonia), this criterion may be altered to allow local parties to participate in the national campaign.
2. Thanks to this innovation, in 2005, for the first time, published data existed on referendum campaign expenses. However, since non-refundable expenses were exempt from declaration requirements they were not included in these data.
3. For the parliamentary election, the ceiling amounts to €38,000 plus €0.15 for each inhabitant in the constituency; for the presidential election, it amounts to €13.7 million for each candidate (€18.3 million for the two candidates who have made it to the second round of the election). For both elections, the candidates can get reimbursement of their actual expenses within a limit of 50 per cent of the ceiling.
4. This pluralism applies not only to the official campaign but also to the general information given on television and radio. According to the directives of the higher audiovisual Council (CSA), when dealing with information related to the subject of the referendum, the audiovisual media should treat all political parties in a fair and impartial way. This means that each party must be given access proportionate to its proportion of the votes or to the number of its representatives in Parliament.
5. Referendums are also possible at the local and regional levels. Regulation of the finances in these referendum campaigns, however, hardly differs to that at the national level.
6. The non-refundable expenses were not taken into account in this data.
7. There were 79 websites for the 'Yes' side and 161 for the 'No' side.

8
Referendums and Spending in Ireland

Karin Gilland Lutz

8.1 Introduction

Ireland is one of the European countries that holds relatively frequent national-level referendums, although it is not in the same league as Switzerland and Italy. The 1937 constitution, *Bunreacht na hEireann*, which created the Irish direct democratic tools that are in existence today, was itself ratified by the very first of the 30 votes that have taken place to date, on 1 July 1937. The most recent vote – at the time of writing – took place on 12 June 2008, and concerned the ratification of the Lisbon Treaty. In between these two dates, issues of great significance to Irish society as well as issues that were not perceived by the electorate – nor, perhaps, by anyone else – to be very important were decided by referendum. High-salience votes include those on EC membership, abortion and divorce rights, and the so-called Belfast Agreement. In contrast, minor reforms to the upper house of the Irish parliament, the *Seanad*, variations in the size of voting districts, and recognition of local authorities count among the voting issues that generated less interest. Notably for political scientists, there were two referendums attempting to change the current Irish electoral system, proportional representation by single transferable vote, to the British first-past-the-post system, but both attempts failed. (Perhaps the Fianna Fáil government's intention to solidify its own position vis-à-vis the other parties was too obvious to appeal to the voters.)

The money–politics nexus – that is to say, the connection between power and money – is a topic that has been very salient in Ireland in recent times – indeed, anyone following Irish news and current affairs in the last seven to ten years must have noticed the myriad of tribunals taking place in relation to various events – these tribunals share the smallest common denominator – they investigate the 'money flow' oftentimes found running from business (builders and property developers figuring remarkably often) to politics, and the possibility that political decisions were made to reflect the recipient's gratitude over these monetary gifts. Although it has been difficult for tribunal judges to prove such links between gifts and decisions (especially given the selective memory loss that suddenly struck most big businessmen and top politicians forced to appear before a tribunal), it has not been difficult to imagine such links, and, indeed, one big player in Irish politics has gone to prison and ruined his political career. To date, however, the money–politics nexus has not touched extensively on the context of referendums. Nevertheless, this sets the backdrop to explaining the lax attitude to money in politics that prevailed until roughly the mid-1990s. Political actors were not able to rely on public funding for their activities, including running election campaigns or indeed referendum campaigns. They could, however, rely on other sources of funding without running the risk of being examined very closely, if at all. Imagery with mafia-like overtones conjured up by media reports from the tribunals (for instance, reports of politicians meeting business people in hotel car parks and receiving brown paper envelopes containing upwards of 50,000 Irish pounds) underlines the culture prevailing at that time.

In the last decade, however, this culture has taken several knocks, on the one hand as the result of what these tribunals revealed about the machinations of Irish politics. Simultaneously, but due to another course of events, namely a series of high-profile court cases successfully taken against the government, the Irish referendum context has become much more tightly regulated than hitherto. These regulations were introduced to establish a level playing field in relation to money as well as in relation to other goods.

The first part of this chapter outlines the legal basis of Irish referendums and provides some flesh on the bones of these legal principles in the shape of some descriptive data concerning issues, turnout, etc. Subsequently, financial and other related regulations are outlined.

8.2   Background and history

The average turnout in Irish referendums is just over 52 per cent, and on 22 out of 30 occasions the government was successful in getting its constitutional amendment bills past the people. Regarding voting behaviour in referendums, Sinnott (1995) shows that the urban–rural, as well as – within urban areas – middle-class–working-class factors, play a role in explaining voting behaviour. Although referendums are supposed to be an opportunity for the voting public instead of elected representatives to make a decision, it is clear that political parties, as well as other actors, play a central role in referendum campaigns. However, as Lyons (2008) has pointed out recently, political parties sometimes have strong incentives not to involve themselves in specific referendum campaigns, especially if they fear that the topic might cause an internal party split. This presumably reduces the extent to which voters simply cast their referendum ballot in accordance with 'their' party's position, as is often thought to be the case in referendums generally.

The historical background of direct democracy in Ireland reflects in many ways the country's history of struggle for independence from Great Britain and political life in the early days of independent Ireland. Although the Irish Republic had existed since 1922, created in the Anglo-Irish Treaty that ended the War of Independence between the colonial power Great Britain and its neighbour Ireland (with the exception of the six counties of Northern Ireland, which remained under British rule), it was only in 1937 that the Irish Republic promulgated a constitution that could truly be called independent. Until then, the constitutional basis of the state was the Irish Free State Constitution of 1922, a document whose contents bore significant traces of British influence. This constitution, too, foresaw elements of direct democracy as part of the Irish political system, at least initially. This was a conscious decision on the part of the political leaders of the time, who wanted to emphasize popular sovereignty in their manifestation and interpretation of Irish independence. Nevertheless, as the Anglo-Irish Treaty itself remained the most contentious issue in Irish politics, and the pro-Treaty government felt concerned that the anti-Treaty opposition might use the constitutional provisions for popular initiatives to further their anti-Treaty objectives, it abolished all direct-democratic measures from the 1922 Constitution in 1928. (Although the War of Independence as well as the Civil War that followed it had been over for several years by 1928, the very foundations of the Free State were still hotly contested, and, some would argue, are still being fought out – these days mainly with words – in Northern Ireland.)

The 1937 Constitution, *Bunreacht na hEireann*, left a great deal virtually unchanged. Most relevant here is of course the reintroduction of a legal basis for direct democracy in Ireland. In fact, the 1937 Constitution makes Ireland one of relatively few countries in Europe where popular consent is required to amend the constitution (Gallagher 1999: 79). Article 46 reads:

1. Any provision of this Constitution may be amended, whether by way of variation, addition, or repeal, in the manner provided by this Article.
2. Every proposal for an amendment of this Constitution shall be initiated in Dáil Éireann as a Bill, and shall upon having been passed or deemed to have been passed by both Houses of the Oireachtas, be submitted by Referendum to the decision of the people in accordance with the law for the time being in force relating to the Referendum.
3. Every such Bill shall be expressed to be 'An Act to amend the Constitution'.
4. A Bill containing a proposal or proposals for the amendment of this Constitution shall not contain any other proposal.
5. A Bill containing a proposal for the amendment of this Constitution shall be signed by the President forthwith upon his being satisfied that the provisions of this Article have been complied with in respect thereof and that such proposal has been duly approved by the people in accordance with the provisions of section 1 of Article 47 of this Constitution and shall be duly promulgated by the President as a law.
   (Note: The *'Houses of the Oireachtas'* is the term used to indicate the two chambers of parliament, the *Dáil* and the *Seanad*).

In 46.2 we also see that only *Dáil Éireann*, the lower chamber of parliament, has the right to propose constitutional changes. Since the political system in Ireland is a parliamentary one, this effectively means that the government – through its control of the *Dáil* – controls the introduction of constitutional change. We moreover see a reference to 'the law for the time being in force relating to the Referendum', a point which will be explored in more detail below. All of the Irish referendums in Ireland to date have been Article 46 referendums.

The Irish Constitution nevertheless does grant an additional possible legal basis for a referendum, but it has remained unused. The lengthy Article 27 of the Constitution sets out the following:

This Article applies to any Bill, other than a Bill expressed to be a Bill containing a proposal for the amendment of this Constitution, which shall have been deemed, by virtue of Article 23 hereof, to have been passed by both Houses of the Oireachtas.

1. A majority of the members of Seanad Éireann and not less than one-third of the members of Dáil Éireann may by a joint petition addressed to the President by them under this Article request the President to decline to sign and promulgate as a law any Bill to which this article applies on the ground that the Bill contains a proposal of such national importance that the will of the people thereon ought to be ascertained.

2. Every such petition shall be in writing and shall be signed by the petitioners whose signatures shall be verified in the manner prescribed by law.

3. Every such petition shall contain a statement of the particular ground or grounds on which the request is based, and shall be presented to the President not later than four days after the date on which the Bill shall have been deemed to have been passed by both Houses of the Oireachtas.

4. 1° Upon receipt of a petition addressed to him under this Article, the President shall forthwith consider such petition and shall, after consultation with the Council of State, pronounce his decision thereon not later than ten days after the date on which the Bill to which such petition relates shall have been deemed to have been passed by both Houses of the Oireachtas.
    2° If the Bill or any provision thereof is or has been referred to the Supreme Court under Article 26 of this Constitution, it shall not be obligatory on the President to consider the petition unless or until the Supreme Court has pronounced a decision on such reference to the effect that the said Bill or the said provision thereof is not repugnant to this Constitution or to any provision thereof, and, if a decision to that effect is pronounced by the Supreme Court, it shall not be obligatory on the President to pronounce his decision on the petition before the expiration of six days after the day on which the decision of the Supreme Court to the effect aforesaid is pronounced.

5. 1° In every case in which the President decides that a Bill the subject of a petition under this Article contains a proposal of such national importance that the will of the people thereon ought to be ascertained, he shall inform the Taoiseach and the Chairman of each House of the Oireachtas accordingly in writing under his hand and Seal and shall decline to sign and promulgate such Bill

as a law unless and until the proposal shall have been approved either

   i by the people at a Referendum in accordance with the provisions of section 2 of Article 47 of this Constitution within a period of eighteen months from the date of the President's decision, or

  ii by a resolution of Dáil Éireann passed within the said period after a dissolution and reassembly of Dáil Éireann.

2° Whenever a proposal contained in a Bill the subject of a petition under this Article shall have been approved either by the people or by a resolution of Dáil Éireann in accordance with the foregoing provisions of this section, such Bill shall as soon as may be after such approval be presented to the President for his signature and promulgation by him as a law and the President shall thereupon sign the Bill and duly promulgate it as a law.

6. In every case in which the President decides that a Bill the subject of a petition under this Article does not contain a proposal of such national importance that the will of the people thereon ought to be ascertained, he shall inform the Taoiseach and the Chairman of each House of the Oireachtas accordingly in writing under his hand and Seal, and such Bill shall be signed by the President not later than eleven days after the date on which the Bill shall have been deemed to have been passed by both Houses of the Oireachtas and shall be duly promulgated by him as a law.

Theoretically, therefore, votes on non-constitutional amendment issues are possible, but a scenario in which this instrument were to be extensively used or even used at all, is unlikely. There are several reasons for this, as discussed in Sinnott (1995: 218–19). One reason is that the mode for electing senators (members of the *Seanad*) makes an anti-government majority in the upper house extremely unlikely (although not entirely without precedent); and that a pro-government *Seanad* would introduce an anti-government bill stretches the imagination somewhat. *Seanad* elections always take place a few months after a *Dáil* election. The 60 senators are elected with the general electorate as such playing no role whatsoever: 43 are elected from five so-called 'panels' (Agriculture, Culture and Education, Industry and Commerce, Labour, Public Administration), where electors are members of county councils as well as major city councils, members of the *Dáil* as well as of the outgoing *Seanad*. Research into the 1997 election shows that these 43 senators were elected by an electorate consisting of 992 people, 794 of whom had a party affiliation (Coakley and Manning, 1999). University graduates elect a further six senators. The remaining 11 are the *Taoiseach*'s (prime minister's) choice. In summary, given that the *Taoiseach* can choose almost 20 per cent of the senators, and that senate elections take place right after *Dáil* elections which lead to the formation of a government, it is unlikely that the composition of the upper house will be anti-government.

A further reason why Article 27 is unlikely to become important is that it is at the President's discretion to agree to act on a petition from a majority of the *Seanad* and a third of the *Dáil*. The presidency as well as the government has tended to be held by the biggest party in the country, *Fianna Fáil*. Moreover, even if the President decides to act, s/he can decide either in favour of a referendum, or in favour of a resolution to be passed by the *Dáil* after the next election. All things considered, then, the chances of an 'active' Article 27 are small.

A legal basis for the Irish electorate on which to stage a vote does not exist.

Having outlined the constitutional background for direct democracy in Ireland, we can now consider the issues that have been decided by referendum in Ireland. Some of these were hinted at in the Introduction, and to a point it would be fair to say that Table 8.1 reflects the major developments in Irish society over roughly the last 50 years. Social or moral issues such as divorce rights (1986, 1995) and the abortion question – in relation to which there have been no less than five referendums to date, between 1983 and 2002 – were very emotional and the campaigns were fought very much in terms of good and evil and basic values. Specific cases of very young girls in their early teens who under unclear/tragic/criminal circumstances became pregnant drove developments forward, as these cases came up against the limits set by the constitution and the Supreme Court was forced to (re-)interpret the constitution in light of these particular cases.

8.3   Financial regulations

A number of fairly recent developments have created a new regime for Irish referendums. Some relate to money itself, others to other goods with monetary value (albeit a value that is usually not easy to estimate) and political institutions regulating the referendum game.

Two court cases played a crucial role here, each brought against the government by a well-known political figure. First, Green Party MEP

Table 8.1   Referendums in Ireland, 1937–2008 (http://c2d.unige.ch/)

	Date	Issue	Turnout (%)	Yes (%)	No (%)
1	12.6.2008	Lisbon Treaty	53.1	46.6	53.4
2	11.6.2004	Citizenship	54	79	21
3	19.10.2002	European Enlargement	49	63	37
4	6.3.2002	Protection of Human Life in Pregnancy	43	50 (49.58)	50 (50.42)
5	7.6.2001	Prohibition of Death Penalty	35	62	38
6	7.6.2001	Adhesion to International Criminal Court	35	64	36
7	7.6.2001	Ratification Nice Treaty	35	46	54
8	11.6.1999	Recognition Local Authorities	52	78	22
9	22.5.1998	Ratification Amsterdam Treaty	56	62	38
10	22.5.1998	Belfast Agreement	56	94	6
11	30.10.1997	Confidentiality Cabinet Meetings	47	53	47
12	28.11.1996	Bail Regulations	29	75	25
13	24.11.1995	Divorce Legislation	62	50 (50.27)	50 (49.73)
14	25.11.1992	Right to Abortion Mother's Life Endangered	68	35	65
15	25.11.1992	Freedom to Travel	68	62	38
16	25.11.1992	Right to Information	68	60	40
17	18.6.1992	Ratification Maastricht Treaty	57	69	31
18	26.5.1987	Ratification Single European Act	44	70	30
19	26.6.1986	Introducing Divorce Legislation	61	37	63
20	14.6.1984	Voting Rights Foreign Residents	47	75	25
21	7.9.1983	Prohibiting Abortion	54	67	33
22	5.7.1979	Representation of Universities in Senate	29	92	8
23	5.7.1979	Adoption Agencies Judicial Powers	29	99	1
24	7.12.1972	Lowering Voting Age to 18	51	85	15
25	7.12.1972	Revoking Catholic Church's Official Privileges	51	84	16
26	10.5.1972	Joining EEC	71	83	17
27	16.10.1968	Size Voting Districts	66	39	61
28	16.10.1968	Electoral Reform	66	39	61
29	18.6.1959	Electoral Reform	58	48	52
30	1.7.1937	Ratification Constitution	76	57	43

Patricia McKenna took a case in 1995 which led the Supreme Court to decide that a government was not allowed to spend public money in one-sided referendum campaigns (on the grounds that the whole point of a referendum is that the people makes 'its' mind up, and thus it is inappropriate that the government of the day uses tax money – the people's own money – in an effort to try to persuade the people in one direction or the other). From this point on, government parties, just like every other campaigner, had to find campaign funds as best it could (*McKenna* v. *An Taoiseach (No.2)* 1995 2IR 10). Secondly, a well-known anti-EU 'opinion maker' took a case against the Broadcasting Complaints Committee and RTÉ (*Radio Telefis Éireann*, public service broadcaster), and after going through several legal instances in a series of appeals the case was decided by the Supreme Court. Its decision laid down that the public service broadcaster was not allowed to give more airtime to one side than to the other in a referendum campaign (*Coughlan* v. *Broadcasting Complaints Commission and RTÉ* 2000 3 IR 1).

These rulings meant that public money could no longer be used for campaigning purposes, and they also signalled the end of free airtime for campaign purposes on RTÉ ('party political broadcasts'). Another significant consequence was the establishment of the Referendum Commission under the Referendum Act (1998), a body that may come into being each time a referendum is held, at the discretion of the Minister for the Environment. (A Referendum Commission has five members, a former Supreme or High Court judge or a current High Court judge; the Comptroller and Auditor General; the Ombudsman; the Clerk of the *Dáil*; and the Clerk of the *Seanad*.) The Commission was originally charged with formulating a 'fair' statement of the referendum issue, as well as with publishing that statement along with balanced pro and con arguments, and also facilitating debate and discussion 'in a manner that is fair to all interests concerned' (Referendum Act 1998, 3.1). These tasks were partially revised in 2001, because the original formula was not felt to work well. Until then, the Referendum Commission had among other things published ads in print and broadcast media with lists of pro and con arguments. For instance, in EU-related votes it was simultaneously argued that Ireland's policy of military neutrality would not be affected by Treaty X, and the very same ad would point out that Ireland's traditional neutrality might indeed be compromised. Instead of providing such pro and con arguments on an issue, which were sometimes felt to be confusing, the post-2001 Commission simply tries to improve voter awareness of the referendum and what the vote is all about.

The McKenna case referred to above did not rule out the possibility of public funding for referendums, but made such funding contingent on both 'sides' in a campaign being accorded equal treatment. Nevertheless, Ireland went down the road of 'no public funding' rather than that of 'equal public funding'. A number of factors might explain this. One might be that parties in Ireland receive comparatively little funding (relative to parties in most other countries), so there is no real culture of publicly funded campaigning. Another reason might be that the 1998 referendum in relation to the Belfast Agreement served as a stark reminder that publicly funded campaigns might, in certain contexts, mean funding groupings or movements representing very extreme and non-democratic positions favoured only by a very small proportion of the population. (More specifically, groups known to favour the 'armed struggle' in the North saw the Belfast Agreement as a move in the wrong direction, in that it would not end the partition of the island of Ireland, but rather reinforce it by involving the Republic of Ireland in the running of Northern Ireland, and thus defusing demands for a united Ireland. Moreover, specific constitutional articles laying claims to the island of Ireland in its entirety were to be dropped if the referendum were passed – which it was – and these republicans were strongly opposed to that.)

A few years after the aforementioned court cases shook up the rules of the referendum game, a parliamentary committee deliberated further on the issues relevant in this chapter (*All-Party Oireachtas Committee on the Constitution*, 2001). It recommended that there should be public funding for referendums, divided equally between those 'in favour' and those 'against'. Nevertheless, it is clear in the Committee's report that this was not actually the majority position of the Committee members; rather, the Committee made this proposal because the McKenna judgment prevented any other way of providing public funding. The majority position was instead that public monies should be paid out on an 'equitable' basis, whatever that might mean. It lies rather close to hand to suspect that it might mean a distribution formula based on the number of seats in parliament a party has, or that that would be a dominant element of an 'equitable' distribution formula. That the situation was deemed as unsatisfactory in many quarters is reflected in the fact that the Committee cited above signalled its intention to review 'aspects of the referendum procedure' (*All-Party Oireachtas Committee on the Constitution*, 2008) concerning the imparting of information to the public during referendum campaigns.

To date, nevertheless, there is no public funding for referendums in Ireland (and there is also no upper limit on spending). It stands to reason, therefore, that campaigners must rely on other means. Although these sources of income are private rather than coming from the public purse, they are subject to certain control mechanisms. The Standards in Public Office (SIPO) Commission was created in 2001 as an independent body, replacing a previous body with a similar function on the basis of the Standards in Public Office Act 2001, a legal act which can be seen very much in the light of the previous years' tribunal discoveries, as described briefly at the beginning of this chapter. Campaigners have to register with the SIPO Commission and submit to it certain information concerning their financial transactions and activities. Specifically, under this regime there are three types of campaigners: political parties, third parties and other persons. While the definition of political parties should not require any further discussion, third parties are defined as 'any person, other than a political party or a candidate at an election, who accepts, in a particular year, a donation (i.e., a contribution given for political purposes) the value of which exceeds €126.97' (Standards in Public Office Commission, 2008: 24). Moreover, third parties are prohibited from accepting anonymous donations exceeding this amount and are prohibited from accepting foreign donations of any value. They are also prohibited from accepting donations exceeding €6,348.69 from a single donor in any one calendar year. Such donations must be returned within 14 days, and must also be reported to SIPO. As an aside, it may moreover be noted in relation to the definition of third parties that in relation to the referendum on the Lisbon Treaty in 2007 the SIPO Commission took legal advice on the particular role of campaigners not based in Ireland. Such actors were deemed not to be subject to these regulations.

Campaigners falling into the 'other persons' category are, in the context of referendum campaigns, any actor participating in the campaign without having received donations specifically for that purpose. Other persons might be individuals spending their own money, or a body or organization mounting a campaign with resources obtained not for the specific referendum purpose. Other persons are not required to register with SIPO or disclose their spending activities.

In contrast, third parties failing to register with SIPO are committing an offence. The Commission, however, as it notes in its 2007 annual report, is unable to prosecute unless it can prove that a potential third party has obtained a contribution (of at least €126.97) for political purposes. Understandably, this is difficult. Accordingly, the Irish system of controls on spending is based on trust to a certain extent, although the Commission proactively approaches individuals or groups it considers potential third parties and requests that they confirm their status in this respect.

Once registered, third parties must furnish the Commission with the following information if possible before, or else after, making use of any funds received:

(i) Its name and address;
(ii) A statement of the nature, purpose and estimated amount of the donations to, and proposed expenses of, the third party in any year; and

(iii) An indication of the third party's connection, if any, with any political party or candidate at a Dáil, Seanad or European election or referendum or otherwise.
(*Source*: http://www.sipo.gov.ie/en/Reports/OtherReports/Third Parties/Involvement/Name,1375,en.htm)

The above pertains not just to gifts of 'cash', but also to donations of property or goods, as well as the free use of property or goods or services, or, indeed, 'the difference between the commercial price and the price charged for the purchase, acquisition or use of property or goods or the supply of any service, where the price, fee or other consideration is less than the commercial price' (cited from the aforementioned website). A relevant definition of 'political purpose' is also provided by the Commission, but it suffices to say here that it covers all activities we would normally think of as campaign activities. These rules apply to third parties as well as political parties, but in this context, it may be noted that if a political party has a loan facility available to it (for instance, from a financial institution or a private individual), SIPO may inquire into the terms and conditions of the loan and also request evidence that it is being, or has been, repaid in accordance with those terms and conditions. Third parties do not have to disclose information on loans to SIPO, but SIPO may require that this information is provided.

Moreover, third parties are required to open a political donations account in an Irish bank or equivalent financial institution, with which all political donations are to be lodged. (Political parties are subject to an ongoing requirement to open and maintain political donations accounts.) By 31 March every year, political and third parties must submit to SIPO a statement of the account (showing what transactions have taken place during the reporting year) together with a statement declaring that all political donations received were lodged to that account and that all amounts debited from the account were used for political purposes. Additionally, one member of each third party or political party must act as the responsible person and sign a statutory declaration that to the best of his/her knowledge and belief, the aforementioned pieces of information are correct. These various pieces of documentation are not available for public inspection. Political parties must additionally submit an annual donations statement outlining the value and nature of all donations in excess of €5,078.95 including the identity and address of the donor. On SIPO's recommendation, the Director of Public Prosecutions may investigate specific donations. Annual donation statements are also laid before the *Oireachtas*.

In other words, SIPO does not receive any detailed information from third parties – the latter are, for instance, not required to disclose from whom they have received political donations. Moreover, SIPO does not receive any particular information from political parties in relation to referendums, although it may be noted that, in general, political parties must disclose the identity of donors giving in excess of €5,078.95. Disclosure of donors seems to be possible only if the campaigners themselves decide to: (a) accept only non-anonymous donations; and (b) publicize the identity of their donors. If this information is to have any effect on the referendum outcome, it must moreover be in the public domain before the day of the vote. In reality, this is far from being the norm. On 20 August 2008, in other words more than two months after the Lisbon Treaty vote, the *Irish Times* found the fact that Sinn Féin disclosed having spent more than €118,000 on its campaign worthy of publication, pointing out that it was the only party to date that had made any voluntary disclosures about its expenditure. Nothing was revealed, however, about the donors behind the party although a party spokesperson is cited in the article as calling for legislation to that effect ('Sinn Féin Spent over €118,000 on Campaign Against Lisbon Treaty', *The Irish Times*, 20 August 2008).

Failure to comply with the regulations outlined above makes campaigners 'guilty of an offence' under section 25(1)(e) of the Electoral Act 1997, as inserted by the 2001 Electoral (Amendment) Act. To date, no cases involving political or third parties have gone to court. As mentioned above, the SIPO Commission does have the authority to approach individuals and groups that come to its attention, and such groups may also contact SIPO. Such a group was the organization Libertas, which came to play a key role in the vote on the Lisbon Treaty in 2007. Libertas is, according to itself, 'a new European movement dedicated to campaigning for greater democratic accountability and transparency in the institutions of the EU and developing innovative policies which can benefit Europe and foster a more positive relationship between those institutions and the citizens for whom they legislate' (http://www.libertas.org/content/view/79/84/).

According to newspaper reports after the 2008 Lisbon vote, Libertas filed accounts with the Companies Registration Office in 2007 showing no income and no expenditure, although it can be shown that during that year, Libertas undertook various activities with clear political purposes in relation to the Lisbon vote – activities that would have incurred costs or at the very least had a monetary value to be reported, as outlined above ('Substantial Amount of Funding for Libertas Came from Ganley',

The Irish Times, 3 October 2008, p. 13). If the SIPO Commission decides to pursue these apparent inconsistencies, it will be the first time the new Irish funding regulations are put to the test in the direct-democratic context.

8.4 Conclusion

As one of the European countries most prone to holding national referendums, Ireland's changed referendum rules in general, and pertaining to spending in particular, makes it an interesting case to anyone interested in the financing issue. These changes can be seen as part of a wider reaction against the unclear and uncomfortable role money has been 'discovered' to play in Irish politics generally. Questions of ethics, trust in blatantly rent-seeking politicians, as well as in the democratic institutions these politicians occupy, were extremely salient in the public domain in Ireland during the years which saw these changes. Nevertheless, there is still no real possibility of 'disclosure', i.e. voters cannot find out who funds a particular campaign. From a theoretical perspective, this is interesting because obviously, then, voters cannot use such information to inform their voting decision. On a practical level, the decidedly weak disclosure regulations look primarily like a minimalist attempt to be seen to 'do something' in a climate that had all political actors clamouring to associate themselves with ethics in public office. It is, for instance, difficult to see how the SIPO Commission could check that campaigners accept no donations from abroad, or that they do not receive donations exceeding the maximum sum of just under €6,500 per year from any single donor. Even if the Commission were to query lodgments of relatively large sums of money, say a few hundred thousand euros, to a third party's account, it apparently would not have the means to examine the campaigner's claim that the lodgment represented many anonymous donations of €100.

In respect of the public funding of referendum campaigns, the likelihood of politicians deciding to introduce public funding is difficult to estimate; it cannot be ruled out that a future government would put a constitutional amendment bill to the people which would, if accepted, overturn the court ruling that public funds would have to be shared equally between 'Yes' and 'No' camps.

References

All-Party Oireachtas Committee on the Constitution (2001) *Sixth Progress Report* (Dublin: Stationery Office).

All-Party Oireachtas Committee on the Constitution (2008) *Press Release* 23 October 2008, http://www.oireachtas.ie/viewdoc.asp?DocID=10187 accessed on 26 October 2008.

Coakley, J. and M. Manning (1999) 'The Senate Elections', in M. Marsh and P. Mitchell (eds), *How Ireland Voted 1997* (Boulder, CO: Westview).

Gallagher, M. (1999) 'The Changing Constitution', in J. Coakley and M. Gallagher (eds), *Politics in the Republic of Ireland*, 3rd edn (London: Routledge in association with PSAI Press).

Irish Times, 3 October 2008.

Lyons, Pat (2008) *Public Opinion, Politics and Society in Contemporary Ireland* (Dublin: Irish Academic Press).

Referendum Act (1998) (Dublin: Stationery Office).

Sinnott, R. (1995) *Irish Voters Decide: Voting Behaviour in Elections and Referendums Since 1918* (Manchester: Manchester University Press).

Standards in Public Office Commission (SIPO) (2008) *Annual Report 2007* (Dublin: Stationery Office).

Websites consulted

http://c2d.unige.ch/.Accessed October 2006.

http://www.sipo.gov.ie/en/Reports/OtherReports/ThirdParties/Involvement/ Name,1375,en.htm. Accessed October 2006.

http://www.libertas.org/content/view/79/84/. Accessed October 2008.

http://www.irishtimes.com. Accessed October 2008.

9
Financing Referendum Campaigns in Italy: How Abrogative Referendum Can Regulate Electoral Financing

Roland Ricci

In the Italian political system, the referendum is an essential institution. It became an inescapable juridical institution following the promulgation of the Republican Constitution of 1948. Overall, as is usual in modern constitutions, the referendum is an instrument to modify the Constitution by enacting laws amending the Constitution and other constitutional laws. Nevertheless, the most important category of referendum in Italian political life is the abrogative referendum which is a legislative referendum.

In 1947 the constitutionalists chose the method of abrogative referendum on popular initiative.[1] This institution played a major role during the political crisis of the 1980s and 1990s. The Italian people have used the process of abrogative referendum to change the electoral system for the members of the upper House of Parliament: the formerly proportional system was replaced by majority ballot. At the same time, the Italian people rejected political corruption by acting to abrogate the public financing of political parties. Following these referendums, both of which took place in 1993, the financing of political activity has concentrated on the reimbursement of electoral spending.

With regard to referendums, both national and regional referendums are financed according to the expenditure of the campaign and the organization of the vote. We find in the Italian political system different forms of referendum: abrogative, confirmative or consultative. The regulation of these referendums depends upon different normative authorities and is composed of specific norms. The main categories of referendum are constitutional referendum, legislative referendum at national and regional levels, and communal referendum. Regulation takes place at two levels: the principles are established at the national level but each category has particular rules enacted by special authority.

We cannot understand the Italian configuration of financing referendum campaigns, however, without studying the influence of referendum use in political elections. The abrogative referendum has become an inescapable instrument of direct democracy. The Italian electors have used this institution to modify the financial norms regulating the activity of political parties because financial questions are at the centre of citizens' concerns. When authorized by the constitutional Court, Italian citizens utilized the abrogative referendum to invalidate the public financing of political parties, replacing this method with the reimbursement of electoral spending. In fact, the principal instrument used to regulate electoral financing is not the law enacted by Parliament but, rather, the law which comes from an abrogative referendum on popular initiative.

9.1   The abrogative referendum in Italy: an inescapable instrument of political life

During preliminary work on the Constitution the question of the legislative referendum was the subject of intense discussion. When the constitutionalists debated the organization of referendums, a number of different conceptions were proposed. In particular, the choice of the authority which could take the initiative of legislative referendum was debated strongly. Finally, the constitutionalists chose popular initiative to allow the people to resolve conflicts between Government and Parliament (Camera dei deputati, Segretariato generale, 1976: 908). This placed the Italian people in the primary position of opposition ahead of political parties, and was the reason behind the choice of popular initiative over presidential initiative.[2]

It was also necessary to place some limits on this new institution. Without paying attention to the details, Article 75 of the Constitution designates these boundaries as follows:

> A popular referendum shall be held to abrogate, totally or partially, a law or a measure having the force of law, when requested by five hundred thousand voters or five Regional Councils.
>
> Referendums are not admissible in the case of tax, budget, amnesty and pardon laws, or laws authorizing the ratification of international treaties.

All citizens eligible to vote for the Chamber of Deputies have the right to participate in referendums.

The proposal subjected to a referendum is approved if the majority of those with voting rights have participated in the vote and a majority of votes validly cast has been reached.

The procedures for conducting a referendum shall be established by law.

Among the norms instituted by this article, we find two kinds of regulations which set down juridical problems: a lacuna and a paradox. The paradox lies in the following statement: the abrogative referendum is an institution brought against the Parliament and its regulation provides that the procedures should be established by the Parliament. We will see that this situation plays an important role in the installation of abrogative referendum in Italy. With regard to the lacuna, this refers to a lack of control: no authority was appointed to ensure the compliance of referendum procedure with the rules stipulated in Article 75 of the Constitution. Further it was impossible to use an abrogative referendum as long as these questions remained unresolved.

The lacuna was filled by the constitutional law no. 1 of 11 March 1953.[3] Article number two of this law added a new competence to the constitutional Court,[4] making the Court the judge of whether or not referendum demands are in accordance with the second paragraph of Article 75 of the Italian Constitution. Nevertheless the second paragraph of the second article of the constitutional law joins the paradox previously mentioned: 'Judgment modalities shall be established by the law which will regulate the procedure of popular referendum.' Thus, it belonged to the Parliament to authorize the popular referendum: in fact, without a specific law enacted by Parliament no referendum could be held. All depended on the will of the Parliament: when it would pass this law and how it would configure its norms. Obviously, Parliament has used this power to prevent Italian citizens initiating abrogative referendum. The law was passed by Parliament in 1970,[5] but only following huge political controversy over the introduction of divorce into the Italian normative system.

The regulation enacted by Parliament in article number 39 of law no. 352 of 1970, was very ambiguous. This article provided: 'If before the date fixed for the referendum, the law or the enactment having the force of law, or their provisions object of the referendum, have been abrogated, the central Office for the referendum shall declare the interruption of the procedure.'

This text allowed the legislator to stop the development of an abrogative referendum by enacting a new law with the content of the previous law which was the law object of the referendum. In such a case, only the form has changed (Bettinelli, 1977: 131), but the norms are the same. To prevent the Parliament from acting in this manner for political reasons, the constitutional Court made a decisive intervention in an important decision of 1978.

The pronouncement was the result of a demand introduced by a committee of promoters for the abrogation of a law.[6] These promoters contested the constitutionality of law no. 352 of 1970 and especially the constitutionality of article number 39. In decision no. 16 of 1978 the Italian Court decided on the unconstitutionality of article 39 of the 1970 law[7] but did not invalidate the law because its absence would prohibit the holding of all abrogative referendum. The constitutional Court preferred to direct an injunction to the Parliament. This norm has fostered the enactment of a new law in which, if the law object of a referendum is replaced by a new text with the same content, the referendum should continue on the new text.

In this way the constitutional judges strongly established the institution of abrogative referendum in Italy. Following this decision the Italian people were able to contest the choices of political parties during the legislative procedure. As expected by the members of the Constituent Assembly, Italian citizens have taken up the referendum as a means of expressing opposition to the political system and, in addition, to the dishonest compromises of parties.

From the beginning of the abrogative referendum on popular initiative, the intention of several promoters' committees was focused on a great problem of Italian political life: the financing of political parties and elections. These committees wanted to remove public financing of political parties in order to suppress abusive usage of this regulation.

9.2 From the public financing of political parties to the reimbursement of election spending

For several decades after the Second World War the Italian political system was characterized by political instability and successive agreements between parties about mutual services: democracy changed into corruption and *partitocracy*. Thus, for the Italian people, the public financing of political parties was not a good measure. Money was not for political projects but for parties.

Only the abrogative referendum was a means able to overthrow the domination of political parties. The first attempt took place in 1978. A referendum was directed to abrogate law no. 195 of 2 May 1974, which established the public financing of political parties. It was an initiative from the Radical party which claimed, and has always claimed, no public financing and no *'lottizzazione'*. In the Italian language, this refers to the practice of giving high functions in public administration and public enterprises to members of political parties.

At this time, the Italian citizens did not agree with the ending of public financing for political parties. Also even if the referendum had been valid, because the majority of electors participated in the vote,[8] on 11 June 1978, the 'Yes' did not win, and the 'No' polled 56.4 per cent of the votes. It was only the first try by the promoters and the question was not closed.

The situation was unstable and the deterioration of relations between citizens and political parties continued. In 1991, Italian political life was shaken by an earthquake. Using the abrogative referendum, the Italian people changed the electoral system for naming the members of the lower House of the Italian Parliament. The abrogation of a few words in the electoral law modified the system. Proportional representation with a preferential vote system turned a single vote system. This abrogation greatly reduced the complexity of the Italian electoral system. Two conditions were necessary for this reversal: the agreement of the Italian constitutional Court and the victory of the 'Yes' vote.

The first condition was uncertain because the promoters of the referendum intended to abrogate an electoral law and because they used the abrogative process to achieve a positive effect. Previously, the constitutional judges, who were in charge of admissibility control, had refused a first demand directed against an electoral law. But, in 1991, they opened the door with decision no. 47 of 1991 for only one of the two demands: the Constitutional court declared the admissibility of the demand directed to abrogate the electoral law of the lower House of Parliament and the inadmissibility of the demand upon the electoral law of the high House.

It is an important decision, historically, in which the constitutional judges established the possibility of using abrogative referendum on electoral laws. The argument which sustained that an electoral law could not be the object of abrogative referendum was rejected by the constitutional Court in accordance with the text of the Constitution. Nevertheless, other requirements had to be satisfied, including the clarity of the demands according to the referendum process: the consultation of electors. The vote might be a conscious vote. Thus, in 1991 other demands calling for abrogative referendums had been rejected because of their lack of clarity. But, after this decision (no. 47 of 1991), abrogative referendums on the popular initiative could be used to abrogate parts of electoral laws, even with a positive result. This was a high point in the history of the abrogative referendum in Italy. Italian citizens were enabled to modify the electoral process.

With regard to the second condition of success after admissibility, the positive vote, the victory of 'Yes' was very important. The highest score in referendum history (95.6 per cent) and participation joined the quorum (62.5 per cent). The object of this referendum was to improve the quality of legislative work through the creation of a stable majority. Despite the instruction of abstention given by several parties, electors chose to break off with *partitocracy*.

This transformation of the electoral and political system continued in 1993. This year saw a second – and decisive – attempt to simultaneously modify electoral law and the financing of political parties.

Among the eight referendums of 1993, a first referendum was proposed to abrogate a part of the electoral law of the high House of the Parliament: it would transform proportional representation into a majority basis vote. The promoters had learnt their lesson from the rejection of an analogous demand in 1991 and their demand passed the control of the constitutional Court. On 18 and 19 April 1993, 77 per cent of electors participated in the vote and the 'Yes' side won, securing 82.7 per cent of the votes.

The promoters of the second referendum had decided on a proposal to abrogate public financing of parliamentary groups. As it was expressed by the constitutional Court,[9] despite the formulation of the question, the citizens could clearly understand that the object of the referendum was to abrogate norms establishing public contributions to political groups. On 18 and 19 April 1993, 77 per cent of the electors participated in the vote and the 'Yes' won with 90.3 per cent of the votes.

After these referendums, a contest can be observed between political parties and Italian citizens regarding the costs of political activity. The first act was the Parliamentary reaction to the referendum of 1993. Following this referendum result a new law had been enacted to regulate electoral campaigns for naming members of the Houses of the Parliament.[10] The legislative Assembly could not remove the effects of the abrogative referendum. Rather, it was possible only to correct, to modify, or to complete the norms resulting from the adoption of the abrogative law.[11]

Parliament was no longer allowed to use public money to directly finance political parties. As a result, a new approach was initiated: from this moment, public contributions have consisted of reimbursing those sums spent by the electoral parties during the electoral campaign. The law has established a new authority to control the regularity of these operations: the electoral mandatory which works with a regional college of electoral guarantee. The electoral mandatory must register every monetary movement during the electoral campaign and must communicate this information to the regional college of electoral guarantee. The law provides a maximum amount for the electoral spending of every candidate and for every political party. After this moment, in Italy, the opposition between political parties and citizens has focused on the level of electoral spending. Political parties have sought ways to increase the amount of reimbursement for electoral spending. At the same time citizens have sought to restrict spending which they consider to be abusive.

The second act was the proposition of a referendum to abrogate all of the public financing of political parties, regardless of the form this financing may take. Such a referendum was initiated in 2000. The promoters of this abrogative referendum planned to remove the reimbursement of electoral spending for elections and referendums. The proposition of this referendum passed the control of the constitutional Court. Despite a winning 'Yes' vote of 71.1 per cent, the participation of electors was only 32.2 per cent.

In fact, abrogative referendums on popular initiatives should act to arbitrate this controversy, one which is always at the centre of Italian political life. That is the reason why abrogative referendums are the principal instrument employed in order to regulate the financing of referendum campaigns.

At present, there is another attempt to suppress the public reimbursement of electoral spending in reaction to the perceived abuse of reimbursements in political practice. Currently, the Italian citizens oppose numerous manipulations made by Italian political parties. Between 1993 and 2008, the amount of public reimbursement on electoral campaigns has increased greatly. Reimbursements are progressively turning into the direct public financing of political parties.

Among manipulations perpetrated by the political parties we find the conversion of reimbursements from Italian lire to euros. In the law of 1993, the amount was 800 lire for every vote; in 2002 it became[12] one euro, that is 1,936.27 lire. At the same time, the law has reduced the level over which reimbursements are possible. This level passed, for election to the lower House of the Parliament, from 4 per cent of the valid votes to 1 per cent.[13] Thus the 'micro-parties' have been allowed to receive reimbursements – even if they are not making any expenditure.

Another problem, always inherent in law no. 156 of 2002,[14] was the level of reimbursement. This amount was fixed at one euro for each elector registered on the electoral roll, for every year of the legislature. So over the course of the parliament each elector brought €5 – even if they had not cast a vote.

The most recent development occurred in 2006. Each year the amount of reimbursement was calculated on the basis of the electoral spending spread over five years, the duration of a legislature. But, secondly, the original version of the law no. 157 of 1999,[15] in case of the dissolution of the chambers of the Parliament, the payment will be interrupted. In 2006, a law on different measures modifying several texts[16] has made a few modifications to the law of 1999. This law has enacted a new norm providing that, in the case of dissolution of the Houses of the Parliament, the payment shall continue. After the dissolution of the Parliament, in February 2008, and the elections in April, newspapers and citizens have been deeply shocked by the doubling of reimbursements – both for the present legislature and for the present legislature.

All of the aforementioned reasons have contributed to the citizens' use of abrogative referendum, in an attempt to modify the legislation on financing electoral spending.

9.3   Financing referendum campaigns by the reimbursement of campaign spending: a solution contested by Italian citizens

To understand the question of the financing of referendum campaigns, it was first necessary to highlight the present situation regarding the financing of election campaigns. The financing of both, referendums and elections, is connected. Currently, the situation is one of pressure for abrogation of the electoral financing law introduced in 2008. Nevertheless, specific legislation on financing referendum campaigns exists and we need to examine it. Then we shall think about the impact of referendum demands on the aforementioned situation.

The norms on financing referendums: the impact of citizens' political distrust

The Constitution establishes only the principles of each category of referendum, with the exception of local referendums on which nothing is said. The norms regulating referendum campaigns are contained in the laws which execute these principles. These norms reiterate those utilized in electoral campaigns.

The norms creating referendum

Article 138 of the Constitution provides a referendum for laws amending the Constitution and other constitutional laws. The process begins with a vote on the law by absolute majority in the two Houses of Parliament. A referendum may be initiated if one-fifth of the members of a House, or 500,000 electors, or five Regional Councils request that a referendum should be held. If the Houses of the Parliament vote in favour of the law on a second occasion, with a majority of two-thirds of the members, the referendum shall not take place.

Of course, in the Constitution, we rediscover the abrogative referendum on popular initiative provided by Article 75. It shall be held to abrogate, either totally or partially, a law or a measure having the force of law, when requested by 500,000 electors or five Regional Councils.

In Article 132, paragraph one, a referendum can be used in the case of a merger between existing Regions, or in the event of a new Region being created which has a minimum of one million inhabitants. It shall be decided by a constitutional law, after consultation with the Regional Councils, when the request has been made by a number of Municipal Councils representing not less than one-third of the populations involved, and when the request has been approved by referendum by a majority of said populations.

In the same Article 132, paragraph two, the referendum concerns the Provinces and Municipalities which request detachment from one Region and incorporation in another. The detachment may be allowed following a referendum and a law of the Republic, which obtains the majority of the populations of the Province or Provinces and the Municipality or Municipalities concerned, and after having heard the Regional Councils.

Finally, the Constitution provides, in Article 123, the possibility of submitting the statutes of the Regions to popular referendum if requested by one-fiftieth of the electors of the Region or one-fifth of the members of the Regional Council within three months of its publication. The statute that is submitted to referendum is not promulgated if it is not approved by the majority of valid votes.

Local referendums can be initiated according to legislative decree no. 267 of 2000. This decree, directed to the administrations of local collectivities, provides – in article number eight[17] – the possibility of holding referendums, requested by citizens, only upon questions within local competences. Regional, and similarly communal, statutes must contain the provisions necessary to implement referendum. Thus these statutes are different and some of them do not adopt the principle of national referendum financing: the reimbursement of campaign spending. It depends upon the provisions. A majority of regions have decided to include different regulations on reimbursements in their statutes. The modalities are not uniform with, in general, a minimum number of signatures and an amount of reimbursement calculated on the basis of the number of signatures or voters and of the price of material expenditures for the vote. Other regional statutes do not provide any reimbursement.

Among these referendums, the most important for Italian political life is the abrogative legislative referendum on popular initiatives, provided by Article 75 of the Constitution. So, as we observed in the first section, it was for the implementation of this referendum, that Parliament enacted law no. 352 of 1970: Norms upon referendum provided by the Constitution and upon legislative propositions by the people. According to this law, however, the financing of referendum campaigns is not an important question.

The norms regulating the campaigns

The object of law no. 352 of 1970 was to allow referendums to take place after the opposition of political parties. So we do not find a large number of provisions regarding financing. Even if the law regulated all national referendums provided by the Constitution, in this period political parties were financed by the Italian State. Thus, this question was not the principal preoccupation of the Parliament. In law the only writings on the financing of referendums concern the indemnification of official persons helping in the collection of signatures,[18] and the distribution of the costs of referendum operations.[19]

After the abrogation of public financing of political parties, a new law organized the reimbursement of referendum spending: law no. 157 of 1999. The title of the law explains its objective: 'New norms in the matter of reimbursements of spending for electoral and referendum consulting, and abrogation of writings about voluntary contribution to political movements and parties.' It was the first law directed explicitly towards the financing of referendum campaigns.

The fourth paragraph of the first article provides that, when an abrogative referendum in accordance with Article 75 of the Constitution is held, and when the referendum is declared admissible by the constitutional Court, an amount is allocated to the committees of promoters. This amount must be within the limits established by the law. The amount is calculated by multiplying by one euro the number of signatures necessary for the declaration of validity: the majority of the citizens listed on the electoral rolls.[20] The law introduces a maximum limit on this amount: €2,582,285 every year. The payment shall be executed before 31 July of the year in which the referendum is held. Finally, this paragraph applies these norms to the referendum provided by Article 138 of the Constitution, in case of enacting laws amending the Constitution or other constitutional laws.

As stated above, the legislation on the financing of electoral campaigns has been transferred to the financing of referendum campaigns. Therefore, the distrust of political parties has had an important influence on legislation in matters related to referendums. The situation continues to evolve because an additional demand of abrogative referendum, introduced in 2008, may modify the manner in which the public finance electoral campaigns. It is a paradoxical aspect of Italian legislation on the financing of referendum campaigns: decisions about referendum campaigns are to be determined by referendums.

Abrogative referendum will decide on the financing of referendum campaigns

The latest developments in the matter of electoral financing have impelled the citizens to counter-attack. In fact, a former minister in the Prodi, D'Alema II and Amato II governments, Willer Bordon, a member of the upper House of the Italian Parliament, has began a political struggle against abusive electoral public spending. In January 2008 he resigned from his political mandate and initiated a campaign to hold an abrogative referendum against law no. 157 of 1999.

The proposal for an abrogative referendum has been deposed to the desk for the referendum at the Supreme Court of Cassation. In fact, the promoters have deposited four questions which intend to abrogate in four different ways the writings of law no. 157 of 1999. The first step of the controls is a technical verification by the desk for the referendum. First, the promoters must deposit the 500,000 signatures necessary for admission of the demands of abrogative referendum according to Article 75 of the Constitution.

The demand was deposed on 24 June 2008. The four questions range from a whole abrogation of the law, to the abrogation of only certain aspects. The first question provides for the entire abrogation of law no. 157 of 1999. This solution possesses an important drawback: the disappearance of regulations on abrogative referendum and, overall, reimbursement of spending by promoters.

The second question aims to reduce spending to an amount that is four-fifths below actual expenditures. The promoters have chosen the abrogation of writings providing the payments every year during the five years of the legislature. The consequence will be to allow only one reimbursement. In this referendum no change is provided in respect of referendum regulation.

The third proposition of the referendum intends to delete the words added by law no. 51 of 2006 and to authorize the reimbursement of electoral spending even when the Parliament has been renewed after dissolution. In this case, the law established a double reimbursement which the referendum would remove. As in the previous question, referendum regulations remain unchanged.

The fourth question concerns the 'privileges' granted by the law on electoral financing. The referendum provides the opportunity to remove textual dispositions on the conditions of the reimbursement of electoral spending: there is no obligation for the political parties and movements to give any banking guarantees; the reimbursements can constitute transferable letters of credit; in the case of irregularity by the eligible parties or movements; and the reimbursements are interrupted until regularization. The referendum intends to delete the lack of guarantees, the transferability of reimbursements and the possibility of regularization. With this referendum there is no change to the principles of reimbursement; the only changes relate to their modalities.

Thus, the aforementioned demands of the abrogative referendum will decide, if the jurisdictional controls are passed, on the validity of law no. 157 of 1999. In the case of victory by a 'Yes' vote on the first question, and if the number of electors reaches a quorum, the entire legislation on the financing of referendums would disappear. However, in previous years no abrogative referendum has achieved the necessary quorum (the vote of the majority of the electors). This has been a recurrent problem in Italy.

Since 1974, 59 referendums have been held. In the first years, between 1974 and 1987, reaching the quorum was unproblematic in the 15 referendums held. Participation was around 80 per cent from 1974 to 1985. However, in 1987 participation decreased to 65 per cent. In 1990, for the first time, participation did not achieve the necessary threshold. Even if the 'Yes' vote won with 92 or 93 per cent in the three referendums, participation did not reach the quorum – achieving only 43 per cent of the electors.

The 21 following referendums again reached the quorum, but not uniformly: 62.5 per cent in 1991, around 70 per cent for the eight referendums held in 1993, between 57 and 58 per cent for the 12 referendums of 1995. But, in 1997, we notice a great decline in the level of electoral participation, which averaged only 30 per cent for the seven referendums. In 1999 participation touched the quorum, at 49.6 per cent, because the object of the demand was politically very important: the modification of electoral law by the abrogation of proportional vote. The following referendums, even those which concerned important political subjects, have not reached the quorum. For the seven referendums held in 2001, participation was 32 per cent; it fell further – to25.5 per cent for the two referendums of 2003. Participation maintained a low average level of 25.7 per cent for the four referendums held in 2005.

The tendency seems strong: the abrogative referendum does not sufficiently interest Italian citizens, whatever the subject in question. For instance, even when the abolition of electoral spending was concerned, in 2000, participation reached only 32 per cent. We cannot foresee the result of the referendums to be proposed in the near future. However recent events, and in particular the initiatives of political parties, seem likely to produce a reaction from the Italian electors.

Notes

1. Constitution of Italian Republic, 31 December 1947, Art. 75.
2. It was the position of C. Mortati (Fagiolo 1992: 955–7).
3. Additional norms to the Constitution upon Constitutional Court.
4. In accordance with the Article 134 of the Constitution: 'The Constitutional Court shall pass judgment on: controversies on the constitutional legitimacy of laws and enactments having the force of law issued by the State and the Regions; conflicts arising from allocation of powers of the State and those powers allocated to State and Regions, and between Regions; accusations made against the President of the Republic and the Ministers, according to the provisions of the Constitution.'
5. Law no. 352 of 25 May 1970: Norms upon referendum provided by the Constitution and upon legislative propositions by the people.
6. It was the law no. 152 of 22 May 1975.
7. Italian constitutional Court, decision no. 68 of 1978, *Giurisprudenza costituzionale*, 1978, part I, pp. 584–6.
8. Article 75 of the Constitution, section 4.
9. Italian constitutional Court, decision no. 30 of 1993.
10. The law no. 515 of 10 December 1993.
11. Italian constitutional Court, decision no. 32 of 1993.
12. Law no. 156 of 2002: article 2, paragraph 2, letter b.
13. Law no. 156 of 2002: article 2, paragraph 2, letter a.
14. Law no. 156 of 2002: article 2, paragraph 3.
15. Law no. 157 of 1999: article 1, paragraph 6.

16. Law no. 51 of 2006: article 39 quaterdecies, paragraph 2, letter a.
17. Paragraphs 3 and 4.
18. Law no. 352 of 25 May 1970, article 8, paragraph 5.
19. Law no. 352 of 25 May 1970, article 8, paragraph 53.
20. Article 75 of the Constitution, paragraph 4.

References

Bettinelli, E. (1977) 'Referendum abrogativo e riserva di sovranità: a proposito dell'articolo 39 della legge 25 maggio 1970 n. 352', in *Scritti in onore di C. Mortati*, Milan: Giuffrè.
Camera dei deputati, Segretariato generale (1976) *La Costituzione della Repubblica nei lavori preparatori della Assemblea costituente*, Roma, 1970–71, reprinted 1976, vol. VII, p. 908.
Fagiolo, G. (1992) *La Costituzione della Repubblica italiana*, vol. 2, Roma: Logos.

10
Financing Referendum Campaigns in Spain

Carlos Closa Montero and Flavia Carbonell Bellolio

10.1 Referendums in Spain in historical perspective

Referendums found their way into Spanish politics only in the 1931 Constitution of the Second Spanish Republic. No previous constitution had considered forms of direct democracy. (A small exception was the local consult for local finances. This was foreseen in Article 69 of the 1987 Statute of Autonomy of Cuba and Puerto Rico.)[1] The Constitution of the Second Republic (1931–1939) balanced two contradictory principles: on the one hand, it favoured a model of representative democracy in which Parliament (*las Cortes*) was the organ *par excellence* of the democratic system. Within this model, referendums and appeals to the people in general were perceived as undermining the authority of Parliament, its democratic quality, and its sovereign position (Garrorena, 1976: 97). On the other hand, drafters of the Republican Constitution assumed a model of *'rationalized parliamentarism'*. This model sought to correct the abuses of an extreme and unstable parliamentary system. Direct participation mechanisms, among others, were perceived as an instrument for this.

The 1931 Constitution resolved this tension by restricting popular consults to consultative referendums (Article 66). However, the Republican parliament did not implement the foreseen referendum legislation and no referendum was convened during the Second Republic. The same Constitution (Article 12) recognized another specific and restricted form of direct popular consultation: the regional plebiscite as a step prior to the adoption of Autonomous Community Basic Law (*Estatuto de Autonomía*). Since these regional referendums would provide a kind of differentiated legitimacy *vis-à-vis* national sovereignty, regions were keen to explore their potential and Catalonia, the Basque Country, and Galicia held referendums on their respective regional statutes.

Table 10.1 Regional referendums under the Spanish Second Republic

Date	Region	Results
3rd August 1931	Catalonia	74,86 % (yes)
5th November 1933	Basque Country	84,05 % (yes)
28th June 1936	Galicia	73,96 % (yes)

The Franco dictatorship (1939–1975) favoured the use of referendums. This was because of the personal plebiscitary possibilities of these consults, and also because the referendum was perceived as a mechanism by which to discredit parliamentary democracy. This view inspired the Law on Referendum in 1945, even though actual usage was scarce. Only two referendums took place, one in 1947 (on the restoration of monarchy as the future form of state; this referendum obtained 93 per cent of votes) and one in 1966 (on the State basic law, 95 per cent of votes) (Aguiar de Luque, 1977: 235ff).

10.2 The 1978 Constitutional regulation of referendums

Referendums played an important role in the transition to democracy (Aguilera de Prat, 1992; López González, 2005). Using the Francoist legislation, the Spaniards approved the Law for Political Reform (1976) which began the democratization process. Drafters of the 1978 Constitution hotly debated forms of direct democracy, although only the conservative AP (Alianza Popular, People's Alliance), inheritor of the Francoist political elite, wholeheartedly supported the extended use of referendums. Parties at the centre and on the left of the political spectrum feared the plebiscitary dimension that referendums had been associated with under Franco's regime. Drafters pondered several models of referendums: referendums for the approval or ratification of laws voted in Parliament, but not yet sanctioned; referendums for consultation regarding political decisions of great importance; and even abrogative referendums for the derogation of laws already in force. Parties on the left were particularly opposed to confirmatory/abrogative referendums. In their view, they proffered the risk of institutional confrontation, the potential to undermine Parliament's sovereignty, and, above all, established the possibility of very serious conflicts between the Government, the King and the Parliament.[2]

Predominant views favoured a stronger role for parliament, and political parties argued that it was necessary to strengthen their role after the de-legitimizing effects of dictatorship. Thus, the final referendum design was a more restrictive one (Pérez Royo, 1988: 21; Equip, 1986) with two modalities: on the one hand, referendums related to the exercise of 'constituent power' either at the national (approval and reform of the Constitution) or regional levels (approval or reform of regional statutes). Referendums were also consultative, with no mandatory character. In further detail, the Constitution considers the following use of referendums:

(a) *Entering into force of the Constitution.* Once drafted and approved in Parliament, the 1978 Constitution was voted in a binding referendum.

(b) *Constitutional reform.* This referendum can be either mandatory (Article 168.3 SC) or optional (Article 167.3 SC), depending on the part of the constitution to be modified. No referendum of this kind has been so far held in Spain.

(c) *Consultative referendum.* For political decisions of great importance or of far-reaching consequence, the King may call a referendum on a proposal from the President of the Government which has obtained previous authorization from the Congress.[3] Typical cases include drastic changes in government policy pertaining to electoral compromises, and unforeseen political events or issues with cross-party cleavages (e.g. moral issues) (Azpitarte and Rodríguez, 2008: 229). Spain has held two consultative referendums: the 1986 referendum on continued membership of NATO, and the 2005 referendum on the EU constitution. (These campaigns and the impact of funding on these campaigns will be discussed respectively below.)

Additionally, the Constitution regulates referendums for the creation and modification of autonomous communities in four different situations:

(i) Access to full autonomy (Article 151.1). Owing to the existence of alternative procedures, only Andalucía held one such referendum, in 1980.

(ii) Approval of the Autonomous Community Basic Law (Article 151.2), of which, four regions have held consults: the Basque Country (1979); Catalonia (1979); Galicia (1980) and Andalucía (1981).

(iii) Amendment of the Autonomous Community Basic Law (Article 152.2). Referendums are required only in those cases in which the

Table 10.2   Results of national referendums in Spain (percentages)

Type	1976 Political reform	1978 Constitution approval	1986 Continued NATO membership	2005 EU Constitution
	Pre-constitutional	Mandatory	Consultative	Consultative
Turnout	77.72	67.11	59.42	41.77
Abstention	22.28	32.89	40.58	58.23
Valid votes	99.7	99.25	98.89	99.14
Void votes	0.3	0.75	1.11	0.86
Blank votes	2.98	3.57	6.61	5.96
Yes votes	94.45	88.54	53.09	76.96
No votes	2.57	7.89	40.3	17.97

Source: Spanish Ministry of Home Affairs http://www.elecciones.mir.es/MIR/jsp/resultados/comunes/listadoElecciones.jsp?tipoEleccion=7& nombreEleccion=Refer%E9ndum (accessed 25 August 2008).

statute was initially approved by means of a referendum. So far, Catalonia (2006) and Andalucía (2006) have amended their statutes by means of referendums.

(iv) Eventual incorporation of Navarra to the Basque Country (Transitory Disposition 4th SC). A referendum has not been used for this purpose.

Apart from Constitutional regulation, a specific 1980 norm[4] regulates referendums in further depth. Some commentators (Oliver, 1989; Linde and Herrero, 1980) have criticized the poor quality of this law which is the result of the specific circumstances surrounding its evolution. The law was urgently required in order to convene a referendum deciding on an initiative unexpectedly proposed in Andalucía. The initiative proposed access to autonomy (see i above). Consequently, the law was drafted in a hurry and without substantial reflection (Oliver, 1989: 144ff).

Referendums are submitted to the general electoral regime in all aspects in which it is applicable.[5] However, popular consultations, celebrated in city councils and referring to issues of a municipal nature, are excluded from the scope of the law on referendums. This means that regulation of these kinds of local consults falls either to regional norms or local rules promulgated at the City Council level.[6]

10.3   Regional and local referendums

At the regional level, the Autonomous Communities may hold referendums on matters different from those regulated in the Constitution – that is, referendums on the region's own policies. Thus, the regions of Asturias, La Rioja, Murcia, Valencia, and Extremadura y Castilla-León have included consults in their regional statutes. More vaguely, the 2006 Catalonia Statute referred to 'instruments of popular consultation' (Article 122) and the reform of the Andalucía Statute included a similar provision. In any case, the competence to authorize a referendum remains with the central state authorities, an aspect explicitly acknowledged in all the aforementioned statutes. To date, no regional referendum (apart from ones referring to reform of the regional statutes) has been held.

More contentiously, in 2006 the Basque government proposed a 'consult'; i.e. a non-binding referendum on a loosely defined rejection of violence and combined with negotiation on the right of self-determination. The central government contested the objectives of the consult. Challenging the Basque government's competence in front of the constitutional court, the Basque government counter-argued that it could consult the citizens by means of a non-binding referendum. The consult was suspended with the Constitutional Court ruling that the Basque government did not have the power to call for a referendum and that this competence belonged to the national authorities.

Local referendums are foreseen in national law and in some regional statutes (for instance, in Valencia). These '*consultas populares*' (popular consultations) are referendums for deciding on 'those issues of municipal competence and local character which have special relevance for the neighbors' interest, excluding the ones related with local funds'.[7] Among these local referendums, the Basque Statute (Article 8) foresees a very specific one for the incorporation of local communities within Basque Country territory which, nevertheless, has historically belonged to neighbouring Castille (Santamaría, 2001: 1456). As with regional referendums, local referendums require previous authorization by the central government. Whilst this may have seemed a reasonable requirement at the beginning of the democratic transition, when the parties wanted to strengthen the Parliament, current changes suggest different regulations. Indeed, in 2004 Parliament saw an initiative to transfer the authorization of 'municipal and supra-municipal' popular consultations to the Autonomous Community Government.[8] The initiative was unsuccessful.

Facing this situation, some city councils have opted to continue citizen consultations by means of specific and sophisticated electronic systems. Consultations on the environmental sustainability of Madrid, carried through by the city council within Agenda 21, are illustrative. However, these consults do not have a decisive character, nor are they organized in a way systematic enough to be considered a kind of referendum mechanism.

10.4   Financial regulations in national referendums

As mentioned above, referendum regulation is subsidiary to general electoral law. Contingent on the actors and the kind of objectives, funding regulations differentiate between *institutional campaigns,* which promote awareness of the call and which are performed by public authorities, and the *non-institutional campaign,* which is carried out by political actors (that is, political parties defending either of the options at stake in a referendum).

Institutional campaigns

Public authorities, whether national or autonomic, perform institutional campaigns which are not regulated explicitly in the law on referendums, but, rather, by general electoral law (Article 50). Accordingly, public authorities convening an electoral process may enact an institutional campaign 'to inform the citizens on the date of the voting, the procedure to vote and the requirements and the steps of the vote by post, without influencing, in any case, the orientation of the vote'.[9] A reform of the law in 1994 specified the content and limits of the campaign: date for the vote, procedure, and also postal voting procedure. The reform implicitly excluded the promotion of participation, as the legislators assumed the thesis that participation affects the results (Azpitarte and Rodríguez, 2008: 238). Some additional regulations are derived from the general regime for institutional publicity and information.[10] The convening public authorities assume the full costs of these campaigns.

Non-institutional campaigns

Actors other than public authorities may conduct campaigns favouring a specific option and these campaigns are labelled non-institutional, as opposed to neutral, institutional campaigns. Political parties are the main players in these campaigns, since they play a central role in Spanish politics: in fact, the Spanish constitution defines parties as the basic instruments of political participation. This means that they also assume a central and pivotal role in any political campaign (including referendums) *vis-à-vis* any eventual nonpartisan player.

For these campaigns, parties may access two different funding sources: the first is regular funding which is established generally for all referendums; the second is extraordinary funding which consists of ad hoc specific state subsidies for a given referendum. So far, extraordinary funding has only been provided in the case of the EU Constitution Referendum.

Regular funding

Central state regulations as well as some regional regulations foresee a certain amount of expense deemed mandatory for the State to provide in the case of referendum campaign. Thus, the referendum options under discussion enjoy 'free spaces' and/or 'advertisement spaces' in the publicly owned media, at both the national and local levels, depending on the scope of the consultation. These spaces are normally measured in minutes of television or radio broadcasts, or in the percentage of pages in written publications.[11] Electoral propaganda will also have a franchise[12] and a special service of postal shipping. Parties and groups obtain these spaces in public media in proportion to the number of deputies obtained in the last general elections or the number of local representatives (in the case of local referendums). Within these publicly subsidized spaces, parties may favour their own option. The law makes no further reference to other expenditures and costs that a referendum campaign can generate. In consequence, each political group must pay all those expenses not expressly considered in the legislation.

Extraordinary economic aids

Extraordinary economic aids are subsidies which the general legislation on electoral campaigns does not contemplate. This kind of funding is granted in cases of particular referendums although the advisory Referendum on the European Constitutional Treaty is the only case in which extraordinary funding has been granted.[13] The approved model has the following characteristics:

– Only political parties and groups with parliamentary representation (i.e. those that obtained seats in the Congress of the Deputies in the last legislative election) may claim subsidies. This excludes parties that lack any presence in Parliament as well as any group and/or association that may have stakes in the referendum but cannot be qualified as a political party. The organ responsible for the concession of extraordinary economic aids is the Minister of Home Affairs which runs the electoral administration.

– Model of funding. Funds are subsidies, granted as an exception within the general law on state subsidies, which oblige the use of competitive calls. The subsidies law creates a special regime, called 'direct concession', according to which a norm may create a specific and different procedure. The legal habilitation was used for the EU constitution referendum, for which a norm Real Ordinance 6/2005, created an extraordinary aid system whose features are described in greater detail below.

– The amount of the subsidy is the lower quantity of the following categories:

(a) Justified expenses. These are the expenses that a given party has justified and that correspond to the 'bankable expenses' (*gastos financiables*) determined by law. Bankable expenses are the following items:

   (i)   Making of envelopes and making of informative, explanatory and broadcasting material;

   (ii)   Direct publicity or indirect publicity to inform and disclose the Treaty in any way and any means that are used in this regard;

   (iii)   Rent of locals for the celebration of informative and broadcasting acts;

   (iv)   Remunerations or bonuses to the non-permanent personnel that lend their services for the performance of these acts;

   (v)   Means of transport and expenses of displacement of the political formations, which must be related to campaign acts;

   (vi)   Correspondence and postage;

   (vii)   Interest on the credits received for these acts;

   (viii)   Those necessary for the organization and operation of the offices and precise services.

(b) Amounts fixed by seats and votes. They correspond to the following fixed amounts:

   (i)   €8,571,428 per seat obtained in the Congress of Deputies.

   (ii)   €0.2442 per vote obtained by each candidature to the Congress. It is necessary that at least one of those members obtained a Deputy seat. The votes obtained in those districts in which 3 per cent of the valid votes have not been reached are not computed here.

In other words, the State pays the amount that the political group has justified according to its expenses in the category 'bankable expenses' but only up to the amount fixed in relation to seats or votes. Parties may request an advanced payment but only up to 75 per cent of the fixed amounts for seats and votes previously indicated.

Other party expenditure

Apart from state subsidies through regular and extraordinary mechanisms, parties are free to expend funds in defence of their favoured option in a given referendum, as are social and political groups lacking parliamentary representation.

Scrutiny of party expenditure

The only two national referendums held had slightly different regulations, although both sets are similar in spirit. The 1986 NATO referendum referred to the electoral law provisions on campaign expenditures, whilst the 2005 referendum established a very tight system for controlling the extraordinary aids (see above) whilst the electoral law would apply for other party expenditures.

Thus, electoral law is the primary instrument regulating the scrutiny of party funding. For this, parties must open special accounts to which all contributions and expenses will be charged. Spanish law prohibits secret donations, without this implying in parallel full publicity for the sources of donations (contributions have a cap of €6,000 per physical or juridical person and donations from foreign sources are prohibited). During the campaign, the Central Electoral Commission may scrutinize the accounts and may ask for all available information from banks on parties' accounts. After elections, the Court of Auditors must check the accounts of those parties, coalitions, or groups that are in receipt of subsidies. Detailed accounts of both income and expenditure for obtaining the subsidies must be presented. Additionally, banks are obliged to provide information.

Interestingly, the regulations remain silent in relation to the expenditures and accounts of parties and/or groups which do not apply for state subsidies. Following the letter of the law, extra-parliamentary groups which do not apply for subsidies would not have their expenditures controlled. In practice, the reliance on parliamentary parties for political participation, in parallel to parties' reliance on state funding for their campaigns means that only a few small ad hoc groups may enter the campaign arena absolutely free of controls on their sources of income and expenditures. During the NATO 1986 referendum, the presence of these small groups was felt and their funding came mainly from very small voluntary contributions. During the 2005 referendum, their presence was almost irrelevant.

10.5 Regulation for funding campaigns in local referendums

In a similar way, norms throughout the autonomous communities and local norms have attempted to regulate the development of popular consultations. Autonomous Communities basic laws and norms, and municipal decrees constitute the set of regulations pertaining to this type of referendum. Despite their wide variety, it is possible to extract some common features regarding the funding of political referendum campaigns.

Institutional campaigns

Some local legislation makes reference to the possibility of carrying out these types of campaigns to promote participation in the referendum, and to provide information on the conditions of this participation (including checking the register, enrolling if not included, postal voting, and so on).[14] The features of institutional campaigns in this case do not differ from those already mentioned with respect to those institutional campaigns in referendums recognized by the Constitution. As is the case with referendums regulated in the constitution, the funding of these types of campaigns is the responsibility of the administration that convenes the referendum (i.e. local administration).

Non-institutional campaigns

The financial regulations in this case are also similar to those concerning the referendums established by the Constitution. Local administration only contributes to the financing of certain issues, that is, it is partial funding. Among these benefits, the most relevant ones are:[15]

  (i) Free spaces in the public media.
 (ii) Reservation of free spaces for the placement of information.
(iii) Free disposal of official or public offices for acts of the campaign.
(iv) Special prices applied to postage and shipping.

The most remarkable difference between this type of referendum and those established by constitutional text relates to the possible beneficiaries of the funding. In local referendums the possibility of funding is also given to political groups not organized as political parties, i.e., local associations or other groups that have promoted the consultation.[16] The incorporation of other political groups leads to a redistribution of the free spaces and places. In the cases under study, that is, under the local laws of Navarra and Andalucía, the principle of equal opportunities between the options in competition is followed.[17]

10.6 Effects of money and financial regulations: the case of consultative referendums

Two of the four nationwide referendums held in Spain are rather particular: (i) the 1976 referendum on political reform marked the transition to democracy and it was held using Francoist legislation under which political parties were banned. (ii) The 1978 referendum on the approval of the Constitution had a similarly extraordinary character, with no established rules on either campaigns and referendums. There are no precise records on campaign expenses but according to some estimations, UCD expended 48 million pesetas (around €3 million), while PSOE expended 40 million (€2.7 million). The PCE informed that they would not spend more than 25 million (€1.5 million). All of these amounts are small in comparison with those invested by the same parties in the electoral campaign of June 1977. Thus, the committee coordinating the campaign against the Constitution calculated that the budget covering its activities was around 70 million (Del Castillo, 1978: 168). In any case, the absence of legal regulation and lack of practice with participatory democratic mechanisms renders both of these referendums unique experiences from which it is difficult to extrapolate.

On the contrary, the 1985 and 2005 referendums can be compared. The first one was a dramatic event which showed the deep division between elites and public opinion on the referendum issue (NATO membership). The second one, in 2005, concerned a highly consensual issue for Spanish public opinion (that is, the EU Constitution and, by extension, EU membership and European integration). What was similar in both cases was the position of political parties: in 1985, the largest and majoritarian party in Congress (202 seats out of 350), the Socialists, supported the 'Yes' side, whilst the conservatives (AP) tactically supported abstention, despite being in favour of the substance of the consult. Left-wing parties (Communist and similar) supported the 'No' side. In 2005, a huge majority of parliamentary parties and MPs supported the 'Yes' side, with no more than ten MPs in opposition. Giving the central role that parliamentary parties play in funding, these data are very important.

The 1986 referendum lacked specific rules for the provision of extraordinary aid to political parties. Consequently, these parties had to pay the expenses out of their own budgets. The PSOE carried out a huge campaign without the reimbursement that takes place in elections and only at the expense of the credits obtained by the treasury of the organization (Soler Sánchez, 2001: 246). The same was true for the other parties and the effect was a certain reluctance to expend the money of those who recommended abstention (AP-CD) or those who maintained an ambiguous position (PNV and CiU). Because of this, transparency in expenditure was a difficult exercise, even though some of those opposed to NATO proposed a mechanism for scrutinizing their expenses.[18]

Now, what was the effect of funding and money on the result? In this respect two aspects of the result deserve attention: firstly, the final outcome overturned the predominant trend of Spanish public opinion against NATO. The affirmative result was both categorical and surprising (Arias, 1988: 37), particularly as opinion polls had consistently showed support for the 'No' side. One month before the election, a CIS poll showed that 32 per cent were against, 32 per cent were in favour and 36 per cent either did not respond or did not know. At the end, 53 per cent of the voters said yes and 40 per cent said no. Secondly, the number of voters saying 'No' (7 million) was much larger than the size of the sum of all voters of parties supporting the 'No' side. Whilst the first factor seems to suggest that the campaign had a major effect, the second lends itself to the opposite option: that issue voting prevailed. The large amount of No votes means that large numbers of Socialist voters did not accept the change of policy and did not follow party cues. In parallel, there is no evidence of massive follow-up in the recommendation of abstention from the conservatives and it seems that many conservative voters did indeed vote on the issue of NATO membership.

Whilst cueing could have played an important role, its impact was conditioned by the confusing clues given by the parties. Only the PSOE and the centrist UCD campaigned openly in favour of the 'Yes', but for Socialists the stance was a total U-turn, since in 1982 PSOE had campaigned against membership of NATO. Other traditional supporters of NATO membership also sent similarly confusing cues: CiU advised its voters to vote freely, PNV sent mixed messages and the largest opposition party, AP-PP, recommended abstention (in contradiction with its substantive support for NATO membership). These confusing cues are reflected in the results: the figure of 6.5 per cent blank votes were the highest ever; and 'No' votes had a plurality of origins: these were predominantly left-wing (Equip, 1986: 205), but there was also some evidence of a punishment vote against the government from conservative sectors (Equip, 1986: 2003).

No doubt, the campaign had an impact on the result. All of the commentators concede that for all practical purposes, the referendum turned into a general vote of confidence on the conduct of the Socialist government, and the strong personal involvement of Prime Minister González turned the referendum into a kind of personal plebiscite (Pérez Royo, 1988: 23; Arias, 1988: 34–8; Equip, 1986). Media pressure in favour of the 'Yes' was high: three of the main papers (*El País*, *Diario 16* and *La Vanguardia*) supported the 'Yes' side, even though two of these (*Diario 16* and *La Vanguardia*) had opposed the holding of a referendum. No media campaigned for the 'No' whilst some, more or less linked to the right side of the political spectrum (for example, *ABC* and *Época*), supported abstention. Moreover, Spanish public television was said to be biased towards a positive vote (Arias, 1988: 38–9) and even the biggest Spanish banks favoured a 'Yes'. In contrast, supporters of the 'No' side had little parliamentary presence and limited material means. Opposition groups gathered under the umbrella of the State Coordinator of Pacifist Organizations (CEOP) which assumed the leadership of the 'No' camp.

Taking into account the large deviation from party cues, the evidence of issue voting, and the large number of 'No' votes, it may be concluded that the campaign did play a role. However, it would be more difficult to assign a leading role to the amount of money spent by either side. Without questioning the imbalance between both, it seems that other factors did play a more prominent role in conditioning the result.

One of the eventual lessons from the 1986 campaign could have been that in the absence of funding for extraordinary expenses, parties that did not stand in strong opposition to the ruling party did not have strong incentives to campaign. Thus, it is probable that the lack of regulation during the 1986 campaign, coupled with the difficulties political parties faced in obtaining funds, induced the regulation of the 2005 campaign. As mentioned earlier, in 2004 the government aimed at an integral reform of electoral law to close the pending issues but, lacking support, it had to develop a specific norm.

The issue in 2005 was less contentious. But this was in itself the main concern for the government: a low turnout would have cast doubts on the result, endangering the (national and European) leadership dividends that the government hoped to reap. Since any attempts to promote participation was forbidden as part of the institutional campaign, the government designed an additional informative campaign whose purpose was to increase awareness of the text (the EU Constitutional Treaty).

The Ministries of Presidency, Home Affairs and Foreign Affairs expended €3 million (Foreign Affairs) and €5 million (Presidency) in the informative campaign,[19] which developed in three main areas (Azpitarte and Rodríguez, 2008: 241). First, public TV broadcast a number of ads (18 ads, including four of 30 seconds and four of 20 seconds). Secondly, the Treaty was distributed in a large number of different versions (in length and format), the newspaper distribution of five million copies being the most significant one. Critics, however, considered this figure to be insufficient (Madroñales, 2005). These copies did not contain either Part III of the Constitution or the Annexes. Thirdly, a number of social bodies and organs collaborated in the diffusion of the referendum and the text through different means. Some of the latter were occasionally 'innovative' – for example, the soft drink 'referendum plus' (sic).

In its information campaign, the government really pushed the limits of neutrality, which implicitly prohibits calls for participation. However, the campaign was challenged in front of the Central Electoral Commission because of the lack of neutrality derived from the slogan chosen – *'The first in Europe'* – which was perceived as being biased and insinuating 'Let's be the first to ratify, i.e. to say yes'. The Central Electoral Commission backed an appeal by *Otra democracia es possible*, the *Foundation Centro de Estudios Jurídicos Tomás Moro* and ERC against the government slogan and forced the government to remove it.[20] According to the ruling, a government campaign should be limited to informing the people objectively about the content of the Constitution and refraining from making any kind of value judgement. On this basis, some have criticized the official campaign for being biased towards ratification (Madroñales, 2005). Government officials, however, claim that the ruling of the electoral commission was by and large supportive of the informative campaign as only the slogan was considered to be biased (Azpitarte and Rodríguez, 2008: 241).

Parties played an important role in the campaign (Santamaría, 2005) and, according to Font, party cues had the largest effect in the 2005 referendum (Font and Rodríguez, 2006). But the parties again supplied confusing cues: thus, only the Socialists showed unambiguous support; at the same time the PP initially issued some critical messages relating to the absence of references to a Christian Europe and Spain's loss of power in the votes of the Council. Some of its leaders insinuated their preference for a negative vote. In tactical terms, the PP did not want to be seen to be acting in support of the Socialist government. For the rest of the parties, centre and right-wing parties sided with the 'Yes' and

Table 10.3   Subsidies in function of either votes or seats for the 2005 Referendum (2004 election results)

	Party	Votes	Seats	Funding on votes	Funding on seats
PSOE	Partido Socialista Obrero Español	11.026.163	164	2.692.589	1.435.204
PP	Partido Popular	9.763.144	148	2.384.159	1.295.211
CIU	Convergencia i Unió	835.471	10	204.022	87.514
ERC	Esquerra Republicana de Catalunya	652.196	8	159.266	70.009
PNV	Partido Nacionalista Vasco	420.980	7	102.803	61.258
IU	Izquierda Unida	1.284.081	5	304.781	43.756
CC	Coalicion Canaria	235.221	3	57.440	26.253
BNG	Bloque Nacionalista Galego	208.688	2	50.961	17.502
CHA	Chunta Aragonesista	94.252	1	23.016	8.751
EA	Eusko Alkartasuna	80.905	1	19.757	8.751
NA-BAI	Nafarroa Bai	61.045	1	14.907	8.751

Source: Own elaboration. Columns Votes and seats: Home Affairs Ministry http://www.elecciones.mir.es/MIR/jsp/resultados/index.htm. For IU the total of subsidies according to votes could be much lower since votes in constituencies under 3 per cent of votes would have to be discounted. IU had a significant number of constituencies in these conditions. The Spanish system selects the lower of the two possible criteria (votes and seats).

left and left-regionalist parties with the 'No', on the grounds of lack of acknowledgement for regional languages and national diversity.

The number of seats and votes secured by the 'Yes' side was well ahead of the 'No' one. Accordingly, funding mirrored this imbalance. The 2005 regulation set the parameters described above. Following these parameters, the calculation of the eventual funding received would be as shown in Table 10.3.

Total Yes (PSOE, PP; CiU; PNV, CC) 332 seats	5.441.013–90,48%	2.905.440–94,85%
Total No (IU, BNG, CHA, EA, NA-BAI) 18 seats	572.688–9,52%	157.520–5,15%

Source: Own elaboration. Madroñales (2005) provides the following figures: nine million Euros, of which 8.1 were to parties supporting the Constitution and 0.1 to parties against.

Clearly, there was a huge imbalance between those parties supporting the 'Yes' and those parties supporting the 'No': the first claimed 95 per cent of subsidies whilst the second could only avail themselves of 5 per cent, but this imbalance roughly reflected their parliamentary strength. The differences were amplified because almost all of the written media supported the 'Yes' and also because civil society organizations received no official subsidies. Social movements which were active against the Spanish involvement in Iraq were mostly on the 'No' side, although by and large civil society had limited participation because of the short period of time from the decision to hold the referendum to the effective date (Losada, 2008). In summary, the campaign was strongly one-sided and not very competitive, with this accounting for the low turnout (Anduiza, 2005; Losada, 2008) with some complaints of unequal access to resources for the respective sides (Madroñales, 2005).

However, even these critics accept that the imbalance between options was not a serious one given the huge imbalance in public support between the two options. Rather, it could be argued that the Gallagher warning makes sense: giving substantial amounts of public money to the weaker side of the two is not so much levelling the field as it is tilting in another direction and creating a different current of opinion (Gallagher, 1996: 248). On the face of it, the Spanish Socialist government managed to take control of the referendum debates, preventing anti-EU campaigners from gaining control of the debates and turning the focus from a symbolic pro-European discourse to materially based anti-European issues (Font, 2008: 302).

10.7 Evaluation of the Spanish referendum model

Most regulation of the referendum model derives from the 1980 Law which most experts consider to be wholly insufficient, mainly for the regulation of non-institutional campaign funding. The velocity and absence of deep analysis in the writing of this law is one of the reasons for this perception (Oliver Araujo, 1989: 145; Aguilera de Prat, 1992: 147ff). Additional norms have to be dictated to address these deficiencies with the occasion of the 1986 NATO referendum[21] and the 2005 EU Constitution referendum.[22] In 2004 and facing the forthcoming referendum, the government wanted to change the general electoral law to allow the official funding of parties during the referendum. The main opposition party opposed, and the government circumvented this by agreeing through an additional norm to an extraordinary budget. The lack of legal norms in a country characterized by its intense taste for legal regulations may be presented as clear evidence of the secondary role that referendums play in current Spanish politics and in the aims of main players.

The regulation of local consultations shares this untidy design. Local norms commonly refer to more general regulation, i.e., to the Law on Referendum, which paradoxically excludes local referendum from the scope of its application, and this creates confusion.[23] The ambiguous local regulations reflect distrust towards any instrument of direct democracy (Font i Llovet, 1985: 126).

The second feature of the Spanish model refers to the pivotal role played by political parties. Political participation is linked inexorably to the primacy of representative democracy, in which political parties are, almost exclusively, the main actors (Ramírez, 1992: 31). Article 6 of the Spanish Constitution declares that political parties are the expression of political pluralism, contributing to the formation and expression of the will of the people and are an essential instrument for political participation. The resulting model was labeled 'the state of parties' (García Pelayo, 1986).

In this context, parties play an important role in referendums as *explicit* clue providers. As Prime Minister Zapatero wrote in his early capacity as a junior constitutional law professor, even if the decision is transferred to the people directly, it does not make sense to charge them with the role of creating 'public opinion' and generating the different options (Rodríguez Zapatero, 1986: 1165), which implies that this function still belongs to parties. However, cues sent by parties do not necessarily follow the issue at stake, as is shown by the referendums in 1986 and 2005. Parties using a campaign with political strategic intentions have a suitable environment to criticize or denounce the activities or decisions of the government, and in order to improve their political position (Gallagher, 1996: 247). This situation can transform the real importance of the referendum into a simple instrument of political party struggles.

As for the model of funding derived from this conception, the absence of regulation for extraordinary campaign expenses runs counter to the explicit role assigned to parties and it creates, in fact, incentives for free-riding. Moreover, the model implies an evident inequality, as the extra-parliamentary forces and small parties are almost impeded in their ability to defend one of the political decisions under consultation (Del Castillo, 1978: 161; Cruz Villalón, 1980: 164). As the 2005 rules established, extra-parliamentary groups may carry out a political campaign, but must support campaign expenditures entirely with their own funds. In contrast, the regulation of local referendums allows for the funding different groups that support different options.

Despite what has been said, it would be premature to conclude that the imbalance of funding in Spanish referendums has had a significant impact upon the results. On the contrary, it would seem that issue voting (particularly in 1986) and cueing from political parties (particularly in 2005) are key factors. As far as parties remain the main actors for political participation, and this is deeply embedded into Spanish politics, it is difficult to judge the model of funding as unfair.

Notes

1. Real Decree (*Real Decreto*) of 25 November 1897.
2. The Communist parliamentary group proposed the suppression of both forms of legislative referendum (ratification and derogation). See the *Journal of the Sessions of the Congress of Deputies* (Commission of Constitutional Affairs and Public Liberties) of 6 June 1978, (81), p. 2937. Quoted in J.L. López González (2005) *El referendum en el sistema español de participación política* (Valencia: Universidad Politécnica de Valencia).
3. Article 161 of the Regulation of the Congress of Deputies of 10 February 1982.
4. Organic Law 2/1980 of 18 January, which regulates Referendum (*OLR*).
5. Organic Law 5/1985, of 19 June, of General Electoral Regime (*LER*).
6. This double regulation can be different in each Autonomous Community as Organic law in some communities states that it is the community authority that has the competence to regulate on this matter. On the contrary, legislation in other communities is silent on this. In those cases, the power to regulate on these topics can be exercised by the Community or by the City Councils.
7. Article 71 Law 7/1985 of 2 April regulating the basis for Local Regime.
8. *Proposition of Law 122/000053* 'Impulse of citizen participation and popular consultations', presented on 23 April 2004.
9. See the Instruction of 31 January 2005, from the Central Electoral Commission, regarding the information campaign that can be developed by public powers with respect to the consultative referendum of the Treaty establishing a Constitution for Europe, once it was convened.
10. Law 29/2005 of 29 December, about Institutional Publicity and Information.
11. See Real Decree (RD) 260/1980, of 8 February, about complementary norms for the celebration of the referendum convened by RD 145/1980, of 26 January; and RD 2364/1979, of 11 October, about the use of the State mass media during the informative campaign of the referendum on the Basic Law of Catalonia.
12. This franchise does not imply offering the service for free. Indeed, according to the Order of 10 February 1986, which dictates norms for the collaboration of Post Services in the celebration of the NATO referendum, special post prices previously fixed will be applied to the shipping of electoral propaganda delivered by political actors (This order refers to another Order of 3 May, by which prices of special postal shipping of electoral propaganda are fixed, and makes it applicable for referendum.) See, more recently, Order FOM/1574/2006, of 22nd May, that dictates norms on the collaboration of Post Services in referendums on the Basic Law of Catalonia.
13. Real Ordinance 6/2005, of 14 January.

14. For example, Article 19 of the Local Law of Navarra or Article 21 of the Law of Regulation of Popular Consultations in Andalucía.
15. Local Law of Navarra and Law of Regulation of Popular Consultations in Andalucía.
16. Article 161 Law Decree that approves the Municipal Law and Local regime of Catalonia.
17. Article 19.4 Local Law of Navarra; Article 20.4 of Law of Regulation of Popular Consultations in Andalucía.
18. Thus, the National Coordinator for Disarmament and Full De-Nuclearization (CEDDT) asked the Ombudsman to audit their sources of funding. Funding for this platform against NATO came from a vote-bonus of 50 pesetas (i.e. €0.30).
19. Oral question information on the cost of the divulgation campaign on the EU Constitution BOCG 23 May 2008 Serie D No. 207 pp. 218–19.
20. Instruction of 31 January 2005, of the Central Electoral Commission.
21. Real Decree RD 215/1986 of 6 February, that fixed application norms exclusively for that referendum.
22. RD 7/2005, of 14 January, that regulates certain aspects of the electoral procedure applicable to the referendum about the Treaty establishing a Constitution for Europe.
23. First Additional disposition of the Regulation of citizen participation in the city of Seville, of 13 October 1999; Article 23 of Organic Regulation of citizen participation in Madrid, 2004. The case of the Seville regulation is paradoxical, because it mandates the application of the Electoral Law. However the Electoral Law indicates expressly that it is not applicable to popular consultations.

References

Aguiar de Luque, L. (1977) *Democracia directa y Estado constitucional* (Madrid: Edersa).

Aguilera de Prat, C.R. (1992) 'El uso del referéndum en la España democrática (1976–1986)', *Revista de Estudios Políticos*, 75: 107–54.

Anduiza, E. (2005) 'Quiénes se abstuvieron y por qué: la participación en el referéndum sobre el Tratado por el que se establece una Constitución para Europa Real Instituto Elcano de Estudios Estratégicos e Internacionales', *ARI N° 34/2005* http://www.realinstitutoelcano.org/analisis/702/Anduiza702.pdf.

Arias, I. (1988) 'Spanish Media and the Two NATO Campaigns', in Federico G. Gil and Joseph S. Tulchin (eds), *Spain's Entry into NATO: Conflicting Political and Strategic Perspectives* (Boulder: Lynne Rienner Publishers), pp. 29–40.

Azpitarte, M. and José Luis Rodríguez (2008) 'La actitud del Gobierno Español ante el Tratado Constitucional. La campaña institucional', in Hans-Jörg Trenz, A.J. Menéndez and F. Losada (eds), *Y por fin somos europeos: La comunicación política en el debate constituyente europeo* (Madrid: Dykinson), pp. 225–52.

Cruz Villalón, P. (1980) 'El referéndum consultivo como modelo de racionalización Constitucional', *Revista de Estudios Políticos*, 13: 145–68.

Del Castillo Vera, P. (1978) 'La campaña del referéndum constitucional', *Revista de Estudios Políticos*, 6: 153–74.

Equip de Sociologia Electoral (1986) 'El referéndum de 12 de marzo de 1986 sobre la permanencia de España en la OTAN y sus consecuencias para el sistema politico', *Revista de Estudios Políticos*, **52**: 183–215.

Font, J. and E. Rodriguez (2006) *The Spanish Referendum on the EU Constitution: Issues, Party Cues, and Second Order Effects*, paper presented at the 64 Annual Meeting of the Midwest Political Science Association, Chicago, 20–3 April.

Font, N. (2008) 'The Politics of the EU in the Constitutional Treaty Referendums', *Perspectives on European Politics and Society*, **9**(3): 301–15.

Font i Llovet, T. (1985) 'El referéndum local en España', *Autonomies – Revista Catalana de Derecho Público*, **2–3**: 123–7.

Gallagher, M. (1996) 'Conclusion', in M. Gallagher and P. Vincenzo (eds), *The Referendum Experience in Europe* (Basingstoke: Palgrave Macmillan), pp. 226–52.

García Pelayo, Manuel (1986) *El estado de partidos* (Madrid: Alianza).

Garrorena Morales, A. (1976) 'Teoría y práctica española de referéndum', *Anales de la Universidad de Murcia/Derecho*, **31**(3–4): 79–108.

Linde Paniagua, E. and Herrero Lera, M. (1980) 'Comentario a la Ley Orgánica de Modalidades de Referéndum', *Revista del Departamento de Derecho Político*, **6**: 83–105.

López González, J. L. (2005) *El referéndum en el sistema español de participación política* (Valencia: Universidad Politécnica de Valencia).

Losada, F. (2008) 'De verdad somos europeos: el debate sobre el tratado constitucional en los medios españoles', in Hans-Jörg Trenz, A.J. Menéndez and F. Losada (eds), *¿Y por fin somos europeos? La comunicación política en el debate constituyente europeo* (Madrid: Dykinson), pp. 277–331.

Madroñales, Juan Carlos (2005) *Spanish Referendum on the EU Constitution Monitoring Report 20 February*, www.masdemocracy.org and http://www .democracy-international.org/fileadmin/di/pdf/monitoring/di-spain.pdf   date accessed, 13 October 2008.

Pérez Royo, Javier (1988) 'Repercussions on the Democratic Process of Spain's Entry into NATO', in Federico G. Gil and Joseph S. Tulchin (eds), *Spain's Entry into NATO: Conflicting Political and Strategic Perspectives* (Boulder: Lynne Rienner Publishers), pp. 20–8.

Oliver Arujo, J. (1989) 'El referéndum en el sistema constitucional español', *Revista de Derecho Político*, **29**: 115–82.

Ramírez, M. (1992) 'El reforzamiento de la participación política', *Revista de Derecho Político*, **36**: 27–45.

Rodríguez Zapatero, J.L. (1986) 'El referéndum consultivo del art. 92 de la Constitución española de 1978: un análisis crítico', *La Ley. Revista Jurídica de Doctrina, Jurisprudencia y Bibliografía*, **1**: 1156–66.

Santamaría, J. (2005) 'Los partidos políticos ante el referéndum de la Constitución Europea', in A. Pizarroso and A. de Miguel (ed.), *El debate sobre la Constitución Europea* (Valencia: Generalitat Valenciana), pp. 151–80.

Santamaría Pastor, J.A. (2001) 'Comentario al artículo 92 de la Constitución Española', in F. Garrido Falla (ed.), *Comentarios a la Constitución* (Madrid: Civitas), pp. 1448–61.

Soler Sánchez, M. (2001) *Campañas electorales y democracia en España* (Castelló de la Plana: Publicaciones de la Universidad Jaume I).

11
Referendum Campaign Regulations in Switzerland

Uwe Serdült

11.1 Overview of Switzerland's direct democratic institutions

As is widely known, Switzerland's political system includes important elements of direct citizen participation for the creation, change, and abolition of binding legal norms (Kriesi, 1993, 2005; Kaufmann et al. 2007; Linder, 2007; Trechsel, 2007; Papadopoulous, 1998). However, most legislation is passed by Parliament without interference from the voters (roughly 95 per cent). In fact, most of the bills going through Parliament are prepared by the executive, namely the public administration. Hence, the literature often refers to the Swiss political system as being a semi-direct democracy.

Historically, direct democratic institutions developed from the bottom up, from the municipal and cantonal level to the national level. Between 1848 and 1873 only mandatory referendums and initiatives aiming at a complete revision of the Federal Constitution were allowed. The optional legislative referendum was introduced in 1874, and the citizen's initiative for partial amendment of the Constitution in 1891. These institutions of direct democracy were advocated by the so-called 'democratic movement' which stood in opposition to the dominant party.

During the twentieth century, only minor modifications were made to direct democratic institutions. The referendum for international treaties, introduced in 1921 and extended in 1977, provided citizen participation in foreign policy decision making. Furthermore, the right of the Federal Assembly to withdraw its decisions from the referendum procedure through the use of the so-called 'urgency clause' (Article 165 of the Constitution) was limited in 1939 and 1949 by the introduction of the abrogative referendum. Six years after the introduction of women's suffrage in 1971, the number of required signatures for an optional referendum was raised from 30,000 to 50,000, and for a citizen's initiative from 50,000 to 100,000 (see also Auer et al., 2006; Linder, 2007). At the cantonal level, citizen's rights have developed considerably since the nineteenth century, and now include legislative initiatives, referendums on administrative acts, as well as referendums on one-time or recurring financial decisions (Linder, 2007; Trechsel and Serdült, 1999).

The most important direct democratic institutions actually in operation at all state levels are the mandatory referendum, the optional referendum, and the citizen's initiative.

The mandatory referendum

A referendum is mandatory for all amendments to the federal Constitution and for membership in some international organizations. (See section 140 of the Constitution.) A vote must be held in such cases and a double majority is required. For adoption, a majority of the popular vote, the votes cast throughout the country, and a majority of the cantons, cantons in which the majority of voters adopted the proposal, is needed. In the case of a split cantonal vote (11.5 of 23 cantonal votes), the bill does not pass.

The optional referendum

Citizens can also challenge parliamentary decisions through optional referendums. Federal laws, generally binding decisions of the Confederation, and some international treaties are subject to an optional referendum. (See section 141 of the Constitution.) In these cases, a popular ballot is held if 50,000 citizens request it within 100 days of a decree's publication. A double majority is not required for an optional referendum. In other words, only a simple majority of the people is needed. Optional Referendums were introduced in the year 1874.

The citizen's initiative

An initiative allows citizens to seek a decision on an amendment that they would like to see added to the federal Constitution. A popular vote takes place if 100,000 signatures are collected in favour of the initiative within the legal timeframe of 18 months. (See sections 138–139b of the Constitution.) For adoption of the initiative a double majority of the people and cantons is again required.

In Switzerland the scope of direct democracy is wide, and the decisions taken on polling day are binding. It is possible to write a citizen's initiative demanding the abolition of the Swiss Army. Such a vote took place in 1989 but did not go through (although an astonishing 36 per cent voted in favour of the initiative), as is the fate of most citizen's initiatives. Of the 254 citizen's initiatives that were handed in between 1848 and in February 2009, 77 were withdrawn by the initiators themselves, 161 were voted on, but only 15 were accepted at the ballot box.

To cite an example as illustration of a normal polling day in Switzerland: a national vote recently took place on the Swiss health insurance system. The initiative – which did not go through – tried to centralize the several dozen existing health insurance companies into one. During the same weekend there were also many cantonal and local referendums, such as the one in Zurich, where the decision to introduce a broadband network, with the help of infrastructure used by local electricity providers, did not go through.

In addition, it might be worth noting that the postal vote (introduced in 1994 at the national level) is the preferred voting channel for most citizens. In bigger cities 80–90 per cent of the voters use postal voting (Luechinger et al., 2007). Voting via the internet is operational in three selected cantons on a trial basis and on average used by about 20 per cent of the voting citizens.

Referendum votes can take place up to four times a year (as a rule of thumb) and are often combined votes at all three state levels (national, cantonal, and municipal). Over time the number of votes at the national level has increased. Since direct democratic institutions are in the first instance a political weapon for parties contesting majorities or, in general, the political opposition, an increase in their use can be interpreted as a period of intensified political struggle, often related to uncertain or unstable economic or social conditions. Such was the case during the 1970s economic crisis, to a lesser degree during the cultural unrest of the 1980s, and then again during the economic recession of the 1990s. During these decades Swiss society and the Swiss economy underwent major transformations. These phases are usually also marked by an increase in party competition.

Switzerland is a federal state. The referendum is used at both the federal and cantonal levels, the latter being to a large extent autonomously regulated by each of the 26 cantons (Auer et al., 2006). In the present chapter, I will focus on the federal level. However, it is important to note that there is mutual influence between the exercise of political rights in the cantons and in the Confederation. On the one hand, the cantons must respect political rights as they are guaranteed by the Federal Constitution. On the other hand, the Swiss Federal Supreme Court has developed important case law on the exercise of political rights in the

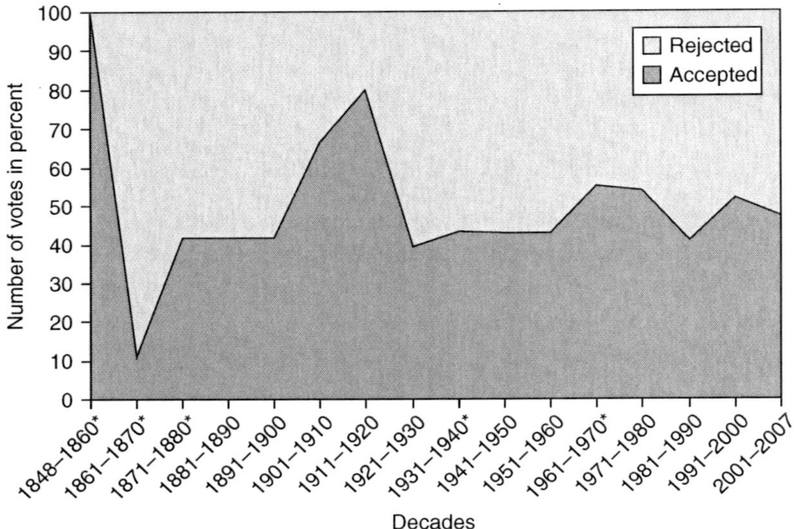

Figure 11.1 Share of rejected and accepted referendums as well as citizen's initiatives per decade

Sources: Federal Chancellery and www.c2d.ch. As one can see in Figure 11.1, at least in modern times the success rate of direct democratic referendums and initiatives together is relatively high and well balanced between the authorities and the people, or organized political interests, respectively.

cantons. Some of this case law deals with referendum campaigns (Auer et al., 2006: notes 887–95; Tornay, 2008). The principles developed by the Swiss Federal Supreme Court, although dealing with cantonal matters, to some extent also serve as guidelines for the federal authorities.[1]

11.2 Referendum campaign rules

With what we have learnt so far one would expect Switzerland, with its long-standing and frequent use of direct democracy institutions, namely the popular initiative, the optional referendum, and the mandatory referendum, to have developed extensive regulations on referendum campaigns, including rules on campaign financing and on media access. Surprisingly, this is not the case (Gruner and Hertig, 1983: 132) and in international comparison Switzerland together with Liechtenstein are quite unique in this respect (Zellweger and Serdült, 2006).

The referendum at the federal level is governed by the provisions of the Federal Constitution[2] and by the Federal Act on Political Rights.[3]

Neither of these contains rules to deal specifically with referendum campaigns. However, several fundamental rights guaranteed by the Federal Constitution have to be considered when examining the legal framework of referendum campaigns. According to Article 34 paragraph 2 of the Federal Constitution, the guarantee of political rights protects the free formation of opinion by the citizens and the unaltered expression of their will. This provision does not impose strict neutrality on political authorities during the referendum debate.[4] Authorities are allowed to take a position and to recommend the approval or the refusal of a referendum question.[5] However, major, active political campaigning by political authorities would be contrary to the constitutional guarantee of political rights,[6] even more so if public funds were to be used for such messages. It is also forbidden to grant disproportionately large public funds to private referendum committees.[7]

Other fundamental rights guaranteed by the Federal Constitution that ensure the fairness of a referendum debate are the freedom of opinion and information, the freedom of the media, the freedom of assembly and the freedom of association.[8]

Rules regarding the financing of referendum campaigns

In Switzerland, there are no specific regulations on the financing of referendum campaigns by political parties and other civil society groups. Thus, whereas the use of public funds for political campaigning is prohibited, campaign spending by political parties and other groups is not limited, and there is no obligation for campaigners to reveal their donors or the amount of money spent on a referendum campaign. In this context we should also mention that the financing of political parties is not regulated in Switzerland. Political parties do not receive any public funds for their activities. As a result, they finance themselves from membership fees, from the donations of party members, non-members, private companies and organizations, as well as from the contributions of office holders (Ladner, 2007). Also, it is worthwhile to restate the fact that direct democracy in Switzerland is at the origin of the formation of mass political parties and not the other way round which has had effects on their self-definition and degree of organization (Gruner, 1969: 22–8).

Clearly, money is also involved before a referendum or an initiative can take place, namely during the phase of signature collection. Here the rule is such that there is no ban on payment of those who collect signatures but on paying those who sign the referendum or the initiative.

As stated, at the federal level, there are no transparency rules at all. Relatively early in the scholarly debate, Gruner (1969: 211) mentioned that party finances are a taboo theme in Swiss politics. Whereas the lack of financial transparency also holds for most of the cantons, two have tried to introduce rules. In the Canton of Ticino, since October 1998 donations of more than 10,000 Swiss francs to political parties have to be published. In the Canton of Geneva, since September 1999 anonymous donations have been forbidden and transparency rules apply not only to political parties, but also to other political groups engaged in campaigns (Balmelli, 2002). For the time being, however, such rules are rather the exception. First experiences in the two mentioned cantons are not very encouraging and they are already thinking of changing the current regulations.

Media access and official information in a referendum campaign

Regarding the access to media by political parties and other civil society organizations engaged in a campaign, there are no rules that would apply solely during referendum campaigns. Contrary to the situation in other member states of the Council of Europe, Swiss law does not determine an official timeframe for the referendum campaign.

Nonetheless, several provisions of the Federal Act on Radio and Television, adopted on 24 March 2006, are particularly important during referendum campaigns.[9] This act mandates all radio and television stations to respect the fundamental rights, to contribute to the free formation of opinion, and to provide varied and objective information for the public. The overall offering of programmes in a region must cover the diversity of events and opinions in a balanced manner. Broadcast information must be objective and representative of the diversity of facts and opinions. Furthermore, personal opinions and commentaries have to be recognisable as such.[10] In addition, political advertising on radio and television is forbidden.[11] Thus any advertising for political parties, any advertising for members of public authorities or candidates to such authorities, and any advertising on the issue of a popular ballot, are forbidden.[12] Last but not least, the sponsoring of news presentations as well as of any programme related to the exercise of political rights is not allowed.[13]

An independent mediator dealing with complaints about such programmes is installed in each of the regions representing one of the three official languages.[14] The mediators' decisions can then be reviewed by an independent authority for radio and television that has been established at the federal level.[15]

As a result, although campaigners do not get free airtime in Switzerland, and notwithstanding the fact that there are no specific rules for referendum campaigns, it seems to be generally recognized by political actors that the regulations set down in the Federal Act on Radio and Television provide for a fair referendum debate in the media.

Kriesi (1994) shows that there is quite a large space for influence with regard to campaigning, especially when the issue at the ballot is complex and the individual level of information possessed by citizens is low.

During a campaign the government is allowed to present its viewpoint and give out a recommendation. The government can explain in an official information brochure, distributed along with the voting material, and has the right to defend its position in a brief TV speech immediately after the main evening news broadcast. In addition, the government usually receives greater space for its own arguments in the information brochure than the adversaries (Kriesi, 1994: 34).

According to Article 34, the authorities have the duty to inform the public about a vote; however, they are not allowed to intervene in a dominating manner. In practice, in democratic political systems, this means that governments have the right and even the duty to participate in public debate. The federal judges have established a few guidelines (Tornay, 2008). Officially submitted information brochures sent to the voters by the government must be objective, whereas neutrality cannot be achieved since the authorities take a position on an issue.

11.3 Scholarly debates and political activities

Can the result of a referendum vote be bought?

In their seminal study on Switzerland, Gruner and Hertig measured the intensity of newspaper ads for 41 votes in three major daily newspapers one week before the poll. According to a linear regression model they estimate that approximately one-third of the variance of the result can be explained by the propaganda dominance of one side (Gruner and Hertig, 1983: 133). Furthermore, propaganda efforts against a proposal seem to be more successful than ones in favour (Gruner and Hertig, 1983: 134). They find enough evidence to conclude that, in principle, referendum results can be bought with money. Irrespective of this conclusion they suggest something should be done. This is because in general they find that an initiative on average has to fight against 'No' propaganda three times as large, and in some extreme cases twenty times as large. They therefore called for a reform (Gruner and Hertig, 1983: 136). However, up until the present time, nothing has changed. Hertig was then also criticized because his data on campaign spending were reliant on estimations.

Typically, some evident counter-examples in which money was not able to buy the end result are cited (see also Schneider and Hess, 1995; Gilland Lutz and Marquis, 2006; Longchamp, 1991: 317). However, at the same time it is suggested that this issue should be monitored closely (Kaufmann et al., 2007: 83–4, 188).

Comparing direct democracy mechanisms and procedures in California and Switzerland, Möckli (1994: 287–8) concludes that money is not the only determinant of the outcome of a vote. He cites some anecdotal evidence listing counter-examples where citizens' initiatives or referendum committees with much less money at their disposal have defeated their much better-funded counterparts (Möckli, 1994: 295). The general trend of the debate on this issue in Switzerland based on empirical research in Switzerland and foremost in comparison to the USA is to say that in general there is no proof that referendum results can be bought (Kriesi, 2005). Summing up, we could say there is evidence of a high correlation but not a deterministic causal relationship between campaign spending and the outcome of the vote.[16]

Detailed analysis for two votes on nuclear power plants measured the advertising space pro and contra campaign committees occupied during the campaign in newspapers (Wymann, 1991). The study once again comes to the conclusion that money alone cannot buy the result. The quantification and measurement of newspaper ads only covers a part of the picture. Seitz (1990, 1992) argues that a professional organization and infrastructure play a crucial role as well.

In the latest piece of empirical research on this issue in Switzerland, Kriesi (forthcoming) draws an analogy to election campaign studies where incumbents are faced with a campaign against challengers and where challengers seem to spend their campaign money more effectively. However, he argues that there is a major problem with this literature, namely, that campaign spending is dependent on expectations of the vote result. Basically, these studies face an endogeneity problem, i.e. why should an incumbent spend more if he or she is almost certain of winning the race for office? In Swiss referendum campaigns a similar situation is faced, usually a parliamentarian majority and the government oppose organized interests (plus sometimes a minority of political parties) as the challengers. Kriesi thus expects campaign spending to be interdependent between opposing groups and to be highest when the race is tight and the outcome uncertain. As Kriesi elaborates the governmental camp (but also the challengers) in Switzerland is almost always confronted with a considerable degree of uncertainty regarding the outcome of the vote. In his empirical analysis he includes all 218 projects submitted to a vote between June 1981 and November 2006. His results show that, in a nutshell, the effect of the governmental camp's spending depends on the expected outcome, and also has to be nuanced regarding the direct democratic instrument, e.g. citizens' initiative, optional or mandatory referendum. Given his results, it seems 'preposterous to claim, as some authors have done, that one can buy success at the polls in a direct democratic vote. It would, however, also be incorrect to claim [...] that campaign spending has hardly any or no influence on the outcome of the vote [...]. As is so often the case, the truth of the matter lies somewhere between these extreme claims' (Kriesi, forthcoming: 26).

Political and judicial activities

Political forces in Parliament, usually from the left party spectrum, have tried to introduce transparency rules on campaign spending or have attempted to tackle the issue indirectly by suggesting that political parties be funded with public funds.[17] So far none of these Parliamentarian initiatives has ever achieved a political majority.

Another possibility in a political system with strong direct democratic elements is, of course, the use of direct democratic mechanisms themselves, such as the popular initiative, in order to bring about change. The only citizen's initiative that has so far tried to influence the rules of the campaign game is quite recent. The citizen's initiative 'Sovereignty of the People instead of Propaganda by the Government' was submitted to a vote on 1 June 2008 and aimed at severely limiting the role of both government and public administration during a referendum campaign. Colloquially, the initiative was therefore called the 'Muzzle Initiative' (Engeli et al., 2008: 22).[18] The text was sponsored by a right-wing citizen's movement called 'Citizens for citizens' and called for a halt to political communication by the government during a referendum campaign, for this was considered to be political propaganda. They argued that the Federal Council, the Swiss executive, should not engage in a campaign trying to win the vote. Instead the Federal Council should not finance, support or engage in information campaigns and propaganda with the exception of the publication of an official explanatory booklet which is sent along with the ballot sheets to every citizen eligible to vote.

The Federal Council itself, as well as both chambers of the Legislature, rejected the citizen's initiative by clear majorities.[19] The political left (Social Democrats SPS including the unions), Christian-Democrats (CVP), the Radicals (FDP) and the Liberals (LP) also issued 'No' recommendations. With the exception of one cantonal section only the right-wing conservative Swiss People's Party (SVP) and the influential political action committee AUNS[20] supported the text. On 1 June 2008, however, all of the 23 cantons and 75.2 per cent of all voters decided against this citizen's initiative (Engeli et al., 2008: 22).

As these political struggles illustrate, the political left continues to demand more transparency and the introduction of party financing from public funds, whereas the political right is rather concerned with limiting the government's and public administration's involvement during referendum campaigns. However, we cannot expect any change of the status quo to come from these activities. There are no clear political majorities for the bills of either side.

An alternative political venue in the Swiss political system is the Federal Court, although much less than in other countries – for example, Germany or the United States of America. There is no formal judicial review at the national level, however, court rulings have occasionally had a political influence in Swiss politics (Rothmayr, 2001) and on direct democracy in the Swiss cantons in particular (Tornay, 2008). Since the Federal Court oversees the Constitutions and legislation in the cantons, its judgements can have an incremental influence from the bottom up even at the national level. I thus present two interesting cases with some relevance for the issue of referendum campaign financing. The Federal Court has acknowledged on various occasions that the intervention of well-financed interest groups can represent a serious threat to democracy and in particular to the citizen's right to free formation and expression of the vote:

> The facts listed by the Federal Court regarding the free formation of the will of the elector relates even more so to referendum votes on concrete objects and not so much to elections: in which case a solution is opposed to another one and the use of considerable financial means can in many instances have a decisive effect on the result of the vote. (Federal Court Ruling 125 I 441: 444; original in Italian)

According to the Federal Court, the public authorities actually have a mandate to inform the public on the issues at stake during a referendum campaign (Tornay, 2008: 232–3). Historically, the Federal Court has over the last five decades shifted gradually from asking the public authorities to retain themselves in a referendum debate to making it almost a duty to be actively involved.

In our first case, in 1999, the Parliament of the Canton of Ticino adopted a new law on political rights to integrate and harmonize legislation that was up to that date dispersed across five different laws.

However, it also added substantially new paragraphs on the transparency of financial donations to political parties, political groups, and individual candidates, so that each donation exceeding 10,000 CHF per annum must be reported and that donations exceeding 5,000 CHF for a candidate during an electoral campaign must also be disclosed with the names of the donors. In addition, the new law introduced in Article 115 paragraph 2, a cap on donations by third parties of 50,000 CHF per campaign and candidate. The rules also applied to referendum campaigns.

As the result of a formal complaint, on 10 July 1999 the Federal Court ruled against this latter regulation, stating that a cap on campaign spending goes against both the principle of equal opportunity and the principle of proportionality (the other two provisions still holding). It would only hurt the less fortunate candidates who depend on third-party financing when they have to compete with a candidate who has sufficient funding of their own. The original idea of the legislator was not to limit an individual candidate's campaign funding; it was mainly preoccupied with the independence of a candidate when third-party financing is too high. This Federal Court ruling will therefore make it more difficult to introduce limits on campaign spending in the future in other cantons and eventually at the federal level.

The principle of a free vote includes the right of each citizen to form an opinion on the issue at stake in a referendum vote. State authorities are therefore not allowed to intervene during elections, and during a referendum campaign only by respecting certain rules, namely those of transparency, legality and fairness (Tornay, 2008: 260–1). Regarding the financing of referendum campaigns the use of public funds to support a private initiative or referendum committee is of particular interest (Tornay, 2008: 266). Federal Court rulings on cases from the cantons of Argovia, Vaud, and Neuchâtel for their lack of transparency can be summed up as follows: regarding the financial intervention of the State during a referendum campaign the Federal Court has, in principle, ruled that public funds must be attributed transparently and that representatives of the public authorities must be an integral member of the private committee they support, otherwise they have no control over what happens with the money (Tornay, 2008: 266–7). The funds a public authority uses to support a private referendum or initiative committee need to have a legal basis, or legitimation by a parliamentarian vote, or at least must be discernible as a separate position in the budget (Tornay, 2008: 268).

Those not so well-known court cases are in the medium to long run probably going to have a bigger effect on future regulations on the use of money in referendum campaigns than parliamentary initiatives, at least on future attempts at regulation regarding the cantonal level.

11.4   Conclusion

Considering the current situation in Switzerland in respect of the financing of referendum campaigns and media access two major trends can be discerned: on the one hand, it becomes very clear that it is highly unlikely that Switzerland will introduce major legislation to regulate this field in the near future. The mainstream argumentation against regulation is that control is too costly and can easily be circumvented. On the other hand, we can see that public authorities were over the years allowed to play a more active role in the democratic process and are even allowed to support private referendum committees as long as certain principles are respected.

Change is therefore not to be expected to come from within the Swiss political system. Instead, sooner rather than later politics in general, and therefore also referendum campaigns, will undergo a transformation through the cultural revolution we are experiencing with the ever deeper invasion of information and communication technologies such as the Internet into our daily lives.

Notes

1. L'engagement du Conseil fédéral et de l'administration dans les campagnes précédant les votations fédérales, Rapport du groupe de travail de la Conférence des services d'information élargie (GT CSIC), Berne, November 2001, pp. 10–12, http://www.admin.ch/ch/f/cf.
2. Articles 138 to 142 of the Federal Constitution of the Swiss Confederation of 18 April 1999; http://www.admin.ch/ch/itl/rs/1/index.htm.
3. Federal Act on Political Rights of 17 December 1976; http://www.admin.ch/ch/e/rs/c161_1.html.
4. Decision of the Federal Supreme Court 121 I 252, 255 f.
5. Compare with Article 11 paragraph 2 of the Federal Act on Political Rights of 17 December 1976.
6. Decision of the Federal Supreme Court 114 Ia 427, 444.
7. Decision of the Federal Supreme Court 114 Ia 427, 443.
8. See Articles 16, 17, 22 and 23 of the Federal Constitution of the Swiss Confederation of 18 April 1999.
9. RS 784.40 ; http://www.admin.ch/ch/f/rs/c784_40.html (French text).
10. Article 4 Federal Act on Radio and Television.
11. Unabhängige Beschwerdeinstanz für Radio und Fernsehen, *Entscheid vom 27. Juni 2003 betreffend Schweizer Fernsehen DRS: Werbespot der Flüchtlingshilfe*, ausgestrahlt am 15. Januar 2003; Eingabe von S vom 28. März 2003; http://www.ubi.admin.ch/presse/2003/de/03082801.

12. Article 10 paragraph 1d Federal Act on Radio and Television.
13. Article 12 paragraph 5 Federal Act on Radio and Television.
14. Article 91 Federal Act on Radio and Television of 24 March 2006.
15. Articles 82 to 85 and Article 94 of the Federal Act on Radio and Television.
16. For the case of election campaigns also check the empirical studies by Schmid (1985) and Wiederkehr (1989).
17. Postulat 94.3435, 5 October 1995, on the role of money in a direct democracy; Parlamentarische Initiative 99.430, 18 June 1999, on transparency of donations for referendum campaigns (both by Andreas Gross, Social Democratic Party of Switzerland). Parlamentarische Initiative 06.406, 20 March 2006, on transparency financing political parties, lobby organizations, and campaigns (by Roger Nordmann, Social-Democratic Party of Switzerland). For motions further back in history see: Moneypulation 1998: 3–9.
18. See also Botschaft über die Volksinitiative 'Volkssouveränität statt Behördenpropaganda', 29 June 2005, 05.054.
19. By 134 'No' to 61 'Yes' votes with three abstentions in the lower chamber, the Nationalrat, and by 38 'No' to 2 'Yes' votes with three abstentions in the upper chamber, the Ständerat. That is not (as in many other countries) the end of the proposal. The vote will take place nevertheless. However, the negative statements of the Executive and the Legislative towards the initiative are a recommendation to the undecided voter (for more on heuristic shortcuts, see Kriesi, 2005) and therefore a symbolic sign of major importance during the campaign.
20. AUNS=For an independent and neutral Switzerland; the movement is politically close and its members largely overlap with the SVP.

References

Auer, A., Malinverni, G., and M. Hottelier (2006) *Droit constitutionnelle suisse* (Bern: Stämpfli).

Balmelli, T. (2002) *Le financement des parties politiques et des campagnes électorales* (Diss. Fribourg).

Botschaft über die Volksinitiative Volkssouveränität statt Behördenpropaganda vom 29. Juni 2005 (05.054), in *Bundesblatt* 2005: 4373–403.

Engeli, I., Anouk L., and N. Alessandro (2008) *Analyse der eidg. Abstimmung vom 1. Juni 2008*. gfs.bern und Institut für Politikwissenschaft, Universität Genf.

Gilland Lutz, K., and L. Marquis (2006) 'Campaigning in a Direct Democracy: Three Case Studies', *Swiss Political Science Review*, **12**(3): 63–81.

Gruner, E. (1969) *Die Parteien in der Schweiz* [Helvetia Politica, Series B, Vol. IV] (Bern: Francke Verlag).

Gruner, E. and H.P. Hertig (1983) *Die Stimmbürger und die 'neue' Politik: Wie reagiert die Politik auf die Beschleunigung der Zeitgeschichte?* [Publikationen des Schweizerischen Nationalfonds aus den Nationalen Forschungsprogrammen, Band 17] (Bern/Stuttgart: Haupt).

Hertig, H.P. (1982), Sind Abstimmungserfolge käuflich? – Elemente der Meinungsbildung bei eidgenössischen Abstimmungen', in *SVPW-Jahrbuch – Annuaire ASSP 22/1982: Medien und politische Kommunikation – Média et communication politique* (Bern: Verlag Paul Haupt), pp. 35–57.

Kaufmann, B., Büchi, R., and N. Braun (2007) *The Initiative & Referendum Institute Europe Guidebook to Direct Democracy in Switzerland and Beyond: 2008 Edition* (Marburg: The Initiative & Referendum Institute Europe).

Kriesi, H. (1994) 'Le défi à la démocratie directe posé par les transformations de l'espace public', in Yannis Papadopoulos, *Présent et avenir de la démocratie directe: Actes du colloque de l'Université de Lausanne* (Genève: Georg), pp. 31–72.

Kriesi, H. (2005) *Direct Democratic Choice: The Swiss Experience* (Lanham, MD: Rowman & Littlefield).

Kriesi, Hanspeter (ed.) (1993) *Citoyenneté et démocratie directe* (Zurich: SEISMO).

Kriesi, H. (forthcoming) *The Effect of Spending in Swiss Direct-Democratic Campaigns.*

Ladner, A. (2007) 'Political Parties', in U. Klöti, P. Knoepfel, H. Kriesi, W. Linder, Y. Papadopoulos and P. Sciarini (eds), *Handbook of Swiss Politics* (Zürich: NZZ Publishing), pp. 309–34.

Linder, W. (2007) 'Direct Democracy', in U. Klöti, P. Knoepfel, H. Kriesi, W. Linder, Y. Papadopoulos and P. Sciarini (eds), *Handbook of Swiss Politics* (Zürich: NZZ Publishing).

Longchamp, C. (1991) Herausgeforderte demokratische Öffentlichkeit: Zu den Möglichkeiten und Grenzen des politischen Marketings bei Abstimmungen und Wahlen in der Schweiz, in *SVPW-Jahrbuch – Annuaire ASSP 31/1991: Direkte Demokratie – Démocratie directe* (Bern/Stuttgart: Verlag Paul Haupt), pp. 303–26.

Luechinger, S., M. Rosinger and A. Stutzer (2007) 'The Impact of Postal Voting on Participation: Evidence from Switzerland', *Swiss Political Science Review*, 13(2): 167–202.

Möckli, S. (1994) *Direkte Demokratie: ein Vergleich der Einrichtungen und Verfahren in der Schweiz und Kalifornien, unter Berücksichtigung von Frankreich, Italien, Dänemark, Irland, Österreich, Liechtenstein und Australien* (Bern/Stuttgart/Wien: Haupt).

Moneypulation ....? Bericht zum Postulat 94.3435 Andreas Gross zur Rolle des Geldes in der direkten Demokratie (1998) (Mimeo).

Papadopoulos, Y. (ed.) (1998) *Démocratie directe* (Paris: Economica).

Rothmayr, C. (2001) 'Towards the Judicialization of Swiss Politics?', *West European Politics*, 24(2): 77–94.

Schmid, U. (1985) *Wahlkampffinanzierung in den USA und in der Schweiz* (Diss. Universität Zürich. Diessenhofen, Rüegger).

Schneider, G. and C. Hess (1995) 'Die innenpolitische Manipulation der Aussenpolitik', *Swiss Political Science Review*, 1(2–3): 93–111.

Seitz, W. (1990) *Prolegomena zur Erstellung eines Abstimmungsbarometers: Eine Untersuchung über die Strukturen und die Finanzierung von Abstimmungskämpfen* (Mimeo Forschungszentrum für schweizerische Politik, Bern).

Seitz, W. (1992) *Geld und Geist in der direkten Demokratie: Ueber den Zusammenhang von Abstimmungsbudget, Abstimmungskampagne und Abstimmungserfolg* (Mimeo, Bern).

Tornay, B. (2008) *La démocratie directe saisie par le juge: L'empreinte de la jurisprudence sur les droits populaires en Suisse* (Zürich: Schulthess).

Trechsel, A. (2007) 'Popular Votes', in U. Klöti, P. Knoepfel, H. Kriesi, W. Linder, Y. Papadopoulos and P. Sciarini (eds), *Handbook of Swiss Politics* (Zürich: NZZ Publishing), pp. 435–61.

Trechsel, A. and U. Serdült (1999) *Kaleidoskop Volksrechte: Die Institutionen der direkten Demokratie in den schweizerischen Kantonen (1970–1996)* (Basel, Genf and München: Helbing & Lichtenhahn).

Wiederkehr, E. (1989) *Der gekaufte Sitz? Werbung und Wahlerfolg: Eine empirische Untersuchung der Wirkung von Zeitungswerbung bei den Nationalratswahlen 1987*, Studien zur Politikwissenschaft, Liz. Universität Zürich, pp. 265–6.

Wymann, C. (1991) *Werbemacht und Direkte Demokratie: Dimensionen und Strukturen von Werbekampagnen vor eidgenössischen Volksabstimmungen, untersucht am Beispiel der Atomschutzinitiative (1979) sowie der Atom- und Energieinitiativen (1984)* (Mimeo, Universität Bern).

Zellweger, T. and U. Serdült (2006) 'Campaign Financing and Media Access Regulation for Referendums', in Venice Commission, *The Preconditions for a Democratic Election*, Collection on the Science and Technique of Democracy, no. 43 (Strasbourg: Council of Europe Publishing), pp. 71–100.

12
Sledgehammers and Nuts?
Regulating Referendums in the UK

Navraj Singh Ghaleigh

12.1   Background and history

Constitutional practice in the United Kingdom and direct democracy

The primacy of the Westminster Parliament in the constitutional arrangements of the United Kingdom[1] is both well known and long established. It entails, amongst other things, the fundamental doctrine of the sovereignty of Parliament. For present purposes, it also contributes to the infrequent use of devices of direct democracy in the United Kingdom. Initiatives – whether direct or indirect – are entirely unknown to our constitutional system, though not unconsidered,[2] as are popular or voter referendums.[3] Legislative or submitted referendums[4] are somewhat more familiar, but deployed only exceptionally. Further, the concept of a *binding referendum* is something of an anathema as a consequence of the aforementioned doctrine of parliamentary sovereignty. Conventionally described as the rule that the 'Queen-in-Parliament' (that is, the House of Commons, the House of Lords and the Crown, acting in concert) may make or unmake *any* law and is alone in having that power, parliamentary sovereignty has traditionally been interpreted to mean that Parliament cannot be legally bound.[5] In the context of referendums, parliamentary sovereignty dictates that the electorate's stated preference can, as a matter of law (though not practical politics), has only ever be advisory. The fine balance between political reality and constitutional formality has been put as follows: 'The Government will be bound by its result, but Parliament, of course, cannot be bound.'[6]

It should not be assumed, however, that debates as to the use of referendums have always been absent. No less a figure than A.V. Dicey (Vinerian

Professor of English Law at Oxford) made the case for referendums to solve questions of major constitutional change. Dicey's argument was of a highly contingent nature, being grounded in debates as to the status of Ireland (which raged from the 1880s to 1918, and beyond), then part of the 'Union' but with aspirations of independence, or 'Home Rule'. A committed Unionist, Dicey's support for referendums was premised upon his belief in the fundamentally conservative instincts of the British electorate. A referendum on Home Rule would, he believed, be defeated and as such the device would operate as 'the people's veto'.[7]

The UK has thus had infrequent recourse to referendums at the national or regional level – the focus of this study.[8] It is worth noting the primary hereof the 'constitutional' referendum of the UK (pertaining to radical changes to the constitution, the establishment of new models of sub-state autonomy and the transfer of soverèign powers to international organizations, etc.) and the absence of ordinary or legislative referendums (pertaining to matters of quotidian policy).[9] For the sake of completeness, some mention should be made of referendums at the local level. The Local Government Act 2000, ss. 34–6 allows for referendums in English and Welsh local authorities for the limited purposes of whether or not to establish a directly elected mayor. Traditionally, such mayors were elected by the local council (which was directly elected) rather than directly by the electorate itself.[10]

Legal basis, frequency, subject matter

> In modern times there has been no single event that has required a comprehensive revision of the constitution and so the United Kingdom has no constitutional text with this special status.[11]

The above quotation can be rephrased into the claim that, unlike almost all comparable polities, the UK has been spared the sort of polity shock (revolution, war, invasion, etc.) that ordinarily requires the general reworking of the system of government and so constitution making. Combining that statement with the Diceyan edict that the referendum device be reserved for matters of considerable constitutional moment, it could be expected that referendums have been rarely deployed in the UK. A recent government discussion paper stated,

> The Government believes that the holding of national referendums should continue to be an exceptional feature of our constitutional arrangements, used in circumstances where these sorts of fundamental issues are at stake. To act otherwise would be to undermine the fundamental principles of representative democracy.[12]

Table 12.1 UK referendums at the national or regional level, to 2008

Year	Issue/Question	Region	Result (underlined)	Turnout	Notes, inc. authorizing legislation
1973	Northern Ireland 'Border Poll' "1. Do you want Northern Ireland to remain part of the UK? Or 2. Do you want Northern Ireland to be joined with the Republic of Ireland, outside of the UK?"	Northern Ireland	<u>Yes</u> Option 1: 98.9% Option 2: 1.1%	57.5%	The electorate was restricted to N. Ireland (that is, did not include the Republic of Ireland). As a result, the N. Irish Catholic/nationalist community boycotted the ballot, accounting for the low 'Option 2' vote. Northern Ireland (Border Poll) Act 1972
1975	Terms of continuing UK membership of the European Economic Community. "Do you think the UK should stay in the European Community (Common Market)?"	United Kingdom	<u>Yes</u> Yes: 67.2% No: 32.8%	64.5%	Referendum Act 1975
1979	(Re-)establishment of a Parliament for Scotland "Do you want the provisions of the Scotland Act 1978 to be put into effect?"	Scotland	<u>No</u>* Yes: 51.6% No: 48.4%	63.8%	·Scotland Act 1978 *Both 1978 referendums were conducted under threshold rules that defined a successful 'yes' vote as requiring the support of 40% of eligible voters.
1979	Establishment of an elected Assembly for Wales "Do you want the provisions of the Wales Act 1978 to be put into effect?"	Wales	<u>No</u>* Yes: 20.3% No: 79.7%	58.8%	Wales Act 1978

1997	(Re-)establishment of a Parliament for Scotland "Question 1: 1. I agree that there should be a Scottish Parliament; or 2. I do not agree that there should be a Scottish Parliament Question 2 1. I agree that a Scottish Parliament should have tax-varying powers; or 2. I do not agree that a Scottish Parliament should have tax-varying powers"	Scotland	Yes, Yes Option 1: Yes: 74.3% No: 25.7% Option 2: Yes: 63.5% No: 36.5%	60.4%	Referendums (Scotland and Wales) Act 1997
1997	Establishment of an elected Assembly for Wales "1. I agree that there should be a Welsh Assembly; or 2. I do not agree that there should be a Welsh Assembly."	Wales	Yes Option 1: 50.3% Option 2: 49.7%	50.1%	Referendums (Scotland and Wales) Act 1997
1998	Establishment of a new scheme of local government for London "Are you in favour of the Government's proposals for a Greater London Authority, made up of an elected mayor and a separately elected assembly?"	Greater London	Yes Yes: 72.0% No: 28.0%	34.1%	
1998	Northern Ireland peace process/Good Friday agreement "Do you support the agreement reached at the multi-party talks on Northern Ireland and set out in Command Paper 3883?"	Northern Ireland	Yes Yes: 71.7% No: 28.9%	81.0%	
2004	Establishment of a regional assembly in NE England "Should there be an elected regional assembly for the North East region?"	North East region of England	No Pro: 22.1% Anti: 77.9%	47.1% (1,889,742 electors)	Political Parties Elections and Referendums Act 2000 Regional Assemblies (Preparations) Act 2003

Table 12.1 lists the entirety of the UK's referendums to the end of 2008, all of which, prior to 2000, took place on an ad hoc legal basis. Reasons for the shortness of the list are proffered above and space precludes their detailed discussion. It is noteworthy that of these experiences, only one has engaged the national electorate – that of 1975.[13]

Arrangements pertaining to the 1975 referendum were set out in detail in a White Paper[14] and included the following: broadcast time would be made available to each campaigning organization free of charge; expenditure limits would not be imposed for fear of restricting freedom of expression; expenditure and donation sources would be publicly disclosed *ex post*; and, limited public funding was to be made available to both sides. This latter arrangement required the passing of the 1975 Referendum Act which permitted the granting of no more than £125,000 to each campaign ('Britain in Europe' and the 'National Referendum Campaign'). The motivation behind public funding – to ensure that both campaigns were supported to a minimum level such that a meaningful contest could take place – was well conceived. The published accounts of both campaigns revealed that the 'Yes' campaign received 369 donations above £100 (from individuals, trade unions, and companies) and raised nearly £1,000,000 whereas the losing 'No' campaign raised a mere £8,610 in donations.[15] Accordingly, public funding accounted for 8 per cent of the former's income and 94 per cent of the latter's, raising inevitable questions about expenditure limits, the campaigning role of government and that of broadcasting.

The 1978 referendums on the re-establishment[16] of a Scottish Parliament and establishment of a Welsh Assembly took place on a different legal basis, with the *Acts* setting out the legislative scheme but only coming into force subject to approval by referendum.[17] Further, the threshold requirement that 40 per cent of the electorate vote positively, meant that the referendum failed not withstanding a majority in favour.[18]

The next round of referendums swiftly followed the 'New Labour' victory of 1997, revisiting the subject matter of the 1978 referendums. Controversy attended the ad hoc funding rules in the Welsh referendum. Having been left without Westminster representation after the 1997 General Election, the Welsh Conservative Party forbore from campaigning in the referendum. As both Plaid Cymru (the Welsh nationalist party) and the Labour Party supported devolution, there was no 'No' campaign until, at the eleventh hour, a disgruntled Labour Party member with the support of a generous individual cobbled together a 'No' campaign. This imbalance 'disturbed' the Committee on Standards in Public Life[19] which, referring to the tiny majority in favor of the proposition, noted that, 'a fairer campaign might well have resulted in a different outcome'. Unfairness arose in the 1997 referendums (and also those of 1978) from the fact that there was no public funding for the two campaigns. Thus the balancing provided by state support in the 1975 poll was absent – a particularly inequitable feature given that the support of the major political parties may be heavily skewed, as in Wales 1997.

The absence of agreed rules of engagement in this and the other recent referendums convinced the Committee that a new regulatory framework was needed for referendums.[20] The key recommendations were that each side in a campaign should be provided with core funding, at public expense[21] and that '[T]he government of the day ... should, as a government, remain neutral and should not distribute at public expense literature, even purportedly "factual" literature, setting out or otherwise promoting its case'.[22] In addition, it was recommended that no spending limits should apply to referendum campaigns as these would be 'administratively impracticable [and] would, or at least might, impose an unwarranted restriction on freedom of expression'.[23]

The provision of public/core funding was debated vigorously in the Cardiff hearings of the Committee where the one-sided nature of the 1997 referendum campaign brought this issue into sharp relief. The Committee was not convinced by the argument that, if one side of the campaign could not raise funds and coordinate itself, this was proof of an absence of public support. Rather it recognized the possibility of there being a mass of unorganized opinion that would be effectively unable to argue its case without public funding. Although the distribution of core funding is left to the Election Commission,[24] the Committee provided no guidance as to how it was to do this.

12.2 Financial regulations

The Report of the Committee on Standards in Public Life was influential on government and led directly to the Political Parties Elections and Referendums Act (PPERA) of 2000. The act thoroughly re-regulates almost every aspect of party funding and electoral law in the UK. It also creates a general scheme regulating all aspects of the conduct of referendums, including the timing of the poll, the mode by which the question is arrived at, who may participate in the campaign, the campaigning role of government, and a detailed scheme of financial controls. The Act further grants a central regulatory role to the Electoral Commission.[25] It nonetheless remains the case that the actual calling of the referendum, the precise stating of the question, the area involved, and the people entitled to vote requires further dedicated, primary legislation.[26] An introduction to the broader issues pertinent to conventional electoral campaigns (which include the establishment of an Election Commission, the registration and accounting requirements of political parties, and the rules controlling the income and expenditure of political parties and third parties) forms a necessary background to the Act's referendum-specific regime.

The general scheme of party and election financing

Prior to the passing of PPERA the UK operated under a regime of party and election funding that was positively antiquated by the standards of other advanced democracies. National campaign expenditure was unlimited, limits on foreign donations were absent, a permanent regulatory body was notable for its absence and the asymmetric rules for companies and trade unions to donate to political parties suggested regulatory partisanship.[27] Most notably for present purposes and as indicated above, when the UK has resorted to referendums, on each occasion, the rules governing their operation have been different. Such shortcomings could be ignored for as long as the UK's electoral practices retained the appearance of substantive competence (and referendums continued to languish in constitutional backwaters). However, throughout the 1980s and increasingly in the mid-1990s such appearances seemed strained. As the long period of Conservative Party hegemony (1979–97) came to an end, a series of party funding scandals created a strategic opportunity for the Labour Party opposition to make the case for a comprehensive reform of party, electoral, and referendum funding. Upon coming into power in 1997, the 'New Labour' government of Prime Minister Blair moved quickly to legislate in this area – although not without a scandal of its own.[28]

PPERA is a comprehensive and detailed act. What follows is a tour of its general highlights only to the extent that they contribute to the specific issue of referendum regulation, dealt with in more detail below.[29]

One of the more striking features of the funding of politics in the UK is that it is a mixed system of public and private money, to an extent unusual in continental Europe and the USA. Whilst there are no direct state subventions or block grants to political parties as such, they do enjoy several forms of discrete and dedicated public support.[30] Mundane, but nonetheless important are facilities such as free postage for one election communication, and free use of schoolrooms for election meetings.[31] The work of the Parliamentary opposition schemes is supported by means of 'Short' and 'Cranborne' schemes (assisting opposition parties in the House of Commons and Lords, respectively)[32] amounting to approximately £3 million per annum. To these long-standing modes of support, PPERA added only 'policy development grants', totalling £2 million per annum.[33]

Broadcasting time, ordinarily a big ticket item in political campaigns, cannot be bought in the UK. Rather it is allocated, free of charge, by broadcasters.[34] Under the terms of its Royal Charter, the BBC is prohibited from carrying paid advertising[35] with the Communications Act 2003 similarly enjoining private broadcasters. This Act creates a regulator called OFCOM which is charged, inter alia, with ensuring that no broadcasters carry any 'political advertising'.[36] The ambit of 'political advertising' is broad[37] and has recently been deemed to include animal rights group's proposed advertisements calling for equal rights for apes.[38]

Partisan political speech finds its way into the broadcast media via the statutory condition (pursuant to which broadcast licenses are issued) that the free airtime made available to political parties by the broadcasters on specific occasions[39] must follow OFCOM's decision on how much time is to be allocated to each particular party.[40] The rules establishing the minimum conditions under which free airtime is provided are published by OFCOM.[41] The actual determinations as to allocations are made by the 'Broadcasters Liaison Group'[42] – a body consisting of broadcasters, OFCOM, and the Electoral Commission (observing only). The determinations of the body are not binding but serve to ensure consistency in allocation across time and consensus across broadcasters.[43] A challenge to these arrangements, in the context of a General Election and on the basis that they unfairly favoured the larger parties, was rejected in *R. v. The British Broadcasting Corporation*.[44]

Whilst the public funding regime was merely amended by PPERA, it is in the area of donations that we first see the great change brought about in 2000. Starting from the definition of a 'permissible donor', the Act tightly defines those that may donate to a political party or candidate, requiring that donors are either on the electoral register, or are a UK registered company or a regulated trade union.[45] The onus is on the receiving party to ensure permissibility, with non-compliance attracting civil penalties. Donations from companies require shareholder consent and those from trade unions require the approval of the membership. There is no limit to the size of a donation, although the reliance of parties on multi-million pound donations has been the source of critical comment[46] with a recent review recommending a donation cap of £50,000.[47]

In terms of expenditure, the UK regulatory regime has controlled the amount that can be spent campaigning at the local level since the nineteenth century. However, regulation failed to match the development of national campaigning techniques and the rise of professionalized political parties such that prior to PPERA, there were no national expenditure limits. This lacuna was perceived as leading to an 'arms race' in funding between the two major parties, to the detriment of other parties, and the big two themselves. Incontinent expenditure is addressed by Part V of the Act which defines campaign expenditure in a detailed fashion[48] and limits it to approximately £20 million per party in the year preceding a General Election.[49] Maintaining the primacy of political parties in British electoral contests, expenditure of third parties is closely circumscribed[50] to approximately £1 million.[51]

Transparency of both income and expenditure is added to the regime by a very detailed set of registration requirements[52] which are supplemented by accounting requirements,[53] duties of donation reporting[54] by parties, as well as expenditure returns.[55] This complicated scheme combines to require parties to disclose publicly, via the Electoral Commission, all donations received by the national party over £5,000, including the precise amount, the name and address of the donor and the date of donation. This information is published quarterly by the Electoral Commission in respect of all parties and published on its website with the data being available in Excel and SPSS formats. During election campaigns, such disclosures are made weekly. As to the Electoral Commission itself, it is a permanent body created by the Act, funded by, but independent from central government, headed up by a college of rigorously non-partisan Commissioners. Its functions include reporting and reviewing elections and electoral practices, the dispensation of policy development grants and a range of powerful enforcement mechanisms.[56]

The referendum-specific scheme

That the rules of each past referendum differed led many commentators to conclude that the lack of consistency compromised fairness and thus legitimacy.[57] In the case of Scotland in 1978 there had long been the sense that the threshold requirement was designed to scupper devolution, whilst in Wales in 1997, the closeness of the result and skewed nature of the expenditure threatened to undermine the entire enterprise of the Welsh Assembly from the offing. Accordingly, Part VII of the Act devotes detailed attention to the conduct of referendums, whilst adopting the general regulations of permissible donations, transparency, and broadcasting as detailed above.

Referendums in the UK are invariably creations of government – that is, in the absence of popular initiatives and given the opposition's limited control of the legislative agenda, only governments have the realistic opportunity to hold a referendum.[58] That being the case, the government's role in the referendum process assumes great moment. PPERA's response is to restrict substantially the capacity of government to engage in the referendum campaign, especially in the pivotal final 28 days of campaigning. In particular, s. 125 PPERA prohibits the publication of promotional materials paid for by local or central government.[59] Although there is no prohibition of the government's position being laid out prior to that date, the rationale is to avoid the 'Welsh scenario' of a poorly funded campaign being outgunned by the resources of the state. Notably, this restriction does not apply to the Commission. Whilst understandable given its likely desire to run voter awareness and engagement campaigns, it is not inconceivable that this will be a source of controversy in the future.

Indeed, the 'Welsh scenario' appears to have loomed large in the mind of the legislator, which appears in PPERA keen to ensure a minimum degree of parity of arms between campaigns in a referendum so as to ensure that all opinions and positions are given a satisfactory airing. The means to avoid distortion resulting from a wholly imbalanced contest is enshrined in s. 108 PPERA which provides for the Electoral Commission to designate one 'Permitted Participant' (PP) from each of the 'Yes' and the 'No' side.[60] A 'Designated Organization' (DO) – essentially a 'lead campaign organisation' – benefits from higher expenditure limits than a PP and, crucially, is eligible for publicly funded assistance to run their campaign. For reasons of equality therefore, the Commission may only designate two or zero permitted participants as DOs. Designated Organizations are eligible for a range of public assistance including a grant of up to £600,000 from the Electoral Commission, sending of referendum addresses for free, the use of public meeting rooms for free, and access to referendum campaign broadcasts. For the purposes of referendums, rules 6,[61] 9[62] and 16[63] of the OFCOM rules are of particular relevance. The same level of cash and non-cash assistance is granted to each DO. Donations to both Permitted Participants and DOs are subject to the general permissibility rules described above. DOs may, however, accept donations from registered political parties – which is likely given their lead role.

In terms of what counts, the term 'referendum expenses' is broadly defined as 'any expenses incurred in connection with promoting or procuring a particular outcome in relation to any question asked at a referendum'.[64] This includes items such as advertising, material production costs, transport etc. and extends to items of notional expenditure such as benefits in kind.

As in General Elections, referendum campaigns are subject to expenditure limits, detailed in Schedule 14 of the Act. Notably, although the Committer on Standards in Public Life did not recommend such limits, the Government was strongly committed to the idea of referendum limits.[65] Expenditure limits varied according to the precise status of the participant. DOs are subject to a referendum expenditure limit of £5 million. Political parties' expenditure limits are determined by their performance at the previous Westminster General Election, ranging from £5 million for parties gaining 30 per cent or more of the vote to £500,000 for those gaining 5–10 per cent of the vote, along a sliding scale. All other permitted participants are capped at £500,000.[66]

Following a referendum, permitted participants are required to submit to the Electoral Commission a fully itemized report of detailed referendum expenses incurred during the relevant period. Reports must be submitted within three months for those expending £250,000 or less; within six months for those over £250,000. The latter must also be independently audited.[67] Although not directly related to the question of financing, the Electoral Commission has responsibilities additional to those above, related to passing comment on the intelligibility of the question, registering PPs, determining the DOs, and generally monitoring compliance.

12.3   Effects of money and financial regulations

Discussions of the effects of referendum regulations must bear one obvious point in mind – that the UK has held only one referendum since the introduction of the PPERA scheme (see Table 12.1). Given its radical departure from the previous scheme, any insights gleaned from earlier referendum experiences will be mainly historical. Further, it may be noted that there is wide divergence between referendum regulation and referendum frequency. On those rare occasions that the device is deployed, one might anticipate a win for the government. Of the eight pre-PPERA referendums, all succeeded bar those of 1979. Whilst the Welsh referendum suffered from a severe lack of popular support,[68] its Scottish counterpart failed only on account of a threshold requirement that was introduced as an amendment to the enabling Bill, by some accounts as a deliberate spoiling measure.[69] The constitutional structure surrounding UK referendums would also suggest that UK governments have the whip hand in the process. After all, the decision to hold a referendum is the government's 'gift', as is the timing of the poll. The question then is whether the regulatory regime established by PPERA is sufficiently robust to preclude the government from deploying its agenda-setting capacities in its own favour in the context of a referendum campaign.[70]

North East Referendum 2004

The test of the new regime arose in the context of the North East Referendum in 2004. Envisaged as the logical extension of devolution to Scotland, Wales and Northern Ireland, the proposition was whether an elected regional assembly should be created for the first time in England. The promotion of English regionalism was very much the 'pet-project' of the then Deputy Prime Minister, John Prescott. Hailing from the north of England and sitting in a Cabinet well stocked with Scots, he took on the task of providing for the English regions that which had been given to other British regions.[71] The North East region was selected as the first of what was envisaged as a series of regional referendums to create such assemblies across England. Polling had suggested very strong local support for the measure. The North East was, in English terms, an unusually coherent region with a strong sense of local pride and an established regional elite. Combined with the financial support of the Labour Party, it was initially assumed that a referendum would be won comfortably.[72]

The result confounded these expectations. A turnout of 47.7 per cent was overwhelmingly opposed to the proposition, with 77.9 per cent voting against. To what extent does this result illustrate the capacity of funding to determine the result?

Table 12.2 details the spending in the campaign of all permitted participants (including political parties and the two Designated Organizations – 'Yes4theNorthEast' and 'North East Says No'). Judged against their maximum expenditure limits, it is notable that none in fact came close to them. This is in contrast to all post-PPERA electoral campaigns where the major political parties and closely fought constituency campaigns come close to the statutory limits.[73] It *may* further suggest that the expenditure thresholds are set too high although one referendum is unlikely to provide sufficient evidence one way or another. It might be expected that a more contentious subject – perhaps on the UK's continuing membership of the EU – would better capture the public's attention and so require more extensive (and expensive) campaigning.

As to the balance of income between the two DOs, the 'Yes' campaign raised more than twice its rival (see Tables 12.3 and 12.4).

The 'No' campaign received minimal support other than from Electoral Commission-administered public funding which amounted to 79 per cent of its total income. As with the 1975 referendum and unlike the Welsh referendum of 1997, public funding enabled the campaign to run

Table 12.2   Spending by permitted participants in the NE Referendum 2004

Permitted participant	Referendum expenditure (£)	Expenditure limit (£)
Yes4theNorthEast Campaign (designated organisation)	361,091	665,000
North East Says No Ltd (designated organisation)	145,008	665,000
Labour Party (The)	124,126	665,000
The Conservative Party	30,243	400,000
UNISON	30,183	100,000
North East No Campaign	28,270	100,000
County Durham Supporters Club	9,044	100,000
Trade Union Congress	4,855	100,000
Friends of Northumberland County (FONC)	4,209	100,000
Liberal Democrats	3,594	400,000
South East Northumberland Unitary Counoil	3,248	100,000
GMB	1,752	100,000
Supporters of Rural Northumberland	846	100,000
British National Party	19	100,000
English Democrats Party	–	100,000
Senior Citizens Party	–	100,000
United Kingdom Independence Party	–	100,000
Mr David Stephens	–	100,000
Total	**746,488**	**4,095,000**

Source: Electoral Commission, 'The North East Regional Assembly and Local Government Referendums', November 2005.

an argument that would otherwise not have had the resources to be run. Claims may be made that an argument that cannot raise funds ought not be given the crutch of public subsidy, but the popular support the 'No' campaign garnered substantially gives the lie to that proposition.

By contrast with its rival, the 'Yes' campaign relied on public support for only 32 per cent of its income, being able to draw on prominent local individuals (Lady Hall is the wife of the former owner of the local football club, Newcastle United), the trade union movement, and private companies. Whilst none of the donations are large in the context of those given in the course of national politics[74] they aggregated to give the 'Yes' campaign a marked income advantage, as well as symbolic support in a region traditionally dominated by unionized heavy industry and passionate about football.

DOs are not the only actors, however – far from it. As Table 12.2 shows, other permitted participants weighed heavily in the campaign, none

Table 12.3 Donations to North East Says No

Donor	Cash	Non-Cash	Public Funds
Lord Steinberg	10,000		
Flowidea Ltd	10,000		
United Kingdom Independence Party		6,399	
Electoral Commission			100,000
Sub-Total	20,000	6,399	100,000
Total		£126,399	

Source: Electoral Commission, *Register of Donations*.

Table 12.4 Donations to Yes4theNorthEast

Donor	Cash	Non-Cash	Public Funds
GMB (trade union)	20,000		
Lady Mae Hall	50,000		
Sovereign Ltd	20,000		
Tyneside Prep'n Cluster Ltd	10,000		
Union (trade union)		20,723	
Nova Int. Ltd		15,000	
Thomsons Solicitors		5,039	
Express Engineering Ltd		9,999	
Express Holdings Ltd		9,999	
Electoral Commission			100,000
Sub-Total	150,000	60,760	100,000
Total		£310,760	

Source: Electoral Commission, *Register of Donations*.

more so than the Labour Party which, as well as being the national government at the time, also regarded the North East region as one of its heartlands. Three other permitted participants expended in the range of £30,000. No others expended significant sums, although it could be expected that the trade unions and supporter's clubs operated in a coordinated manner. Accordingly, it will be no surprise that expenditure broadly followed income, with expenditure by answer as per Table 12.5. Whereas the donation income of the two DOs gave the 'Yes' campaign an advantage of £184,361 (amounting to 42 per cent of all donations),

Table 12.5 Expenditure by 'Answer'

'Yes' Campaign	£542,102
'No' Campaign	£204,386

Source: Electoral Commission, *Register of Expenditure*.

Table 12.6 Expenditure by type

Participant	**Amount (£)**
Designated organization (2)	506,099
Political party (4)	157,982
Trade union (3)	36,790
Misc. campaigning groups (5)	45,617
Total	746,488

Source: Electoral Commission, *Register of Expenditure*.

in terms of expenditure, the additional intervention of other permitted participants slightly raised the 'Yes' campaign's advantage to £337,716 (amounting to 45 per cent of all expenditure). This is as expected by PPERA – the lead role of DOs was merely mirrored by the activities of other permitted participants.

In terms of the balance of campaign expenditure by type of organization, DOs obviously dominated. This is very much as intended by PPERA – DOs are both provided with the greatest public support and subject to the greatest regulatory attention. Given the 'party-focused' nature of general British politics, it is unsurprising that political parties weigh in next, with the Labour Party accounting for the majority of party expenditure.

The reasons for the resounding defeat of the NE referendum are inevitably numerous. According to Tickell et al.,[75] there were short-comings in the 'Yes' campaign's strategy. Local MPs appeared lukewarm towards the project and when under pressure from the growing 'No' campaign, 'went negative' with disastrous consequences. From the perspective of funding, however, it is noteworthy that despite having a sizable advantage in every category of income and expenditure, the 'Yes' campaign was unable to translate this into a victory. The key regulatory mechanism here was equal public support for each DO. In the absence of this, the 'No' campaign – lacking traditional channels of support in its region from the Labour Party, prominent business people, and the trade union movement – would have been starved of funding and unable to mount its late, ultimately successful, challenge. The absence of such a provision caused much anxiety in relation to the Welsh referendum of 1997,[76] which passed with the slimmest of majorities on the basis of an overwhelming financial advantage in favor of the government supported campaign.

One concern that arises after the NE referendum relates to spending limits. Whilst there is parity between DOs and limits on what other permitted participants can expend, PPERA does not prevent one or more wealthy individuals from splitting their donations between a large number of permitted participants. Were this to occur, the system of spending limits would be subverted and equality of campaigning would be undermined. Moreover, such a strategy could also undermine the primacy of DOs. Designed to operate as the 'lead campaigning bodies', they are subjected to the greatest degree of regulatory scrutiny in the PPERA scheme. However, were a large number of well-funded permitted participants to actively campaign on one side of a future referendum they may be able to dominate a campaign, outwith the structure of DOs and the protections that come with it. Whilst this was not an issue in the current case study, it could be foreseen to be a meaningful issue in more contentious referendum settings.

12.4 Concluding remarks

The UK occupies a paradoxical position vis-à-vis referendums. It scarcely uses them but has at its disposal a comprehensive regulatory scheme when it does. A sledgehammer to crack a nut? The riposte is that on those rare occasions that they are deployed, the subject matter is of great significance. Each of the episodes detailed in Table 12.1 can be framed as an attempt to resolve a question of first order status – they are modes of arriving at constitutional accommodation and as such 'address the location or distribution of ultimate authority within the polity and in doing so, implicate the sovereign relations between people and government'.[77]

Indeed, in the near future a referendum on the status of Scotland within the Union is expected. The Scottish National Party minority executive in the devolved Scottish administration has promised such a referendum in 2010. Such an 'autonomy referendum' is unknown to the UK, though more familiar in polities such as Quebec.[78] What is distinct about the promised poll is that it threatens the very basis of the United Kingdom.[79] It also raises questions as to the competence of the Scottish Parliament (can it call such a referendum, within its devolved powers?), whether the UK government would be bound by and indeed, what the financing arrangements for any such referendum might be.[80] However, any presumed axiomatic advantage to the government in UK referendums seems to be somewhat more complicated. The government's capacity to dictate when and on what a referendum will be held, combined with its general agenda setting powers might be expected to drive results, but the detailed scheme of referendum financing has been shown (albeit only on one occasion) to be able to resist such determinist outcomes.

Notes

1. Other reasons for the United Kingdom's non-use of devices of direct democracy range include an adherence to the Burkean tradition of representative democracy – see Balsom, D. in Gallagher and Uleri (eds), *The Referendum Experience in Europe* (Macmillan, 1996) and the absence of the sort of challenge to representative democracy led by the Populists in the USA of the 1890s and Progressives thereafter – see E. Gerber (1999) *The Populist Paradox* (Princeton University Press).
2. See L. Maer *Citizens' Initiatives*, House of Commons Library Standard Note, SN/PC/04483 (2008).
3. Understood as the device whereby upon the collection of the requisite signatures, a law already passed by the legislature is subjected to approval/rejection by the electorate.
4. Understood as the device whereby the legislature places a proposed law for dis/approval before the electorate.
5. Understandings of parliamentary sovereignty in this form originate from the constitutional theory of A.V. Dicey, canonically articulated in his *Introduction to the Study of the Law of the Constitution* (1885). The nature of parliamentary sovereignty is now commonly agreed to have been modified both by the UK's membership of the European Union, as well as the incorporation of the European Convention of Human Rights into domestic law by the Human Rights Act 1998 and the process of asymmetric devolution exemplified by the Scotland Act 1998.
6. Edward Short, Lord President and Leader of the House of Commons, House of Commons, Official Report, 11 March 1975, col. 293.
7. See M. Qvortrup (2002) *A Comparative Study of Referendums: Government by the People* (Manchester University Press), chapter 2; and V. Bogdanor (1985) 'Dicey and the Reform of the Constitution', [1985] *Public Law*, 652.
8. See Table 12.1 below.
9. The balance of use of 'ordinary' and 'constitutional' referendums is markedly different in the UK than in the USA and Canada in particular. For the significance of this distinction, see S. Tierney 'Constitutional Referendums: A Theoretical Inquiry', [2009] *Modern Law Review* 360.

10. At the time of writing (August 2009), 37 such referendums had been held with 25 being rejected, and 12 succeeding. The Local Government Act 1972, as amended, contains little used provisions permitting local petitions – see Local Authorities (Conduct of Referendums) (England) Regulations 2007/ 2089.

11. See Leyland, P. (2007) *The Constitution of the United Kingdom: A Contextual Analysis* (Hart).

12. Ministry of Justice (2008) *A National Framework for Greater Citizen Engagement: Discussion Paper* (London).

13. See D. Butler and U. Kitzinger (1976) *The 1975 Referendum Campaign* (London, 1976). Although the UK joined the EEC in 1972 under the Conservative Party, the incoming Labour administration of 1974 had pledged to hold a referendum on continuing membership.

14. *White Paper Referendum on United Kingdom Membership of the European Community*, 26 February 1975, Cmnd 5925.

15. See *Accounts of Campaigning Organisations*, Cmnd 6251 (London, 1975).

16. Prior to the Union with England and Wales of 1707, Scotland had enjoyed its own Parliament.

17. This scheme has led some scholars to characterize the 1978 referendum as conclusive or mandatory rather than merely advisory, with a 'yes' vote 'possessing binding legal force' whilst conceding that 'being legislatively supreme, the UK Parliament could of course override the result ... [but the political pressure to comply] would be overwhelming.' – S Tierney, *Constitutional Law and National Pluralism* (Oxford, 2004), p. 288. A contrary view on the political calculus, as held by the responsible Minister, Michael Foot, is found in K.O. Morgan, *Michael Foot: A Life* (London: Harper, 2008), pp. 365–6 and attendant footnotes.

18. For details, see O. Gay (2004) *Thresholds in Referendums*, House of Commons Library Standard Note, SN/PC/2809 (2004).

19. This independent non-Parliamentary committee was charged with looking at matters of party funding by the Blair government in 1998. It reported in 1999 – *The Funding of Political Parties in the United Kingdom* (London, 1999), Cm. 4057.

20. Ibid., Recommendations 83–93.

21. Ibid., Recommendations 83–4.

22. Ibid., Recommendation 89.

23. Ibid., vol. 1, paras 12.45–12.47.

24. Ibid., Recommendation 85.

25. The Act is available at http://www.opsi.gov.uk/Acts/acts2000/ukpga_20000041 _en_1 and is considered in detail below.

26. In the case of the 2004 North East referendum, such details were provided by the Regional Assemblies (Preparations) Act 2003.

27. Such shortcomings did not go without academic comment. For a particularly influential intervention, see Ewing, K.D. (1987) *The Funding of Political Parties in Britain* (Cambridge University Press).

28. For details of the pre-history of PPERA, see N.S. Ghaleigh (1999) 'Funding of Political Parties in the United Kingdom: The Case for Cherry-Picking', *Public Law*, 43; L. Klein (1999) 'On the Brink of Reform: Political Party Funding in Britain', 31 *Case Western Reserve Journal of International Law*, **31**, 1.

29. For more detailed accounts see, K.D. Ewing (2001) 'Transparency, Accountability and Equality: the Political Parties, Elections and Referendums Act 2000', *Public Law*, 542–70; K.D. Ewing (2007) *The Cost of Democracy* (Oxford); K.D. Ewing and N.S. Ghaleigh (2007) 'The Cost of Giving and Receiving: Donations to Political Parties in the United Kingdom', *Election Law Journal*, (1): 56–71.
30. See generally, J. Fisher (2000) 'Economic Performance or Electoral Necessity? Evaluating the System of Voluntary Income to Political Parties', *British Journal of Politics and International Relations*, **2**: 179.
31. Representation of the People Act 1983, ss. **91**, 95.
32. Ibid., s. **72** (8).
33. PPERA 2000, s. 12.
34. PPERA, s. 11. Challenges to the allocations of the broadcasters have been raised unsuccessfully by smaller parties. *R. v. BBC and Independent Television Commission, ex p. Referendum Party* [1997] EMLR 605. Further, in the Scottish referendum of 1978, referendum broadcasts were deemed to violate the statutory duties of the Independent Broadcasting Authority, and so prohibited. See *Wilson* v. *IBA* 1979 S.C. 351.
35. See Royal Charter for the Continuance of The British Broadcasting Corporation, Cm 3248, 1996.
36. Communications Act 2003, s. 319(2)(g).
37. Communications Act 2003, s. 221(2).
38. *R. (on the application of Animal Defenders International)* v. *Secretary of State for Culture, Media and Sport* [2008] UKHL 15.
39. Communications Act 2003, s. 333(1)(a).
40. Ibid., s333(1)(b).
41. OFCOM Rules on Party Political and Referendum Broadcasts, 14 October 2004, see http://www.ofcom.org.uk/tv/ifi/guidance/ppbrules/ppbrules.pdf.
42. See http://www.broadcastersliaisongroup.org.uk/index.html.
43. See further, *The Electoral Commission, Party political broadcasting: Report and Recommendations* (London, 2003).
44. See note 34 above.
45. PPERA 2000, s. 54.
46. Ewing and Ghaleigh (2007).
47. Review of the Funding of Politics, chaired by Sir Hayden Phillips, http://www.partyfundingreview.gov.uk/. On account of the impact such a cap would have on the traditional relationship between the Labour Party and the trade union movement, the Government has declined to legislate in accordance with this recommendation in the Political Parties and Elections Act (2009).
48. PPERA, s. 72.
49. Ibid., s. 79.
50. Ibid., Part VI.
51. Ibid., s. 94.
52. Ibid., Part II.
53. Ibid., Part III.
54. Ibid., ss. 62–7.
55. Ibid., ss. 80–4.
56. See generally, Part I, PPERA.

57. See remarks of Professors Vernon Bogdanor and James Mitchell to the Committee on Standards in Public Life, supra, Volume 2, p. 10, para 86 and Volume 2, p. **469**, para 5816.
58. Indeed, for these reasons, Kaufmann categorizes UK referendums merely as 'plebiscites' as they do not fulfill the criterion of power sharing – see B. Kaufmann and P. Frankhauser (2005) 'Initiative and Referendum Institute Europe', *Guidebook to Direct Democracy: In Switzerland and Beyond* (Amsterdam, 2005).
59. There is a caveat for materials that are 'specifically requested', so as to avoid the anomaly of government not being able to supply information to a citizen that has requested it!
60. A 'Permitted participant' (a 'PP') is defined in s. 105 PPERA as a person or entity who has notified the Electoral Commission of its intention to expend more than £10,000 on the campaign during the specified 'referendum period' s. 102 – spending above that level without having so notified is a criminal offence.
61. 'Referendum broadcasts will be carried by all of the broadcasters named above in the case of a UK referendum, or by the relevant ITV regions in the case of regional referendums.'
62. 'Referendum broadcasts will be allocated to referendum organizations designated by the Electoral Commission (see the Political Parties, Elections and Referendums Act, 2000).'
63. 'UK referendum broadcasts and general election broadcasts by the Conservatives, Labour and Liberal Democrats must be carried on national radio between 5.00 p.m. and 9.00 p.m. Other broadcasts must be transmitted between 6.00 a.m. and 10.00 p.m.'
64. PPERA, s. 111.
65. This was at the time no doubt motivated by the fact that the sorts of issues likely to be put to a referendum, especially the question of the Single Currency, excited a number of wealthy individuals who would be willing to support the 'No' campaign (and other referendum participants) to such an extent that they may outspend the 'Yes' parties.
66. All figures assume UK-wide referendums. Amounts would be scaled down by electorate for regional polls.
67. See ss.120–4 PPERA.
68. See the discussion in *The Funding of Political Parties in the United Kingdom*, chapter 12.
69. See generally O. Gay (2004) *Thresholds in Referendums*, House of Commons Library Standard Note, SN/PC/2809 (2004).
70. See C. Walker, C. (2003) *The Strategic Use of Referendums: Power, Legitimacy and Democracy* (Basingstoke: Palgrave).
71. See Statement to the House on the Elected Regional Assembly Referendum in the North East, HC Deb., vol. 426 (151), cols 587–8, 8 November 2004.
72. See A. Tickell et al. (2005) 'The North East Region Referendum Campaign of 2004: Issues and Turning Points', *Political Quarterly*, 76: 488–96.
73. See the Electoral Commission's own post-election reports at www.electioncommission.gov.uk.
74. See Ewing and Ghaleigh (2007). Seven-figure donations are routinely given to each of the major UK political parties.

75. See n. 72 above.
76. See n. 68 above.
77. See T. Tierney, ibid., note 9.
78. See S. Tierney (2004) *Constitutional Law and National Pluralism* (Oxford) for a detailed discussion.
79. See N. MacCormick (2000) 'Is There a Constitutional Path to Scottish Independence?', *Parliamentary Affairs*, 53: 721–36.
80. The regulatory scheme detailed at 12.2 and 12.3 above 'held in pursuance of any provision made by or under an Act of Parliament' – PPERA s. 101 (2)(a). The prospective Scottish Independence Referendum of 2010 will be held pursuant to an act of the Scottish Parliament, not the Westminster one, and as such falls outwith the ambit of the PPERA and into a legal vacuum whereby the above detailed scheme does not apply. At the time of writing (August 2009), no indication has been given as to the relevant rules under which the 2010 Referendum will operate and any such rules will require explication in an Act of the Scottish Parliament.

13
Referendum Campaign Regulations in Europe and Latin America

Tobias Zellweger, Uwe Serdült and Irène Renfer

Over the last few years, the use of nationwide referendums has become more frequent. This is true not only for Europe but also for Latin America. Indeed, in the case of Europe we have noticed an increasing use of direct democracy mechanisms in Eastern Europe as well as a growing use of referendums on European integration. Regarding Latin America, we can observe an increase of national referendums since the 1990s. As a consequence, there is a growing need to ensure that referendums meet with minimum democratic requirements. In order to define such a referendum standard, the Council of Europe's Venice Commission adopted the Code of Good Practice on Referendums in March 2007. This chapter gives an overview of the national regulations on referendum campaigns, with a focus on campaign financing and on media access, two aspects of important preliminary conditions for democratic referendums. Beginning with a presentation of the relevant regulation in Switzerland, which surprisingly does not include extensive regulation on referendum campaigns, the chapter then turns to regulation in the member states of the Council of Europe as well as in Latin American states with at least one referendum experience since 1995. Distinguishing both the form and content of regulation, the chapter discusses countries that are typical in terms of campaign financing and media access rules respectively. There is a wide variety of national regulation on referendum campaigns both in Europe and in Latin America.

In the analysis of regulations that follows, we have distinguished different groups of countries regarding campaign financing rules as well as media access rules. In the field of campaign financing we have found four groups of countries: those with no regulations at all; others which prohibit the use of public funds for campaigning; states who distribute some advantage to campaigners, but without granting direct financial support;

and, finally, those countries that grant public funds. Regarding rules on media access we have determined five kinds of regulations: no regulation at all; general provisions on fair access rules during a campaign; the prohibition of political advertising; free airtime for political parties only; and free airtime for all campaigners, including citizens' groups.

13.1   Introduction

Over the past two decades Europe has seen an increasing use of national referendums. Several reasons are responsible for this development. Democratic revolutions in post-communist states have led to the adoption of new constitutions, many of which have been adopted by the use of a referendum. Furthermore, ongoing integration within the European Union has given rise to numerous referendums on European issues (Hug, 2002; Marxer, 2004). Referendums took place on different treaties, including Maastricht, Amsterdam and Nice, although not in all member states. The adoption of the euro was also voted on in some member states. More important still, in many of the new member states, the decision to join the EU was made by the people. For instance, all new member states joining the EU on 1 May 2004, excluding Cyprus, had submitted the question of whether to join to a national referendum. More recently, referendums took place on the Treaty establishing a Constitution for Europe. It is true that the rejection of the Constitution in the French as well as the Dutch referendums has almost put an end to the holding of future referendums on this question in other member states. Only Luxembourg has held a referendum on the issue since the French and Dutch 'No', the other member states having ratified the Treaty by parliament or postponed the referendum to an uncertain date in the future. Nonetheless, on the European scene, the referendum seems to have become an instrument that is employed more and more frequently (IRI, 2004/2005).

Similarly, since the 1990s, we have seen an increase of national referendums in Latin American states (Lissidini et al., 2008; Welp and Serdült, 2009), be it referendums triggered from below, or, as is more frequent, those initiated from above (Altman, 2006). Unlike Europe, this phenomenon cannot be explained by the formation of a supranational organization, the joining of which states could have submitted to a referendum. However, as in the case of the former Soviet Union, many Latin American states have also known democratic revolutions over the past decades. In the 1980s, military regimes gave way to elected civilian governments. The institutions of representative democracy replacing those regimes have sometimes failed to respond to the people's hopes.

As a result, a general sense of dissatisfaction or pessimism about democratic government has evolved. The constitutional revisions that have occurred in this context have often provided for some degree of direct democracy (Barczak, 2001). Whatever the precise reasons, it is clear that the number of nationwide referendums has been increasing over the last two decades, both in Europe and in Latin America.

However, the quantity of referendums by itself does not prove that decision making has necessarily become more democratic. It is well known that referendums can be, and historically have been, misused (Wheatley, 2008). Quite obviously, therefore, one has also to look at the quality of referendums. The variety of referendum modalities in the various states that use this instrument makes referendum evaluation a difficult task. Even if limited to the European context, such an evaluation is tricky. It is even more so if one takes into account referendum campaigns in other parts of the world. In examining the conditions for a referendum to be qualified as democratic, many aspects have to be taken into account. In the first place, there are the institutional requirements for a referendum to be held. Does the Constitution provide for a mandatory referendum? Can a referendum be called for by a certain number of citizens (referendum from below), and, if so, under what conditions? Does the referendum depend on the will of parliament, the government, or the head of state (referendum from above)? Is the outcome of the referendum binding or not? The modalities that apply to a referendum are equally important. Citizens should be given objective information on the question they are going to answer. Thus, the campaign preceding the voting has to allow for a public debate to take place under fair and free conditions. Respect for the rule of law and for fundamental rights is a preliminary condition for such a public debate. Furthermore, safeguards may be necessary in order to allow different viewpoints to be expressed. All political parties and civil society organizations should be given the opportunity to participate in the referendum campaign. In addition, the wording of the referendum question must be clear and unambiguous to the citizen. After the referendum day, judicial review of irregularities should be possible. These are only a few of the various criteria that are relevant when it comes to evaluating whether a specific referendum is free and fair, and thus democratic.

13.2   Focus on financing rules and media access

With the increasing number of referendums organized in European states we can also observe efforts undertaken to analyze and qualify them (Hug, 2002). To cite two recent studies, we can mention the *Initiative &*

Referendum Monitor 2004/2005 drawn up by the Initiative and Referendum Institute Europe, as well as the *TEAM Referendum Monitoring Report*.[1] However, these approaches faced the obstacle that, at the time of drafting, no 'referendum standard' or 'code of good conduct' generally accepted by European states existed.

Efforts to adopt such referendum standards have been undertaken within the Council of Europe since the mid-1990s. The Committee of Ministers adopted a recommendation to member states on referendums and popular initiatives at the local level on 15 February 1996.[2] Appended to this recommendation are guidelines on referendums and popular initiatives at the local level. Regarding the minimum rules with which states should comply for constitutional referendums, the Council of Europe's Venice Commission adopted guidelines for constitutional referendums at its 47th Plenary Meeting in July 2001.[3] The Green Paper presented to the Council of Europe that was drafted within the framework of the project 'Making Democratic Institutions Work in 2004' recommended the preparation of a handbook on referendums and initiatives, similar to the Venice Commission's 'Code of Good Practice in Electoral Matters' (Schmitter and Trechsel, 2004). More recently, in April 2005, the Parliamentary Assembly of the Council of Europe adopted a recommendation on 'Referendums: Towards Good Practices in Europe',[4] inviting the Committee of Ministers to draw up a recommendation to member states containing guidelines on referendums in general. However, the Committee of Ministers declared that for the time being, there was no need to prepare a draft recommendation at the intergovernmental level given that the Venice Commission was, in parallel, preparing recommendations on referendums. The Committee of Ministers explained that it would await the results of the Venice Commission's efforts to which it could then give political support by way of a declaration – if deemed necessary – as it had done before on the Code of Good practice in Electoral Matters.[5]

Indeed, at its 64th Plenary Session in October 2005, the Venice Commission adopted an opinion on the Parliamentary Assembly's recommendation, in which it declared itself willing to support and assist any work by the statutory bodies of the Council of Europe on matters concerning referendums.[6] The Venice Commission conducted studies on referendums in order to formulate detailed recommendations on the subject matter.[7] Based on these studies, the Venice Commission and the Council for Democratic Elections were able to adopt, in October 2006, the Guidelines on the Holding of Referendums,[8] which finally led to the adoption in March 2007, by the same organs, of the Code of Good

Practice on Referendums.[9] This new document, considered to be 'the little brother of the Code of Good Practice in Electoral Matters' (Garrone, 2006), relies on and completes the Council of Europe's previous work in the field of financing political parties and electoral campaigns.[10] Its content is presented in further detail below.

A recommendation on the legal, technical and procedural elements of nationwide referendums was also adopted in 2006 by the Association of European Election Officials (ACEEEO), a nongovernmental organization whose main aim is to contribute to democratic and fair elections in Central Europe.[11] Less detailed than the Council of Europe's Code of Good Practice, the ACEEEO's recommendation simply states, concerning the campaigning for and against the question put to referendum that 'nationwide referendums initiated by the government shall never be supported by campaigns financed from the state budget' and that 'the state budget shall cover only those expenditures emerging in connection with the conduction of the election process'.[12] This very short recommendation nevertheless points out a central element of a fair referendum campaign: the neutrality of state organs. Unfortunately, this basic rule is not always met by national legislation on referendum campaigns.

Regarding the Latin American case, we are not aware of any similar undertakings towards transnational referendum guidelines. For the time being, the emergence of mechanisms of direct democracy in national constitutions in the region (in most cases) is too recent to expect international efforts on a Latin American scale with the purpose of developing a generally accepted referendum standard.

The present chapter aims to examine the preliminary conditions of democratic referendums. We have chosen to focus on two aspects that, in our opinion, are central to the preliminary phase of a referendum, or the referendum campaign. These two aspects are the rules on campaign financing and the rules on media access during the campaign. Our analysis is based on the existing regulations in the states under examination. It is very possible that in some states the practice differs from the regulation. For example, the absence of a specific regulation applying to referendum campaigns does not necessarily mean that the campaign practice is unfair. Vice versa, it does not exclude the possibility that the practice in states with an exhaustive set of regulations is unfair either.

Our focus is on the holding of a campaign in view of a nationwide referendum. Thus we do not distinguish the different types of referendums, and it does not matter for our purposes whether a referendum has been initiated by the people, from below, or by the authorities in power, from above. Furthermore, we do not distinguish binding from non-binding referendums. We even include campaigns in view of the collection of signatures for a popular initiative not necessarily leading to a ballot, but only submitting proposals to the legislature for consideration. Such campaigns are common in Argentina for instance and can play an important role.

By campaign financing regulation, we mean any rule having an impact on the financing of the various actors' political campaigning during referendum campaigns. The political actors include state organs, political parties, all kinds of civil society organization and individual citizens. Campaign financing regulation thus covers any regulation on the granting of public funds to political actors for their campaigns, and any regulation on the provision of selective and task-bound benefits for campaigners, such as the free use of public premises for campaign messages or special fees applying to campaign mailing. Campaign financing regulation also covers spending limits for campaign activity as well as transparency rules, such as the obligation to reveal the identity of donors or the amount of campaign spending.

The precise impact of the money available to campaigners on the outcome of a referendum is not very clear. In Europe, not much research has been done on the subject. Hertig has argued that the outcome of a referendum can be bought if enough money is spent (Hertig, 1982). Others have criticized the lack of precision in this study and painted a more balanced picture (Papadopoulos, 1998). It seems obvious, however, that to a certain extent, money does matter during referendum campaigns, and even more so for the collecting of signatures in the case of a referendum instigated by a popular initiative or in the case of an optional referendum.

By media access regulation we understand any rule having an impact on the political actors' use of mass media for political campaigning during referendum campaigns. Media access regulation thus covers rules on the granting of free airtime for political actors engaged in a referendum campaign, rules fixing the conditions of political advertising in the media as well as rules on fair media access during referendum campaigns, such as the obligation for public or private broadcasters to guarantee a balanced presentation of the various political opinions expressed during the campaign.

In the Code of Good Practice on Referendums, the Venice Commission fixed a number of minimum rules, amongst others, on equality of opportunity between the supporters and opponents of the proposal being voted on, notably as concerns the coverage by the media as well as public subsidies and other forms of backing during the campaign period. The

Code of Good Practice on Referendums, although not a legally binding document, is meant to apply to all referendums – national, regional, and local – regardless of the question they concern (CDL-AD(2007)008: 15). It consists of guidelines on the holding of referendums on the one hand, and the draft explanatory memorandum on the other. In our opinion, the Code of Good Practice constitutes a useful reference for the evaluation of national legislation pertaining to referendum campaigns, even for non-European referendum legislation. Therefore, we recall the rules related to campaign financing and media access outlined in the Code of Good Practice before examining national regulations on these issues in chosen European and Latin American states.

Extract from the Venice Commission's Code of Good Practice on Referendums

 I. Referendums and Europe's electoral heritage

[…]

2.2. Equality of opportunity

    a. Equality of opportunity must be guaranteed for the supporters and opponents of the proposal being voted on. This entails a neutral attitude by administrative authorities, in particular with regard to:
        i. the referendum campaign;
        ii. coverage by the media, in particular by the publicly owned media;
        iii. public funding of the campaign and its actors;
        iv. billposting and advertising;
        v. the right to demonstrate on public thoroughfares.
    b. In public radio and television broadcasts on the referendum campaign, it is advisable that equality be ensured between the proposal's supporters and opponents.
    c. Balanced coverage must be guaranteed to the proposal's supporters and opponents in other public mass media broadcasts, especially news broadcasts. Account may be taken of the number of political parties supporting each option or their election results.
    d. Equality must be ensured in terms of public subsidies and other forms of backing. It is advisable that equality be

ensured between the proposal's supporters and opponents. Such backing may, however, be restricted to supporters and opponents of the proposal who account for a minimum percentage of the electorate. If equality is ensured between political parties, it may be strict or proportional. If it is strict, political parties are treated on an equal footing irrespective of their current parliamentary strength or support among the electorate. If it is proportional, political parties must be treated according to the results achieved in the elections.

e. Financial or other conditions for radio and television advertising must be the same for the proposal's supporters and opponents.

f. In conformity with freedom of expression, legal provision should be made to ensure that there is minimum access to privately owned audiovisual media, with regard to the referendum campaign and to advertising, for all participants in the referendum.

g. Political party and referendum campaign funding must be transparent.

h. The principle of equality of opportunity can, in certain cases, lead to a limitation on spending by political parties and other parties involved in the referendum debate, especially on advertising.

i. Sanctions must be imposed in the case of breaches of the duty of neutrality.

[...]

3.1. Freedom of voters to form an opinion

[...]

b. Contrary to the case of elections, it is not necessary to completely prohibit intervention by the authorities in support of or against the proposal submitted to a referendum. However, the public authorities (national, regional, and local) must not influence the outcome of the vote by excessive, one-sided campaigning. The use of public funds by the authorities for campaigning purposes must be prohibited.

[...]

II. Conditions for implementing these principles

[...]

3.4. Funding

a. The general rules on the funding of political parties and electoral campaigns must be applied to both public and private funding.
b. The use of public funds by the authorities for campaigning purposes must be prohibited.

[...]

III. Specific rules

[...]

4. Specific rules applicable to referendums held at the request of a section of the electorate and to popular initiatives (where they are provided for in the Constitution).
    [...]

    e. Payment from private sources for the collection of signatures for popular initiatives and requests for referendums should, as a rule, be prohibited. If permitted, it must be regulated, with regard to both the total amount allocated and the amount paid to each person.

    [...]

13.3 Country selection

Naturally, we base our report on the situation of campaign financing and media access only on those states that conduct referendums. In order to delimit our task, we include countries holding referendums between January 1995 and April 2007. Geographically, the present study covers all member states of the Council of Europe as well as all Latin American states.[13]

Among the 47 member states of the Council of Europe[14] and the 17 states of Latin America, 41 have organized at least one referendum within

Table 13.1 Number of referendum texts voted on in 32 European states and in 9 Latin American states, January 1995 to April 2007

No. of Texts	No. of Countries	Countries
1	15	Costa Rica, Cyprus, Czech Republic, Estonia, Georgia, Luxembourg, Malta, Moldova, Montenegro, Netherlands, Romania, Serbia, Spain, Sweden, The Former Yugoslav Republic of Macedonia
2	4	Albania, Denmark, France, Panama
3	2	Armenia, Latvia,
4	5	Brazil, Guatemala, Hungary, Portugal, Ukraine
5	2	Uruguay, Venezuela
6	1	Lithuania
7	2	Bolivia, Poland
8	1	Slovakia
9	1	Azerbaijan
11	1	Slovenia
11	1	San Marino
12	2	Ireland, Liechtenstein
16	1	Colombia
29	1	Ecuador
35	1	Italy
111	1	Switzerland

this time frame.[15] Looking more closely at the number of issues voted upon in referendums, we can see that 15 countries have voted on one issue, 22 countries on between two and 12, and four countries on a greater number (see Table 13.1). **Italy** with 35 and **Switzerland** with 111 texts are clearly the 'leaders' in referendum practice among Council of Europe member states, followed by **Ecuador** in Latin America where 29 texts have been voted on.

However, the simple count of texts voted upon might be a bit misleading. For current referendum practice and regulation in this area the number of polls conducted is probably the more important figure (see Table 13.2). We should thus expect that countries with a relatively high frequency of polls within the last twelve years should have developed a considerable body of regulation regarding media access and campaign financing and vice versa, that countries with a low number of referendum polls have less-developed rules.

As Table 13.2 shows, we can thus form three categories of countries. Countries with a low level of referendum practice have organized one

Table 13.2 Number of polls conducted in 32 European states and in 9 Latin American states, January 1995 to April 2007

No. of Polls	No. of Countries	Countries
1	17	Costa Rica, Cyprus, Czech Republic, Estonia, Georgia, Guatemala, Luxembourg, Malta, Moldova, Montenegro, Netherlands, Romania, Serbia, Spain, Sweden, The Former Yugoslav Republic of Macedonia, Ukraine
2	8	Albania, Azerbaijan, Bolivia, Brazil, Colombia, Denmark, France, Panama
3	6	Armenia, Hungary, Latvia, Lithuania, Poland, Portugal
4	3	Ecuador, Uruguay, Venezuela
5	2	San Marino, Slovakia
8	1	Italy
9	2	Ireland, Slovenia
11	1	Liechtenstein
37	1	Switzerland

to two polls (25 countries in total), mainly in order to ratify a new constitution, to sanction important changes in the constitution, or in relation to EU or NATO membership. Countries with three to 11 polls use direct democratic instruments more frequently and also to decide important political matters other than constitutional, territorial or supranational issues (15 countries). Switzerland, with 37 polls during the observed timeframe, represents the well-known exceptional case and forms the third category.

13.4 Results

In this section we will first present the regulations on campaign financing and on media access in the outlier country, Switzerland.[16] Then in the two following sections we will proceed to an analysis based on the data we collected. At the current stage of data collection we intend to come up with ideal types of countries for referendum campaign regulation and media access rules respectively.

The Swiss case

One would expect Switzerland, with its long-standing and frequent use of direct democracy institutions, namely the popular initiative, the optional referendum, and the mandatory referendum, to have developed extensive regulations on referendum campaigns, including rules on campaign financing and on media access. Surprisingly, this is not the case.

Switzerland is a federal state. The referendum is used at both the federal and cantonal levels, the latter being to a large extent autonomously regulated by each of the 26 cantons (Auer et al., 2006). In the present essay, we shall focus on the federal level. However, it is important to note that there is some kind of mutual influence between the exercise of political rights in the cantons and in the Confederation. On the one hand, the cantons must respect political rights as they are guaranteed by the Federal Constitution. On the other hand, the Swiss Federal Supreme Court has developed important case law on the exercise of political rights in the cantons. Some of this case law deals with referendum campaigns (Auer et al. 2006: notes 887–95). The principles developed by the Swiss Federal Supreme Court, although dealing with cantonal matters, to some extent also serve as guidelines to the federal authorities.[17]

The referendum at the federal level is governed by the provisions of the Federal Constitution[18] and the Federal Act on Political Rights.[19] None of these contain rules dealing with referendum campaigns in particular. However, several fundamental rights guaranteed by the Federal Constitution have to be considered when examining the legal framework of referendum campaigns. According to Article 34 paragraph 2 of the Federal Constitution, the guarantee of political rights protects the free formation of opinion by the citizens and the unaltered expression of their will. This provision does not impose strict neutrality on political authorities during the referendum debate.[20] Authorities are allowed to take a position and to recommend the approval or the refusal of a referendum question.[21] However, any kind of political campaign by political authorities would be contrary to the constitutional guarantee of political rights,[22] even more so if public funds were to be used for such messages. It is also forbidden to grant public funds to private referendum committees.[23]

Other fundamental rights guaranteed by the Federal Constitution that ensure the fairness of a referendum debate are the freedom of opinion and information, the freedom of the media, the freedom of assembly and the freedom of association.[24]

However, there is no specific regulation on the financing of referendum campaigns by political parties and other civil society groups. Thus, whereas the use of public funds for political campaigning is prohibited, campaign spending by political parties and other groups is unlimited, and there is no obligation for campaigners to reveal their donors or the amount of money spent on a referendum campaign. In this context we should also mention that the financing of political parties is not regulated in Switzerland. Political parties do not receive any public funds for their activities. As a result, they finance themselves from membership fees, from donations of party members, non-members, private companies and organizations, as well as from contributions from office holders (Ladner, 2004). On the federal level, there are no transparency rules at all. Whereas this is generally also the case at the cantonal level, two cantons have introduced transparency rules. In the canton of Ticino, donations of more than 10,000 Swiss francs to political parties have to be published. In the canton of Geneva, anonymous donations are forbidden and transparency rules apply not only to political parties, but also to other political groups engaged in campaigns (Balmelli, 2002). But for the time being, such rules are still exceptional.

Regarding the access to media by political parties and other civil society organizations engaged in a campaign, there are no rules applicable during referendum campaigns only. Contrary to the situation in other member states of the Council of Europe, Swiss law does not determine an official timeframe for the referendum campaign.

Nonetheless, several provisions of the Federal Act on Radio and Television, adopted on 24 March 2006 are particularly important during referendum campaigns.[25] This act mandates all radio and television stations to respect fundamental rights, to contribute to the free formation of opinion and to provide varied and objective information for the public. The overall offering of programmes in a region must cover the diversity of events and opinions in a balanced manner. Broadcast information has to be objective and representative of the diversity of facts and opinions. Furthermore, personal opinions and commentaries have to be recognizable as such.[26] In addition, political advertising on radio and television is forbidden.[27] Thus any advertising for political parties, any advertising for members of public authorities or candidates to such authorities, and any advertising on the issue of a popular ballot, is forbidden.[28] Last but not least, the sponsoring of the news presentations as well as of any programme related to the exercise of political rights is not allowed.[29]

An independent mediator, who deals with complaints about programmes, is installed in each of the regions representing one of the three official languages.[30] The mediators' decisions can then be reviewed by an independent authority for radio and television established at the federal level.[31]

As a result, although campaigners do not get any free airtime in Switzerland, and notwithstanding the fact that there are no specific rules for referendum campaigns, it seems to be recognized by political actors in general that the regulations set down in the Federal Act on Radio and Television provide for a fair referendum debate in the media.

Referendum campaign financing in European and Latin American countries

Regarding campaign financing regulation we can distinguish two dimensions: *form* and *content*. The formal characteristics of a regulation can be ordered according to the degree of institutionalization. By institutionalization we mean a process over time, during which norms and rules are transformed into binding, sanctionable elements of a political system, mostly in the form of a legal framework. The more differentiated and binding the regulation, the higher the degree of institutionalization. On the lowest level of this cascade of institutionalization there is the case of no regulation at all. One stage further, we can observe the informal application of already existing laws, in most cases electoral laws, for a referendum, because this is the closest to a referendum regulation there is at hand. Going one step further there is case-law-based regulation and then ad hoc regulation (by parliament or the government) for each referendum. For countries with only limited referendum experience this is the type of formal arrangement we would expect. It might also occur if referendums have to be organized under time pressure or, for the first time in the history of a country, without any pre-knowledge of whether there would be sufficient use of referendums in the future to justify the drafting of a separate law. The referendum law (or any equivalent regulation with reference to other already existing laws) represents the final stage of institutionalization.

With regard to the *form* of referendum rules, the recently adopted Code of Good Practice on Referendums states that 'apart from rules on technical matters and detail (which may be included in regulations of the executive), rules of referendum law should have at least the rank of a statute'. Also, 'the fundamental aspects of referendum law should not be open to amendment less than one year before a referendum, or should be written in the Constitution or at a level superior to ordinary law'. Thus, according to the Code of Good Practice, only the last level of institutionalization is fully satisfying for referendum laws, *ad hoc* legislation being suspicious because of its adoption in view of one particular referendum.

Regarding the *content* of existing regulation we can distinguish again between countries with no regulation at all, those that forbid the use of public funds for campaigning, those that distribute task-bound selective benefits to campaigners, and those that provide public funds for campaigns (be it for political parties only or for campaigners as well).

In the last category, we can distinguish states that provide public funds for campaigners on an ad hoc basis from those that have institutionalized public support. In addition, it is necessary to check existing regulations for clauses setting a limit on campaign spending and certain transparency rules for campaigners.

Among the states that have no regulation at all on the financing of referendum campaigns is **Luxembourg**. The absence of campaign-specific regulation in this state can be explained by the fact that the recent referendum on the Treaty establishing a Constitution for Europe in July 2005 was the first referendum to be held there since 1937.[32] Likewise, in post-communist **Romania**, where only two referendums have been held, one on the approval of the Constitution in 1991 and another on the revision of the Constitution on 19 October 2003, there are no rules on campaign financing. **Serbia**'s Law on Financing of Political Parties of 2002 applies only to election campaigns but not to referendum campaigns. The Law on referendums and people's initiatives of 1994 only deals with the organizational costs of the referendum and contains no rules on the financing of political messages by authorities, political parties, or other actors.[33] As a result, Serbia has no legislation on the financing of political campaigning in view of referendums. **Uruguay**'s Referendum Law also has no rules about the financing of political campaigning by political actors,[34] and the financing is in charge of the promoters (Risotto, 2007). In **Guatemala** finally, instruments of direct democracy figure in the national constitution but have never been implemented by law. There are no rules on campaign financing.

Several states prohibit the use of public funds for campaigning. **Swiss** regulation, which falls into this category, has already been examined above. **Slovenia** has rules on the financing of electoral campaigns, but the act on referendums does not provide an analogous solution for referendum campaigns. Therefore, in **Slovenia**, public funds must not be used to back political messages by campaigners, nor for an official and neutral information campaign. According to the Slovenian Electoral Authority, there are projects to legislate in this field. In **Malta**, the Referenda Act[35] states that the General Elections Act and the Electoral Polling Ordinance shall apply to the conduct of referendums, except for some specified provisions. The Electoral Polling Ordinance provides for the return of election expenses to electoral candidates.[36] However, according to the second schedule of the Referenda Act, these provisions do not apply to referendums. As a result, no public funds are used for referendum campaigns in **Malta**. In **Poland**, the Act on nationwide referendums states that those engaged in referendums shall cover the expenses out of their own resources and in accordance with provisions relating to their finan-cial activities.[37] **Venezuela** has not adopted specific rules for referendum campaigns, but has extensive rules on recalls.[38] The Act on Publicity and Propaganda for Recalls prohibits the use of public funds for political campaigns.[39] Likewise, the **Costa Rican** Act on Referendums prohibits public authorities to use their funds for campaigning, or to finance polit-ical campaigning by private actors.[40] Finally, under the **Argentinean** Popular Initiative Act, no public funds may be used for the campaign. Furthermore, donations from foreign governments, foreign companies, trade unions, employer associations and professional associations are prohibited.[41]

A number of states distribute task-bound, selective benefits to cam-paigners, without granting direct financial support to them. In this field, **Portugal** has far-reaching legislation.[42] Political parties and citizens' groups that have registered for the campaign are entitled to free political advertising, on public and private television and radio stations, as well as in public buildings.[43] The modalities of such free advertising are fixed by the law. For example, the municipalities have to provide places for campaigners to display their campaign posters.[44] Also, public buildings can be used for campaigning events. The hiring of theatres for politi-cal meetings is regulated by the law, including a limit on the hiring fee. Hiring can be imposed on the private owners of theatres. The hiring of offices as headquarters for the organization of a particular group's cam-paign is also regulated by law. The campaigners are also entitled to have a telephone installed free of charge.[45] In **Macedonia**, tax exemptions are granted for activities connected with a referendum.[46] In **Moldova**, local administrative authorities establish and guarantee a minimum number of designated areas for campaign posters and provide places for orga-nizing and holding campaign meetings.[47] We are not aware of similar regulations in **Latin American** states providing for the distribution of task-bound, selective benefits to campaigners, other than the granting of airtime on radio and television.

A last group of states grant public funds to political actors for their campaign activity. In most cases this is done on an ad hoc basis. In **Spain**, the law on the regulation of referendums[48] allows public funding only for the government's impartial informative campaign. Nonetheless, in January 2004 parliament approved an extraordinary budget for the funding of political parties engaged in the referendum campaign on the European Constitution. The funds were distributed among the political parties represented in parliament, but no funds were granted to civil soci-ety organizations engaged in the campaign. Similarly, public funds have been used for political campaigning during the most recent referendums held in the **Netherlands** and in **Estonia**, in both cases on an ad hoc basis. In **Estonia**, public funds went to the government's impartial information campaign, but were also distributed among political parties and other civil society campaigners, representing both the 'No' and the 'Yes' campaigns. **Sweden**, which does not have many referendums, devised a very precise formula for how to divide public money between official 'Yes' and 'No' camps during the referendum on EU membership in 1994.[49] Only a few states have institutionalized direct financial support to campaigners. Under **San Marino**'s law on referendums and legislative popular initiatives, both the official 'Yes' and the official 'No' committees received public funds for their campaign activity during the referendum campaign.[50] In **Montenegro**, the regular referendum law of 2001 has been complemented by the ad hoc Law on the Referendum on State-Legal Status of the Republic of Montenegro of 1 March 2006, which gave way to the referendum on independence from Serbia. This law granted €1,000,000 for both sides of the campaign. In order to benefit from public funds, political parties had to register for the campaign, and NGOs had to associate themselves with political parties already registered and representing either the 'Yes' or the 'No' option.[51] All activities linked to campaigning are exempt from any fees whatsoever. Public authorities, on the other hand, must not use public funds or infrastructure for campaigning purposes. Again, there seem to be no rules providing for the distribution of public funds for campaigners in the examined **Latin American** states.

Independent of prohibiting the use of public funds for campaigns or of granting direct or indirect public support to campaigners, some states have adopted clauses setting a limit on campaign spending and certain transparency rules for campaigners.

In **Poland**, the act concerning nationwide referendums states that any political message for or against a draft proposal, published in the press or by television or radio, shall bear an indication of who is paying for the campaign and who is donating the funds. Ignoring this rule exposes the person responsible to a fine.[52] In **Portugal**, there is a limit on the amount campaigners are allowed to spend on campaigning. The Referendum Act refers to the spending limit applicable in the case of elections to the national parliament and governed by the act on the financing of political parties and electoral campaigns.[53] The spending limit is calculated on the basis of the minimum wage.[54] Furthermore, political parties and citizens' groups are responsible for keeping accounts of referendum spending. These accounts have to be presented to the National

Election Commission within 90 days of the publication of the referendum results.[55] In **Spain**, there are restrictions on the campaign spending of political parties, but there is no control over other campaigners' spending. All private donations have to be paid into special bank accounts and donors have to reveal their identity. A donation may not exceed €6,000. In **Montenegro**, the total sum of private donations may not exceed the amount designated by the Law on the financing of political parties. The identity of donors who provide financial support to campaigners has to be disclosed and parties have to report their campaign spending.[56] Under the **Colombian** Law governing the legislative and the constitutional referendum, campaigners are entitled to receive private funding on the condition that campaign spending is revealed. Control is confined to an officially accounted reviser. Citizens are entitled to request that the names and number of donors having contributed a sum higher than the minimum wage be published. There is an upper limit to private funding, fixed every year by the National Electoral Council.[57] **Ecuador**'s law governing popular consultations and recalls does not pronounce itself on campaign financing.[58] However, there is a specific law on electoral campaigns that also applies to referendum campaigns. It states the principle that campaign spending is limited.[59] The exact amount political parties or other campaigners are allowed to spend on campaign activity is determined in an ad hoc decree adopted for each referendum.[60] In **Argentina**, the Popular Initiative Act limits donations to the campaign in view of the collection of signatures to 30,000 pesos. Anonymous donations are allowed only up to the sum of 50 pesos.[61]

Media access during referendum campaigns in European and Latin American countries

Five basic types of regulation regarding media access rules during referendum campaigns are revealed by our examination: no regulation at all; general provisions about fair access rules during a campaign; the prohibition of political advertising; free airtime for political parties only; and free airtime for all campaigners, including citizens' groups. Furthermore we can make a distinction between regulation applying only to the public media sector, and to regulation applicable to both public and private sectors.

Representative of the group of states that have no regulation at all on media access by campaigners are **Luxembourg, Slovenia, Ecuador** and **Guatemala**. As explained above, in **Luxembourg** the absence of regulation may be due to the rare use of the referendum there. This is also true for Guatemala which has had only one single poll since 1995.

In **Slovenia**, the lack of regulation is more surprising, since referendums are held quite regularly. However, rules for electoral campaigns exist, and according to the electoral authority, airtime is granted by the media during referendum campaigns too. The absence of regulation is also unexpected in **Ecuador**, where five polls on 29 issues have been held during the examined timeframe. We can also count **Costa Rica** in this group, which has virtually no rules on media access. Legislation states only that foreigners are prohibited from intervening in the political campaign and that the publication of opinion polls is forbidden on the two days prior to voting.[62]

Some states have general provisions regarding fair access rules during a campaign, albeit without granting free airtime for political advertising. In **San Marino**, for instance, radio and television programmes are guaranteed and supervised by the secretary of state for internal affairs during the referendum campaign. Different views have to be presented in a balanced manner.[63] In **Uruguay**, the Electoral Court provides for objective information on radio and television, as well as in the newspapers, but must abstain from political campaigning.[64] **Venezuela**, despite having no rules on referendum campaigns, adopted an Act on Recalls in 2004 which contains rules on political campaigns. Thus the National Electoral Council secures equal media access for political organizations and registered citizens' groups. Space for political information, debates, publicity and other forms of campaigning is distributed on equal terms.[65] The content of campaign speeches during recall campaigns is widely regulated by the Act on Elections and Political Participation as well as by the Act on Publicity and Propaganda for Recalls.[66] Anonymous campaigning and political campaigning in public buildings and churches are prohibited. Television airtime is limited to two minutes per channel a day and television broadcasters must reveal the airtime used and campaigning costs incurred by each campaigning group. The campaign must cease 48 hours prior to the vote. In **Ukraine**, the Law on All-Ukrainian and Local Referendums states that citizens, political parties, public organizations, mass movements and labour collectives shall have the right to free campaign publicity. To implement this right, the interested persons and organizations shall be provided with premises for meetings, and be ensured of the possibility to use mass media. The mass media shall cover the referendum campaign and are guaranteed unrestricted access to all assemblies and meetings related to the referendum.[67]

Other states have forbidden political advertising on radio and television. We have already analyzed **Swiss** legislation above. In **Liechtenstein**, too, media law prohibits political advertising on radio and television. Notwithstanding the prohibition of political advertising, there can be general provisions on fair media coverage of a campaign. **Serbia**'s legislation is less clear on the prohibition of political advertising in electronic media as regards referendum campaigns. In principle, the Law on Advertising of 2005 and the law regulating elections of people's deputies prohibit political advertising in electronic media outside of the election campaign period. Since there is no exception made for the referendum campaign, political messages during referendum campaigns are allowed only via printed media, billboards, pamphlets and gatherings.[68]

Another group of states only grant free airtime to political parties. In the **Netherlands**, political parties represented in parliament can use the time allocated to them on radio and television for the referendum campaign. In **France**, too, only the parties represented in parliament and those whose participation appears justified in view of the nature of the question at hand may express their views. However, both private and public media must provide supporters and opponents of the draft proposal with fair coverage.[69] In **Slovakia**, access to the media is allowed only for political parties that are represented in the national parliament.[70] Under the **Argentinean** Referendum Act, officially recognized political parties are granted free airtime in the mass media. For this matter, the electoral law applies analogously.[71] However, there are actually no rules concerning campaigns in view of non-binding popular initiatives, which are more frequent in **Argentina** than referendums. A recent reform introducing such rules was rejected.

Quite extensive rules have been developed by those states that grant free airtime in the media to all campaigners, including both political parties and other civil society groups. In these cases, it is common for the official campaign period to be limited by the law. In **Portugal**, starting with the publication of the decree fixing the referendum date, any kind of commercial political advertising in the media is forbidden.[72] Any journalistic information on the referendum published in state-controlled media has to respect strict neutrality and treat political opponents equally.[73] Private media outlets have to inform the National Election Commission on their reporting of the referendum. They also have to ensure fair journalistic treatment of the campaigning parties and citizens' groups.[74] The journals of political parties, associations and citizens' groups are exempted.[75] During a **Portuguese** referendum campaign, registered political parties and citizens' groups have the right to free airtime on radio and television, both private and public.[76] Half of the slots have to be distributed among the parties represented in the national parliament, the other half are to be distributed among the other campaigners. The order in which the political advertisements are presented is drawn by lottery. In particular cases, such as campaigners calling for violence or engaging in commercial advertising, free airtime can be suspended or withdrawn. In **Poland**, referendum campaigners who have previously registered with the National Electoral Commission have the right to campaign on radio and television. Both the recording and broadcast of a referendum programme are free of charge. The referendum programmes are broadcast on nationwide and regional channels. The total broadcasting time is fixed by law, and is divided equally among the entitled referendum campaigners. The sequence of referendum programmes to be broadcast each day is determined by lottery. In addition to publicly funded broadcasting, entitled campaigners may broadcast paid referendum advertisements on radio and television during the referendum campaign.[77] The rates for paid advertisements are regulated by law and broadcasters cannot refuse to transmit such referendum programmes. On the other hand, the broadcasters are not responsible for the contents of the advertisements. In **Montenegro**, free airtime is also granted to campaigners.[78] In order to benefit from the statutes of a subject of the referendum campaign, political parties have to register for the campaign, and NGOs have to associate themselves with political parties already registered and representing either the 'Yes' or the 'No' option.[79] The official campaign lasts at least 75 days.[80] Whereas all media shall assist voters during the referendum process in making an informed choice on the option they will favour, in particular by means of specific information programmes and public debates involving both referendum options, public service broadcasters have to provide equal presentation of different referendum options, which includes granting free airtime to campaigners.[81] Paid political advertising is allowed but must be clearly indicated as such. In accepting paid advertising, private media must not discriminate between supporters of the two referendum options.[82] In **Brazil**, the Referendum and Popular Initiative Act provides for free public media access for both political parties and suprapartisan groups set up by civil society.[83] Likewise, according to ad hoc regulation in **Panama**, political parties and groups have to register for the campaign with the Electoral Authority in order to benefit from free airtime. Airtime is distributed on equal terms amongst major political parties on the one hand, and amongst various groups representing the 'Yes' and 'No' camps on the other hand.[84] Finally, **Colombia** has set down quite extensive rules in the Law governing the legislative and the constitutional referendum. During the 30 days preceding the popular vote, promoters, political parties and other movements with legal personality are granted airtime in each national television channel at least twice. The national government can request to be granted airtime at least three times during this timeframe.

The Electoral Organization supervises the 'Yes' and the 'No' campaigns and is responsible for objective information. All kinds of media can be used for the political campaign. Those media outlets that are willing to broadcast political messages have to treat all campaigners on equal terms.[85]

13.5 Final remarks

The data collection and framework of analysis we have put forth in the preceding sections of this chapter represent the intermediate results of an ongoing project within the Centre on Direct Democracy (C2D). We can already affirm that there is a wide variety of regulations among the examined states with regard both to campaign financing and to media access. In addition, the data analyzed show that many combinations are possible between the different regulation types we have described. Furthermore, most states do not fully comply with the rules on funding and media as set down in the Code of Good Practice on Referendums elaborated by the Venice Commission, even though the Code sets only a minimal standard formulated in rather open terms. Quite often national regulations do not cover all of the relevant points and sometimes they provide for solutions which are to some extent contradictory to the Code itself. Whereas in several states, the referendum campaign is not regulated at all, most of the states have adopted some basic rules on one or more aspects of political communication. However, states having adopted comprehensive legislation providing full equality of opportunity to all participants in the campaign, be they political parties or other citizens' groups, with regard to both media access and campaign financing, are rather exceptional. It is true that from the absence of perfect regulations one should not necessarily conclude that referendum campaigns are unfair, since the contemporaneous application of electoral laws as well as a particular state's political culture are also important. In addition, the variety of political systems and circumstances does not allow the specification of one single standard that would be valuable for all states. Nevertheless, in comparison to the attention that has been given globally to the regulation of electoral campaigns, the regulation of referendum campaigns has been to date relatively neglected. There is still room for improvement. Efforts towards a better realization of equality of opportunity amongst different political parties and civil society groups must also consider the impact of new ICTs on contemporary referendum campaigns – an aspect which has hardly been taken into account to date.

Notes

1. TEAM Referendum Monitoring Report – Version II presented at the European Referendum Monitoring Workshop in Tartu, Estonia, 26–8 September 2003, http://www.teameurope.info.
2. Recommendation No. R (96) 2.
3. European Commission for Democracy through Law (Venice Commission), *Guidelines for Constitutional Referendums*, CDL-INF (2001) 010.
4. Parliamentary Assembly Recommendation 1704 (2005), *Referendums: Towards Good Practices in Europe*.
5. CM Documents, *Referendums: Towards Good Practices in Europe, Parliamentary Assembly Recommendation 1704(2005), Reply Adopted by the Committee of Ministers on 9 November 2005 at the 945th meeting of the Ministers' Deputies*, CM/AS(2005)Rec1704 final, 10 November 2005.
6. European Commission for Democracy through Law (Venice Commission), *Opinion on Parliamentary Assembly Recommendation 1704 (2005) on Referendums: Towards Good Practices in Europe*, CDL-AD (2005) 028.
7. European Commission for Democracy through Law (Venice Commission), *Referendums in Europe – an Analysis of the Legal Rules in European States*, CDL-AD (2005) 034.
8. European Commission for Democracy through Law (Venice Commission), *Guidelines on the Holding of Referendums adopted by the Council for Democratic Elections at its 18th Meeting (Venice, 12 October 2006) and the Venice Commission at its 68th Plenary Session (Venice, 13–14 October 2006)*, CDL-AD(2006)027rev.
9. European Commission for Democracy through Law (Venice Commission), *Code of Good Practice on Referendums Adopted by the Council for Democratic Elections at its 19th Meeting (Venice, 16 December 2006) and the Venice Commission at its 70th Plenary Session (Venice, 16–17 March 2007)*, CDL-AD (2007)008.
10. For references, see Parliamentary Assembly Recommendation 1704 (2005), *Referendums: Towards Good Practices in Europe*, at section 10.
11. ACEEEO unites election officials from 18 states: Albania, Armenia, Belarus, Bosnia and Herzegovina, Bulgaria, Croatia, Georgia, Hungary, Latvia, Lithuania, Macedonia, Moldova, Poland, Rumania, Russia, Slovakia, Turkey and Ukraine.
12. Recommendation on the legal, technical and procedural elements of nationwide referendums, adopted by the General Assembly Meeting of the ACEEEO's 15th Anniversary Conference in Riga, Latvia, 31 August–2 September 2006, http://www.aceeeo.org/conferences/2006/index.html.
13. The goal of our ongoing research project is to cover every democracy in the world which has recent referendum experience. Thus, the choice of Europe and Latin America only reflects the state of our research and is not to be understood as a deliberate choice due to the types of direct democracy practiced in these areas of the world. The term 'Latin American states' is understood to include all Hispanic states in Central and South America, including Brazil.
14. After its split from Serbia and Montenegro in 2006, the Republic of Montenegro became an independent member of the Council of Europe on 11 May 2007, raising the number of member states to 47.

15. Counting the Argentinean political campaigns in view of non-binding popular initiatives, the number of states having known political campaigns within the examined timeframe rises to 42.
16. You can find the dataset we used for this article under the data section on www.c2d.ch.
17. *L'engagement du Conseil fédéral et de l'administration dans les campagnes précédant les votations fédérales*, Rapport du groupe de travail de la Conférence des services d'information élargie (GT CSIC), Berne, November 2001, pp. 10–12, http://www.admin.ch/ch/f/cf.
18. Articles 138 to 142 of the Federal Constitution of the Swiss Confederation of 18 April 1999; http://www.admin.ch/ch/itl/rs/1/index.htm.
19. Federal Act on Political Rights of 17 December 1976; http://www.admin.ch/ch/e/rs/c161_1.html.
20. Decision of the Federal Supreme Court 121 I 252, 255 f.
21. Compare with article 11 paragraph 2 of the Federal Act on Political Rights of 17 December 1976.
22. Decision of the Federal Supreme Court 114 Ia 427, 444.
23. Decision of the Federal Supreme Court 114 Ia 427, 443.
24. See articles 16, 17, 22 and 23 of the Federal Constitution of the Swiss Confederation of 18 April 1999.
25. RS 784.40; http://www.admin.ch/ch/f/rs/c784_40.html (French text).
26. Article 4 Federal Act on Radio and Television.
27. Unabhängige Beschwerdeinstanz für Radio und Fernsehen, *Entscheid vom 27. Juni 2003 betreffend Schweizer Fernsehen DRS: Werbespot der Flüchtlingshilfe,* ausgestrahlt am 15. Januar 2003; Eingabe von S vom 28. März 2003; http://www.ubi.admin.ch/presse/2003/de/03082801.
28. Article 10 paragraph 1 d Federal Act on Radio and Television.
29. Article 12 paragraph 5 Federal Act on Radio and Television.
30. Article 91 Federal Act on Radio and Television of 24 March 2006.
31. Articles 82 to 85 and Article 94 of the Federal Act on Radio and Television.
32. The referendum of July 2005 was governed by the Act on nationwide referendums of 4 February 2005 (Loi du 4 février 2005 relative au référendum au niveau national).
33. See Transparency Serbia, Preposition of the Constitution of the Republic of Serbia and fight against corruption, http://www.transparentnost.org.yu/english/ACTIVITIES/FOS/09102006.htm.
34. Law 16.017.
35. Article 10 of the Referenda Act of 20 July 1973; http://www2.justice.gov.mt/lom/home.asp.
36. Article 50 of the Electoral Polling Ordinance.
37. Article 47 of the Act of 14 March 2003 on nationwide referendum (Dziennik Ustaw [Journal of Laws of the Republic of Poland] No. 57, item 507 and No. 85, item 782); http://www.pkw.gov.pl/gallery/00/8.pdf.
38. Most of them were adopted when Venezuela had to face the Chavez Recall in 2004.
39. Article 7 of the Act on Publicity and Propaganda for Recalls (Normas sobre publicidad y propaganda de los procesos de referendo revocatorio de mandatos de cargos públicos de elección popular, Resolución No. 031114–775, 14 November 2003).

40. Article 20 Referendum Act (Ley No. 8492, Regulación del Referéndum).
41. Art. 12 Ley 24.747 Iniciativa legislativa popular, 19 diciembre de 1996.
42. Referendum Act of 3 April 1998 (Lei no. 15-A/98 de 3 de Abril: Lei Orgânica do Regime do Referendo).
43. Article 46 of the Referendum Act.
44. Article 52 of the Referendum Act.
45. See articles 65 to 70 of the Referendum Act.
46. European Commission for Democracy through Law (Venice Commission), Referendums in Europe – an Analysis of the Legal Rules in European States, CDL-AD (2005) 034, p. 18.
47. Article 163 read in combination with article 47 paragraph 6 of the Electoral Code of Moldova of 21 November 1997; http://e-democracy.md/en/legislation/electoralcode/vi/.
48. Ley orgánica 2/1980 de 18 de enero, sobre regulación de las distintas modalidades de referéndum.
49. Information provided by the Swedish Electoral Authority.
50. Article 36 of the Law on referendums and legislative popular initiatives of 28 November 1994 (Legge no. 101 del 28 novembre 1994: Nuove norme in materia di referendum e iniziativa legislativa popolare); http://www.elezioni.sm/src/elezioni/index.php?id=170.
51. Articles 27, 28, 29 and 34 Law on the Referendum on State-Legal Status of the Republic of Montenegro of March 1, 2006.
52. Article 46 and Article 82 of the Act on nationwide referendum.
53. Lei no. 56/98 de 18 de Agosto: Financiamento dos partidos politicos e das campanhas eleitorales.
54. Article 19 of the Act on the financing of political parties and electoral campaigns.
55. Articles 73 to 75 of the Referendum Act.
56. Articles 34 and 41 Law on the Referendum on State-Legal Status of the Republic of Montenegro of March 1, 2006.
57. Articles 97 and 98 of the Law governing the legislative and the constitutional referendum (Ley 134 de 1994 que regula los mecanismos de participación ciudadana).
58. Reglamento para consulta popular y revocatoria del mandato, Registro Official No.366 - 11 - 07 - 2001.
59. Art. 10 Ley Orgánica del Control del Gasto Electoral y de la Propaganda Electoral, Registro Oficial no. 241.
60. See, for example, Resolución PLE-TSE-2-14-2007.
61. Art. 12 Ley 24.747 Iniciativa legislativa popular, 19 diciembre de 1996.
62. Articles 20–21 Law 8492.
63. Article 7 of the Ordinance on Electoral Campaign Discipline of 14 March 1997 (Regolamento per la disciplina della campagna elettorale, del 14 marzo 1997).
64. Democracia directa y referéndum en América Latina, Cuadernos CNE, CNE Bolivia 2004, p. 67.
65. Article 3 Resolución 030925–465.
66. Ley Orgánica del Sufragio y Participación Política / Resolución 031114–775.
67. Article 8 Law on All-Ukrainian and Local Referendums of 1994, as amended in 2001.

68. See Transparency Serbia, Preposition of the Constitution of the Republic of Serbia and fight against corruption, http://www.transparentnost.org.yu/english/ACTIVITIES/FOS/09102006.htm.
69. Décret no. 2005-238 du 17 mars 2005 relatif à la campagne en vue du référendum; Décision CC 'Génération écologie' et autres, 7 avril 2005, cons. 4, JO du 9 avril 2005, p. 6458.
70. Law on Referendum No. 564/1992 Coll.
71. Article 11 Law on Referendum (law 25.432).
72. Article 53 of the Referendum Act.
73. Article 54 of the Referendum Act.
74. Article 55 of the Referendum Act.
75. Article 56 of the Referendum Act.
76. See articles 57 to 64 of the Referendum Act.
77. Article 56 of the Act on nationwide referendum.
78. OSCE/Office for Democratic Institutions and Human Rights, Needs Assessment Mission report ahead of the 21 May referendum in Serbia and Montenegro, Warsaw, 14 March 2006, p. 5, http://osce.org/odihr-elections/documents.html.
79. Article 27 Law on the Referendum on State-Legal Status of the Republic of Montenegro of March 1, 2006.
80. Article 4 Law on the Referendum on State-Legal Status of the Republic of Montenegro of March 1, 2006.
81. Articles 43–45 Law on the Referendum on State-Legal Status of the Republic of Montenegro of March 1, 2006.
82. Article 49 Law on the Referendum on State-Legal Status of the Republic of Montenegro of March 1, 2006.
83. Article 8 Referendum and Popular Initiative Act (Law 9.709).
84. Decreto no. 10 de 18 de julio de 2006.
85. Articles 91–96 Law no. 134/1994.

References

Altman, D. (2006) '*Mecanismos de Democracia Directa como Agentes de Responsabilidad Vertical y Legitimidad Democrática en Uruguay.' Latin American Program of the Woodrow Wilson Center for Scholars – Junior Post-Doctoral Scholars in the Study of Democracy*, Unpublished mimeo.

Auer, A., G. Malinverni and M. Hottelier (2006) *Droit constitutionnel Suisse, Vol. I, L'Etat*, 2nd edn (Berne: Stämpfli).

Balmelli, T. (2002) *Le financement des partis politiques et des campagnes électorales* (Fribourg: Editions universitaires).

Barczak, M. (2001) 'Representation by Consultation? The Rise of Direct Democracy in Latin America', *Latin American Politics and Society*, **43**(3): 37–59.

Corte Nacional Electoral de Bolivia, *Democracia directa y referéndum en América Latina*, Cuadernos CNE, 2004.

Costello, C. (2005) 'Peoples' Vengeances – Ireland's Nice Referenda', *European Constitutional Law Review*, **1**: 357–82.

Delley, J.D (2001) 'La professionnalisation des campagnes référendaires', in F. Hamon and O. Passelecq, *Le référendum en Europe – Bilan et perspectives* (Paris: Harmattan).

Fabiano, L. (2005) 'Italy', in Thomas D. Grand (ed.), *Lobbying, Government Relations and Campaign Finance Worldwide: Navigating the Laws, Regulations and Practices of National Regimes* (Oxford: Oceana Publications), pp. 281–95.

Garrone, P. (2006) *The Work of the Venice Commission in the Field of Referenda: Towards a Code of Good Practice for Referenda,* Paper presented at the CEEEO jubilee annual Conference and General Assembly meeting, Jurmala, 30 August– 2 September 2006, http://www.aceeeo.org/conferences/2006/programme .html.

Grabowska, M. (2002) 'Polish National Referendum Act: The Accession Referenda', *Yearbook of Polish European Studies,* **6**: 181–205.

Hug, S. (2002) *Voices of Europe: Citizens, Referendums and European Integration* (Lanhar, MD: Rowman & Littlefield).

Hertig, H.P. (1982) 'Sind Abstimmungserfolge käuflich?', *Annuaire suisse de science politique,* **22**(1): 35–58.

Ladner, A. (2004) 'The Political Parties and the Party System', in Ulrich Klöti, Peter Knoepfel, Hanspeter Kriesi, Wolf Linder and Yannis Papadopoulos (eds), *Handbook of Swiss Politics* (Zurich: NZZ Publishing).

Lissidini, A., Welp, Y. and Zovatto, D. (coord.) (2008) *Democracia directa en Latinoamérica* (Buenos Aires: Prometeo).

López, A.C. (2006) *The Spanish Consultative Referendum on the Treaty Establishing a Constitution for Europe,* Paper presented at the CEEEO jubilee annual Conference and General Assembly meeting, Jurmala, 30 August–2 September 2006, http://www.aceeeo.org/conferences/2006/programme.html.

Madroñal, J.C. *Spanish Referendum on the EU Constitution, Monitoring Report,* Mas Democracia, March 2005, http://www.masdemocracia.org.

Moraru, A. and E. Iorga (2005) *Legislation and Control Mechanisms of Political Parties' Funding: Czech Republic, Poland, Romania, Ukraine,* Institute for Public Policies (IPP), Bucharest, October 2005, http://www.ipp.ro.

Nijeboer, A. (2005) 'Peoples' Vengeances – The Dutch Referendum', *European Constitutional Law Review,* **1**: 393–405.

Papadopoulos, I. (1998) *Démocratie directe* (Paris: Economica).

Rodolfo González Risotto, *Democracia Directa: El Caso de Uruguay,* Paper presented at the Internacional Conference on Direct Democracy in Buenos Aires, March 2007, http://www.dd-la.ch/download/Gonzalez_Rodolfo.pdf.

Schmitter, P.C. and A.H. Trechsel (eds) (2004) *The Future of Democracy in Europe – Trends, Analyses and Reforms* (Strasbourg: Council of Europe Publishing).

Supreme Court of the United States (2003) *Senator Mitch McConnel v. Federal Election Commission, Brief of Amici Curiae international experts in support of appellees/cross-appellants,* No.02–1674, 5 August.

Welp, Y. and U. Serdült (eds) (2009) *Armas de doble Filo. La participación ciudadana en la encruciajada y La democracia directa en América Latina* (Buenos Aires: Prometeo).

Wheatley, Jonathan, Direct Democracy in the Commonwealth of Independent States: The State of the Art, *C2D Working Paper Series* no **28**, Aarau. www.c2d.ch.

Wilfried, M. (2004) *Wir sind das Volk: Direkte Demokratie – Verfahren, Verbreitung, Wirkung*, Liechtenstein-Institut, Beiträge Nr. 24/2004, http://www.liechtenstein-institut.li.

Council of Europe Documents

European Commission for Democracy through Law (Venice Commission), *Guidelines for Constitutional Referendums*, CDL-INF (2001) 010.

European Commission for Democracy through Law (Venice Commission), *Opinion on Parliamentary Assembly Recommendation 1704 (2005) on Referendums: Towards Good Practices in Europe*, CDL-AD (2005) 028.

European Commission for Democracy through Law (Venice Commission), *Referendums in Europe – an Analysis of the Legal Rules in European States*, CDL-AD (2005) 034.

Parliamentary Assembly Recommendation 1704 (2005), *Referendums: Towards Good Practices in Europe*.

CM Documents, *Referendums: Towards Good Practices in Europe, Parliamentary Assembly Recommendation 1704(2005), Reply Adopted by the Committee of Ministers on 9 November 2005 at the 945th Meeting of the Ministers' Deputies*, CM/AS(2005) Rec1704 final, 10 November 2005.

European Commission for Democracy through Law (Venice Commission), *Guidelines on the Holding of Referendums adopted by the Council for Democratic Elections at its 18th Meeting (Venice, 12 October 2006) and the Venice Commission at its 68th Plenary Session (Venice, 13–14 October 2006)*, CDL-AD(2006)027rev.

European Commission for Democracy through Law (Venice Commission), *Code of Good Practice on Referendums adopted by the Council for Democratic Elections at its 19th Meeting (Venice, 16 December 2006) and the Venice Commission at its 70th Plenary Session (Venice, 16–17 March 2007)*, CDL-AD(2007)008.

14
Conclusion

Karin Gilland Lutz and Simon Hug

That money plays a role in politics is hardly news. It is also widely known that its role in election campaigns varies quite considerably across countries (e.g., Katz, 1996). Much less is known, however, especially comparatively, on the role of money in referendum campaigns. This is in part due to the rather limited number of countries that have provisions at the national level to allow for referendums. In part it is also due, however, to the research questions pursued in the literature, most of which have focused on other aspects of referendums.

The earlier literature, as is discussed by Stratmann (2009), focused considerably on the question of whether one could buy success in referendum campaigns. As both Stratmann (2009) and Smith (2009) remind us in their chapters, the evidence presented in the literature – mostly on the states in the United States – is mixed. The picture is largely mixed because of the inferential problems, as Stratmann (2009) nicely illustrates. Referendum campaigns might attract very little money, simply because the result of the vote is a foregone conclusion. Stratmann (2009) convincingly argues that this requires more theoretically founded empirical analysis. His analysis, Smith (2009) argues, finds positive effects of campaign spending on success, but the substantive effect is rather small.

While the question of whether successes at the ballot box may be bought is certainly interesting in itself, the question has also to be considered in a broader context. Even if successes may be bought, does this possibility make voters worse off, or are they, perhaps, better off, since the victor has the same preferences as the voters themselves?

From this interrogation arises the question of how campaign spending affects voters. Stratmann (2009) frames this more recent debate by discussing how voters may obtain information through the campaign. Hence, informative campaigning results in the voters being better informed about the policy location of the proposal and the status quo. Persuasive campaigning, on the other hand, wishes to convince voters of particular consequences linked with the adoption (or rejection) of a proposal.[1]

Work by Lupia (1994)[2] has emphasized that campaign expenditure might offer cues to voters about the consequences of their votes. For a set of widely discussed initiative proposals in California, Lupia (1994) also finds evidence supporting this hypothesis.[3]

Whether referendum campaigns can play such a beneficial role for voters is very dependent on what information voters obtain concerning campaign spending. Here, the way in which the campaign spending is regulated becomes of central importance. Hence the chapters in this book attempted to shed a first, comparative light on the regulations present in a dozen countries which use referendums. As the broad overview by Zellweger, Serdült and Renfer (2009) clearly demonstrates, the differences across the countries covered across the European and American continents are quite dramatic. While at the national level the regulations vary between next to nonexistent in Switzerland (Serdült, 2009),[4] to a carefully designed set of rules in Great Britain (Ghaleigh, 2009). It might have struck more than one reader of this book that these two cases suggest an inverse relation between the frequency with which referendums are used and the extent of regulation of referendum campaigns.[5]

All of the other countries covered in this book and covered in Zellweger, Serdült and Renfer (2009) fall somewhere between these two extremes. Luxembourg, as Zellweger, Serdült and Renfer (2009) discuss, is very similar to the Swiss case,[6] while in Italy voters themselves have reduced to some degree the regulation of referendum campaigns (Ricci, 2009).

In most of the other countries covered (Auers, Ruus and Krupavicius, 2009; Closa Montero and Carbonell Bellolio, 2009; Gilland Lutz, 2009; Hamon, 2009; Hobolt, 2009) some regulation of referendum campaigns and their financing exists, but most at the same time provide for finances coming directly from the state, either directly to the campaigns or through political parties. Generally, political parties play a central role in most countries, but their expenditures in referendum campaigns are generally only slightly transparent, as are their sources.

As the chapters dealing with national regulations have clearly demonstrated, the extent of transparency in expenditures, possibly with the exception of Great Britain (Ghaleigh, 2009), is quite far from the regulations existing in most states in the USA (Smith, 2009), or Canada for that matter (Johnston, 2009). Hence, very few of the contributors were able to offer detailed information on the expenditures that political actors had during referendum campaigns. In addition, the availability of this information is in most cases not as easy as in most US states (Smith, 2009). Hence, while there might be good theoretical reasons to expect that expenditures in referendum campaigns are informative (see Lupia, 1994), in practice very few referendum campaigns (especially at the national level) are regulated in such a fashion that voters might learn something from spending patterns.

Thus, it cannot come as a surprise that the contributors can offer mostly only speculation on what effects spending and the regulation thereof have in referendum campaigns. While in some cases quite unbalanced spending patterns might have tipped the balance in favour of a particular outcome, whether this tipping was the result of a more informed electorate or not, is hard to assess. Only the more systematic studies carried out at the subnational level in the USA (for instance, Lupia, 1994; Bowler and Donovan, 1998) and the more recent study on national votes in Switzerland (Kriesi, 2005)[7] offer some evidence on how expenditures affect the information of voters.

Hence, while the present volume has offered an overview over the regulation of referendum campaigns and their finances in many countries, it has also highlighted the considerable research gaps that still exist. While for some national and subnational contexts we have quite detailed information on the role that money plays in referendum campaigns, in others such information is cruelly lacking. Against this lack of solid empirical findings on a rather central aspect of referendums, it is surprising that numerous scholars indiscriminately advise constitutional framers to introduce referendums in new or revised constitutions, without considering the details of financial regulation. Hence, both scholars and politicians should spend more time on thinking and researching about the effects of any such regulations.

Notes

1. Stratmann (2009) also discusses negative campaigning and campaigns that reduce the uncertainty of voters.
2. The theoretical underpinnings are discussed in a broader context in Lupia and McCubbins (1998).
3. Empirically, Bowler and Donovan (1998) provide additional evidence in support of this role of campaigns at the level of US states. Both Christin, Hug and Sciarini (2002) and Kriesi (2005) have attempted to assess the role of cues

in referendum votes in Switzerland. Given that expenditure information is, however, not available in Switzerland (Serdült, 2009), cues in terms of voting recommendations and ads in newspapers are employed.

4. Both (Serdült, 2009) and Zellweger, Serdült and Renfer (2009) rightly emphasize that Switzerland has tightly regulated access to TV and radio, where for referendum campaigns, ads cannot be placed.

5. Zellweger, Serdült and Renfer (2009) suggest that the absence (or weak) regulation of campaigns in countries with only few votes is largely due to the inexperience these countries have in respect of consulting their voters. Whether there is a general relationship between frequency of use and extent of regulation is, however, debatable.

6. Zellweger, Serdült and Renfer (2009) explain this by the fact that the referendum on the EU treaty establishing a constitution for Europe was the first in the post-Second World War period. One might also venture as explanation that both Switzerland and Luxembourg have strongly developed bank secrecy laws.

7. Given that Switzerland does not require any transparency on expenditures, the latter are often measured on the basis of information on ads in newspapers (see also Hertig, 1982). This is obviously a very indirect measure of expenditures, and studies relying on such measures have to be taken with a grain of salt.

References

Auers, D., J. Ruus and A. Krupavicius (2009) 'Financing Referendums and Initiatives in the Baltic States', in K. Gilland Lutz and S. Hug (eds), *Financing Referendum Campaigns* (Basingstoke: Palgrave Macmillan).

Bowler, S. and T. Donovan (1998) *Demanding Choices* (Ann Arbor: University of Michigan Press).

Christin, T., S. Hug and P. Sciarini (2002) 'Interests and Information in Referendum Voting. An Analysis of Swiss Voters', *European Journal of Political Research*, **41**(6): 759–76.

Closa Montero, C. and F. Carbonell Bellolio (2009) 'Financing Referendum Campaigns in Spain', in K. Gilland Lutz and S. Hug (eds), *Financing Referendum Campaigns* (Basingstoke: Palgrave Macmillan).

Ghaleigh, N.S. (2009) 'Sledgehammers and Nuts? Regulating Referendums in the UK', in K. Gilland Lutz and S. Hug (eds), *Financing Referendum Campaigns* (Basingstoke: Palgrave Macmillan).

Gilland Lutz, K. (2009) 'Referendums and Spending in Ireland', in K. Gilland Lutz and S. Hug (eds), *Financing Referendum Campaigns* (Basingstoke: Palgrave Macmillan).

Hamon, F. (2009) 'The Financing of Referendum Campaigns in France', in K. Gilland Lutz and S. Hug (eds), *Financing Referendum Campaigns* (Basingstoke: Palgrave Macmillan).

Hertig, H.P. (1982) 'Sind Abstimmungserfolge käuflich?', *Annuaire suisse de science politique*, **22**(1): 35–58.

Hobolt, S. B. (2009) 'Campaign Financing in Danish Referendums', in K. Gilland Lutz and S. Hug (eds), *Financing Referendum Campaigns* (Basingstoke: Palgrave Macmillan).

Johnston, R. (2009) 'Regulating Campaign Finance in Canadian Referendums and Initiatives', in K. Gilland Lutz and S. Hug (eds), *Financing Referendum Campaigns* (Basingstoke: Palgrave Macmillan).

Katz, R.S. (1996) 'Part Organizations and Finance', in L. Lawrence, R.G. Niemi and P. Norris (eds), *Comparing Democracies: Elections and Voting in Global Perspective* (London: Sage), pp. 107–33.

Kriesi, H. (2005) *Direct Democratic Choice: The Swiss Experience* (Lanham, MD: Lexington Books).

Lupia, A. (1994) 'Shortcuts Versus Encyclopedias: Information and Voting Behavior in California Insurance Reform Elections', *American Political Science Review* 88(1): 63–76.

Lupia, A. and M.D. McCubbins (1998) *The Democratic Dilemma: Can Citizens Learn What They Really Need to Know?* (New York: Cambridge University Press).

Ricci, R. (2009) 'Financing Referendum Campaigns in Italy: How the Abrogative Referendum Can Regulate Electoral Financing', in K. Gilland Lutz and S. Hug (eds), *Financing Referendum Campaigns* (Basingstoke: Palgrave Macmillan).

Serdült, U. (2009) 'Financing Referendum Campaigns in Switzerland', in K. Gilland Lutz and S. Hug (eds), *Financing Referendum Campaigns* (Basingstoke: Palgrave Macmillan).

Smith, D. (2009) 'US States', in K. Gilland Lutz and S. Hug (eds), *Financing Referendum Campaigns* (Basingstoke: Palgrave Macmillan).

Stratmann, T. (2009, forthcoming) 'Campaign Spending and Ballot Measures', in K. Gilland Lutz and S. Hug (eds), *Financing Referendum Campaigns* (Basingstoke: Palgrave Macmillan).

Zellweger, T., U. Serdült and I. Renfer (2009) 'Referendum Campaign Regulations in Europe and Latin America', in K. Gilland Lutz and S. Hug (eds), *Financing Referendum Campaigns* (Basingstoke: Palgrave Macmillan).